T0319955

Embracing Entrepreneurship Across Disciplines

Embracing Entrepreneurship Across Disciplines

Ideas and Insights from Engineering, Science, Medicine and Arts

Edited by

Satish Nambisan

Professor of Entrepreneurship & Technology Management, University of Wisconsin-Milwaukee, USA

Edward Elgar
PUBLISHING

Cheltenham, UK • Northampton, MA, USA

Published by
Edward Elgar Publishing Limited
The Lypiatts
15 Lansdown Road
Cheltenham
Glos GL50 2JA
UK

Edward Elgar Publishing, Inc.
William Pratt House
9 Dewey Court
Northampton
Massachusetts 01060
USA

A catalogue record for this book
is available from the British Library

Library of Congress Control Number: 2015933451

This book is available electronically in the **Elgar**online
Business subject collection
DOI 10.4337/9781782549963

ISBN 978 1 78254 995 6 (cased)
ISBN 978 1 78254 996 3 (eBook)

Typeset by Columns Design XML Ltd, Reading
Printed and bound in Great Britain by T.J. International Ltd, Padstow

Contents

Figures

Tables

Contributors

R. Joseph (Joe) Anderson has been with the History Programs of the American Institute of Physics (AIP) since 1993 and is presently Director of AIP's Niels Bohr Library & Archives and Associate Director of the Center for History of Physics. Previous positions include Director of the Library and Archives of the Balch Institute for Ethnic Studies and archivist at the Yale University Department of Manuscripts and Archives. He has an MA in American history (Ohio University) and a MALS specializing in archives administration (University of Wisconsin-Madison) and is a fellow of the Society of American Archivists. He has published in *The American Archivist*, *Isis* and other journals.

Gary D. Beckman is Director of Entrepreneurial Studies in the Arts at North Carolina State University, where he developed and administers the nation's first campus-wide Arts Entrepreneurship minor. Before arriving at NC State, he developed the country's first Music Entrepreneurship minor at the University of South Carolina's School of Music. He also edited the field's first essay collection, *Disciplining the Arts: Teaching Entrepreneurship in Context* and edits the *Journal of Arts Entrepreneurship Research* and the *Journal of Arts Entrepreneurship Education*. Gary's articles on arts entrepreneurship, arts leadership education and intellectual entrepreneurship appear in *Planning for Higher Education*, *Symposium*, *Metropolitan Universities Journal*, *Arts Education Policy Review*, *The Journal of Arts Management, Law, and Society* and a number of essay collections. Gary earned a PhD in Musicology from The University of Texas at Austin, a MA in Musicology from the University of New Hampshire and a BA in Music from the University of Southern Maine.

Angela Myles Beeching directs the Center for Music Entrepreneurship at the Manhattan School of Music, where she serves on the faculty. Previously, she directed music career programs at New England Conservatory and at Indiana University, where she launched Project Jumpstart, an innovative student-centered and student-driven music entrepreneurship program. Angela also maintains a thriving consulting practice and is author of *Beyond Talent: Creating a Successful Career in*

Music. Published by Oxford University Press, the book is used as a text at scores of music schools throughout the US and, in translated editions, in Japan and (forthcoming) China. She's contributed chapters to a number of other volumes and her articles have appeared in *Inside Arts*, *The Strad*, *Classical Singer* and *Chamber Music* magazines. A Fulbright Scholar and Harriet Hale Woolley grant recipient, Angela holds a doctorate in cello performance from Stony Brook University.

Robert W. Brown, PhD, is Institute Professor and Distinguished University Professor in the physics department of Case Western Reserve University. His present association with a dozen manufacturing companies in Ohio is a culmination of a long career in industrial design, applied research and entrepreneurial physics education. His teams have worked in astroparticle physics, MRI, electromagnetics, inverse methods, rf ablation, heat transfer, radiation physics, nonlinear dynamics, EEG, MEG, susceptometry, muscle models, superconductivity and sensor development. Robert co-founded a pioneering Master's Program in Physics Entrepreneurship at Case, and has advised more than 50 PhD and MS graduates. Robert has co-authored a 944-page textbook that has become the "daily companion of the MRI scientist." He has received four national teaching honors, is a Fellow of both the American Physical Society and of the American Association of Physics Teachers and has chaired or co-chaired four regional and international conferences during the last decade.

Orville R. Butler is currently founder and CEO of Dragon Eagle LLC, a cross-cultural training and consulting startup that assists companies seeking to succeed in doing business in and with China. From 2005 to 2013, he was a historian at the Center for History of Physics, American Institute of Physics, where he co-authored *History of Physicists in Industry: Final Report* (2008) and *Physics Entrepreneurship and Innovation "You Can't Rely on Large Companies Anymore"* (2013). He has a PhD in History of Technology and Science (Iowa State University), an M.Juris in International Trade Law (Bond University, Australia), an MA in History and Philosophy of Science (University of Notre Dame) and a BS in Physics (Walla Walla College). He is co-author of *History of Kennedy Space Center* (Florida, 2007) and *Manufacturing the Future: A History of Western Electric* (Cambridge, 1999) in addition to several articles dealing with aspects of the inter-relationship between science/ technology, culture, and business.

Lisa Canning is a main street creative entrepreneur. With a love for the arts, entrepreneurship, creativity and innovation, Lisa has developed, and helped others develop, ventures at the intersection of their creativity and business ideas for over 30 years. Her passion is creating organizations that maximize value potential while realizing their highest purpose using their creativity. As a pioneer in arts entrepreneurship who launched her first entrepreneurial venture at 17 from her dorm room at Northwestern University, Lisa has created not one but six multi-million dollar ventures. Each has experienced double digit growth using her imagination and creativity. As co-founder of an innovative online education and giving platform designed to help small to medium size enterprises raise money and build new thinking, business and sales skills, her focus is to help grow ideas into products and services for sustainable living and global trade.

James D. Hart is Director of Arts Entrepreneurship and Assistant Professor of Practice at the Meadows School of the Arts, where he manages two minors, Arts Management and Arts Entrepreneurship. James is the founder and former dean of TITAN Teaterakademi (The International Theatre Academy Norway), an accredited conservatory for theatre entrepreneurship in Oslo. James serves as co-chair for the special interest group Entrepreneurship in the Arts for the United States Association for Small Business and Entrepreneurship (USASBE), and is a co-founder of the Society for Arts Entrepreneurship Education (SAEE). Artistically, James earned recognition as an actor, director, writer and producer. He earned his MFA in acting from the Yale School of Drama.

Andrew Kant is Program Manager for the Drugs, Devices and Diagnostics (4D) Strategic Initiative at NC TraCS Institute within the University of North Carolina-Chapel Hill. Previously he was Assistant Director of Carolina KickStart, a startup accelerator at UNC-Chapel Hill, focused on commercializing faculty research through venture creation. Andrew was an Oak Ridge National Laboratory Fellow at the Food and Drug Administration's National Center for Toxicological Research. He holds a BS from University of Massachusetts-Dartmouth and an MS from UNC-Chapel Hill.

Doug Melton is Program Director for Entrepreneurial Engineering at the Kern Family Foundation of Wisconsin. He works with universities to develop engineering programs that foster entrepreneurial mindsets in undergraduates. It is work that is informed by his previous roles. As a former faculty member at Kettering University, he helped develop a campus-wide program for entrepreneurship. His 17 years of teaching electrical and computer engineering with a specialization in signal processing and communications emphasized industry connections. Prior to serving as a faculty member, Doug directed the research and development activities of Digisonix Incorporated, a spin-off company with a startup culture. His team created adaptive, multi-channel system identification, signal processing and control strategies for aircraft, vehicles and air handling systems. The active sound and vibration control products, intellectual property, and projects he managed ranged from DSP development tools to production DSP systems for OEM products.

Arlen Meyers, MD, MBA, is Professor of Otolaryngology, Dentistry and Engineering at the University of Colorado Denver and President and Chief Medical Officer of Medvoy (a healthcare referral management and physician–doctor network – www.medvoy.com). He leads several global bioentrepreneurship education, research and practice initiatives, serving as the founding CEO and President of the Society of Physician Entrepreneurs (www.sopenet.org) and as the Director of the Certificate Program in Bioinnovation and Entrepreneurship at the University of Colorado. He is a former Harvard-Macy fellow, and in 2010 he completed a Fulbright Fellowship at Kings Business, the commercialization office of technology transfer at Kings College in London. He serves on the editorial boards of the *Journal of Commercial Biotechnology* and the journal *Technology Transfer and Entrepreneurship*.

Satish Nambisan is Professor of Entrepreneurship & Technology Management at the Sheldon B. Lubar School of Business, University of Wisconsin-Milwaukee (UWM), where he also directs the entrepreneurship and technology management initiatives. He holds a joint position as Professor of Mechanical Engineering in the College of Engineering & Applied Sciences at UWM. He conducts research in the areas of entrepreneurship, technology and innovation management, product development, and technology strategy. His current work focuses on open innovation; entrepreneurship in innovation ecosystems; customer co-innovation and value co-creation; and information technology and product/service innovation. His research has been published in a wide range of top-tier business journals including *Harvard Business Review*, *MIT Sloan Management Review*, *Management Science*, *Organization Science*, *Academy of Management Review*, *Research Policy*, *MIS Quarterly* and *Stanford Social Innovation Review*. He is the author of *The Global Brain: Your Roadmap for Innovating Faster and Smarter in a Networked World* (Wharton School Publishing). He serves on the editorial boards of several business and management journals.

Cam Patterson is the Chief Operating Officer of the New York Presbyterian Hospital at Weill Cornell Medical Center. Previously, he was the

Associate Dean of UNC Healthcare Entrepreneurship, Chief of Cardiology and Physician-in-Chief of the UNC Center for Heart and Vascular Care and a healthcare investor who has launched two startups. He was Director of UNC McAllister Heart Institute. Cam is the Ernest and Hazel Craige Distinguished Professor of Cardiovascular Medicine. He is an Established Investigator of the American Heart Association and a Burroughs Wellcome Fund Clinical Scientist in Translational Research. Cam's research programs include the areas of angiogenesis and vascular development, cardiac hypertrophy, protein quality control and translational genomics and metabolomics. He holds an MBA from the University of North Carolina (UNC) and an MD from Emory University.

Joyce Thomas, MFA, IDSA, is an inventor, innovator and educator with a passion to empower people through good design. Professionally, she has worked across interdisciplinary boundaries integrating marketing, engineering and consumer needs into creative products. She has utilized empathic research strategies in her product designs that have accounted for more than $4 billion in retail sales and been awarded 59 patents worldwide. Joyce is a visiting assistant professor of industrial design at the University of Illinois Urbana-Champaign, teaching design thinking and studio courses. As Chief Creative Officer for the ThomasSchumerGroup she is helping to develop and provide entrepreneurship education and innovative product solutions for a diverse group of small businesses.

1. Entrepreneurship perspectives: an introduction

Satish Nambisan

I. INTRODUCTION

In the past decade or so, the study of entrepreneurship has expanded well beyond its traditional home in business schools. Scholars and educators in fields such as engineering, medicine/healthcare, science, arts/music, design, and architecture have shown great interest in entrepreneurship and indicated their potential to bring unique perspectives and insights on this topic. Terms such as 'engineering entrepreneurship,' 'design entrepreneurship,' 'life sciences entrepreneurship,' 'health entrepreneurship,' and 'arts entrepreneurship' (and the academic communities built around these topics in the respective fields) reflect this rapidly emerging research and pedagogical interest on issues related to entrepreneurship among scholars outside the business field. Indeed, entrepreneurship-related programs and courses tailored to the different fields and domains continue to be created in many schools and universities.

These initiatives have also given rise to diverse field- or discipline-specific perspectives of entrepreneurship. While there are some differences among these 'entrepreneurship perspectives,' there is also considerable opportunity to cross-fertilize and/or integrate unique ideas and insights on entrepreneurship from the different fields.

Such an opportunity currently remains largely untapped. There are numerous books and articles on entrepreneurship written by scholars in the business academia. However, given their primary focus (on business and management areas) and the nature of their audience (largely business school academics and students), there is very limited attention paid to entrepreneurship as interpreted in non-business fields such as engineering, science, arts, design, and health/medicine.

More recently, scholars and practitioners in non-business fields too have written books and articles on entrepreneurship – for example, on arts entrepreneurship;[1,2] on engineering entrepreneurship;[3] and on health-care entrepreneurship.[4] However, most such books have (understandably) provided a rather narrow treatment of the concept of entrepreneurship as relevant to that particular field. Thus, there is a critical need (and considerable potential) to adopt a broad-based focus on entrepreneurship – one that integrates ideas, insights, and themes from across diverse fields.

II. GOALS AND OBJECTIVES OF THE BOOK

The primary objective of this book is to bring together these diverse field-specific perspectives on entrepreneurship and to build a broad cross-disciplinary understanding of entrepreneurship in ways that will advance the education and practice of entrepreneurship in all fields and disciplines. The book chapters incorporate and build on the different perspectives of entrepreneurship (that exist in fields such as engineering, science, arts, design, medicine/health, etc.) and speak to a broad audience of entrepreneurship scholars in the different fields.

There is another important reason for developing such an integrative or cross-disciplinary perspective of entrepreneurship. Over the last several years, innovation activities (development of new products and services) in fields such as engineering, science, information technology/ information science, and medicine have increasingly become inter-disciplinary. For example, in markets such as medical devices, e-medicine, consumer electronics and applications, biotechnology, energy, and so on, entrepreneurial (and innovation) activities have involved extensive collaboration among professionals in two or more of the above mentioned fields. A good example in this regard is e-medicine: many new ventures in this area have founders from fields such as information science, medicine, engineering, business, and arts/design. This indicates that there is a natural affinity among the above fields – at least with regard to innovation and entrepreneurship – and that it is imperative to adopt (research, educate, and practice) a cross-disciplinary view of entrepreneurship. This book is thus intended to offer a timely forum for entrepreneurship scholars in the different fields to come together and contribute towards such a more cross-disciplinary under-standing of entrepreneurship. Overall, it is my hope that this book will help research and practice in entrepreneurship in the following ways:

- Facilitate the development of cumulative knowledge on entrepreneurship by building on core themes and concepts identified in the different fields;
- Provide the opportunity to share entrepreneurship-related insights and best practices across fields;
- Support the development of entrepreneurship educational materials that can be shared across fields;
- Inform the development and evaluation of entrepreneurship policies and programs that cross or impact multiple disciplines or fields.

Before describing the individual chapters, a quick note on how this book may be used in entrepreneurship-related courses and programs. It can be used as a primary or secondary textbook for introductory courses on entrepreneurship in different schools and disciplines as it would enable students to understand the core aspects of entrepreneurship as practiced in their particular field and at the same time gain a broader perspective of entrepreneurship.

III. ORGANIZATION OF THE BOOK

Given the diverse entrepreneurship-related contexts, concepts, and ideas that exist in the different fields, the emphasis of the individual chapters is on drawing on such rich material and at the same time articulating the core concepts and insights in a way that would be understandable to a broad set of audiences (scholars, practitioners, and policy makers in all of the above fields and disciplines).

The book consists of ten chapters organized as follows. Following this introductory chapter (Chapter 1), we start with the engineering perspective of entrepreneurship and then move on to other fields.

In Chapter 2 ('Engineering entrepreneurship: developing an entrepreneurial mindset'), Doug Melton (Kern Entrepreneurship Education Network – KEEN) presents a framework for fostering an entrepreneurial mindset among engineers. KEEN is a collaboration of around 19 U.S. universities that strive to instill an entrepreneurial mindset in undergraduate engineering and technology students. KEEN's mission is to graduate engineers who will contribute to business success and in the process transform the American workforce. From his perch as the program director of KEEN, Doug examines the need for entrepreneurship education in engineering schools and suggests a more coherent approach in this regard. In particular, he focuses on how engineering education should focus on developing an 'entrepreneurial mindset' among students and coupling that with engineering thinking and skills. He also describes Entrepreneurially Minded Learning (EML), a student-centered pedagogy in which students learn about a subject through the experience of identifying opportunities to create value. He identifies a set of EML skills that bring the emphasis to value creation and to the 'know-why' along with the 'know-how' in engineering education. Much of the entrepreneurship mindset framework that Melton presents here can be applied to entrepreneurship education in other disciplines and contexts.

In Chapter 3 ('Challenges in faculty entrepreneurship in the sciences: becoming an entrepreneur but staying at the university'), Robert Brown (Case Western Reserve University – CWRU) expands on the growing importance of entrepreneurship education in the sciences. Drawing on his rich and extensive experience as an entrepreneur and as an academic in physics, Brown describes a model of faculty entrepreneurship – one that addresses the conflict of fulfilling faculty responsibilities and goals while meeting the demands of a new business. His approach (validated by his own personal experience across the past four decades or so) emphasizes two key factors: (1) the importance of identifying a major business partner(s) from a network of colleagues, which springs from industrial contacts and former students; and (2) the importance of finding viable business ideas through research collaboration in industry. Brown also describes an innovative graduate program in physics entrepreneurship that he founded and championed at CWRU. He concludes with a set of key insights on how a young faculty in the sciences can build a career as a full-time faculty and an entrepreneur.

In Chapter 4 ('Physics entrepreneurship: an evolution from technology push to market pull'), Orville Butler and Joseph Anderson (American Institute of Physics) present an illuminating set of findings on entrepreneurship in the sciences from an extensive four-year study, supported by the National Science Foundation, that they conducted on physicist entrepreneurs. Drawing on interviews with more than 140 physics entrepreneurs and visits to 91 high technology start-ups, Butler and Anderson provide a fascinating account of the evolving character of scientist entrepreneurs. Starting from the basic question of who is a physicist (or scientist) entrepreneur, they go on to address many other interesting questions including whether entrepreneurship in the sciences is a learned behavior or an inherited characteristic and how 'technology push' entrepreneurs differ from 'market pull' entrepreneurs. They conclude by providing some insights into how we can prepare physicists (or more broadly scientists) for entrepreneurial pursuits.

Next, we turn to entrepreneurship in medicine, healthcare, and more broadly in the life sciences.

In Chapter 5 ('Bioentrepreneurship: opportunities and challenges'), Arlen Meyers (University of Colorado Denver) examines the topic of bioentrepreneurship. Bioentrepreneurship is the pursuit of entrepreneurial opportunities in bio or life sciences leading to biomedical and health innovation. Myers presents the basic concepts of bioentrepreneurship, how it applies to other domains, and makes the case that innovation is the main sustainable competitive advantage for health service organizations and national health systems. He also describes in detail the innovative Master's program that he created and leads at UC Denver in the area of bioentrepreneurship.

In Chapter 6 ('Healthcare entrepreneurship: the changing landscape'), Cam Patterson and Andrew Kant (University of North Carolina at Chapel Hill) continue this discussion by focusing on healthcare entrepreneurship. This is an area that has exploded in recent years, fueled by the continuous need to improve quality of life for patients and strong R&D efforts at for-profit and non-profit entities. In this chapter they explore various challenges and rewards for healthcare entrepreneurship. They also consider the different initiatives and programs that can be adopted to foster entrepreneurial pursuits in medical schools and other healthcare educational institutions.

Next, we turn to entrepreneurship in arts, music, and design.

In Chapter 7 ('The entrepreneurial musician: the Tao of DIY'), Angela Myles Beeching (Manhattan School of Music) considers how musicians are redefining entrepreneurship and offers highly insightful case studies along with perspectives on the 'gift economy,' musician entrepreneurial mindset and opportunities, and on the ramifications for entrepreneurship educators. As she notes, there is a Brave New World out there for musicians – thanks to new technologies (for example, file sharing, online recording and streaming), musicians face a destabilized profession that demands entrepreneurial approaches. An increasing number of conservatories and university music programs have added entrepreneurship courses and programming in a range of formats and services to address this emerging need. While schools may employ diverse pedagogical approaches, they need to be guided by the six key development areas for music entrepreneurs that Beeching identifies. There are lessons and insights here not just for entrepreneurship programs in music schools but in other fields as well – particularly on the relevance of fostering an entrepreneurial mindset when technologies and new business models disrupt professions and fields.

In Chapter 8 ('Educating arts entrepreneurs: does, can or should one size fit all?'), Gary Beckman (North Carolina State University) and James Hart (Southern Methodist University) argues for a consensus among arts entrepreneurship educators on the field's desired student outcomes and curricular design. They note that without such a consensus, arts entrepreneurship classrooms will remain largely based on educator personal experience and individual research. After providing a brief history of arts entrepreneurship, Beckman and Hart flesh out the educational outcomes for arts entrepreneurship programs and illustrate that using a fictional vignette. In doing so, they also tease out some of the differences among programs targeting fine arts students and music/theatre students. Following that, they consider in detail the pedagogical approach that might be helpful in serving these outcomes. The authors conclude by identifying significant trends in the development of arts entrepreneurship training programs in a cross-disciplinary context (having a mixed classroom of arts and non-arts majors – including business majors).

In Chapter 9 ('The value of creativity: implications for industrial design and design entrepreneurship'), Joyce Thomas (Beckman Institute of Design) and Lisa Canning (Arts Entrepreneurship) examine the role of entrepreneurship in industrial design and the lessons for the broader community of entrepreneurship educators. In recent years, design thinking – that has its roots in industrial design – has found wide acceptance among entrepreneurs and innovators in different fields including business, engineering, and sciences. Thomas and Canning explore the emerging topic of industrial design entrepreneurship and its implications for the broader field of arts entrepreneurship. They describe the different roles that industrial designers play in start-ups and then provide an extensive account, with examples, of promoting entrepreneurship education in industrial design schools.

In the final and concluding chapter, Chapter 10 ('Towards a cross-disciplinary understanding of entrepreneurship'), I bring together the unique perspectives and insights on entrepreneurship from the different fields (as described in the various chapters) and offer a framework to advance a more cross-disciplinary understanding of entrepreneurship. The objective is to help develop (through future research and practice) a more comprehensive and coherent approach to entrepreneurship education in all fields – one that acknowledges the unique context of each field and at the same time draws on the strengths of various perspectives and approaches.

Our efforts at developing a broader view of entrepreneurship (in both education and practice) is very much a work in progress and we are probably only at the beginning stages. However, our success in fostering entrepreneurial thinking skills among all students – across all disciplines – will be contingent on us adopting such a broader perspective of entrepreneurship. I hope that this book will help us take a first step in this direction.

NOTES

1. Scherdin, M. and Zander, I. 2011. *Art Entrepreneurship*. Cheltenham, UK and Northampton, MA: Edward Elgar.
2. Roberts, J.S. 2004. *Arts Entrepreneurship: The Business of the Arts*. Bloomingdale, IL: United Press Services.
3. Allen, K. 2009. *Entrepreneurship for Engineers and Scientists*. Upper Saddle River, NJ: Prentice Hall.
4. Pareras, L.G. 2011. *Innovation and Entrepreneurship in the Healthcare Sector: From Idea to Funding to Launch*. Phoenix, MD: Greenbranch Publishing.

PART I

Engineering, science, and technology entrepreneurship

2. Engineering entrepreneurship: developing an entrepreneurial mindset

Doug Melton

I. INTRODUCTION

The purpose of this chapter is to define *entrepreneurial mindset* and relate how it is particularly important within the field of engineering. A mindset is an outlook and collection of attitudes applicable when approaching any situation. Entrepreneurial mindset is at the root of entrepreneurial behavior. In contrast, a traditional study of entrepreneurship may focus on innovations, obtaining resources and funding, and following entrepreneurial business practices and processes. While these are valuable, an individual's entrepreneurial mindset is the true engine of value creation.

Many researchers have attempted to identify core entrepreneurial attributes, behaviors, and mental models.[1] These types of studies focus on the personal agency of the entrepreneur. Our focus is upon the underlying entrepreneurial mindset that can be applied in any situation, becoming an entire outlook on life. It can be applied in any context, within a new venture or within an existing organization. In particular circumstances, an entrepreneurial mindset might lead to entrepreneurship in the traditional sense of the word. We demonstrate how this broad and succinct definition of entrepreneurial mindset is particularly suited to engineering.

It is valuable to acknowledge that over the past several decades there has been significant debate about the value of studying the personal attributes of the entrepreneurs themselves. While personality plays a moderate role, a study indicates that there is little ability to predict entrepreneurial intentions or entrepreneurial performance based on personality traits.[2] To gain a foothold in the study of entrepreneurs, some researchers study their behavior, accounting for individual context and career paths. To avoid the trap of trying to create a comprehensive list of personal attributes, we limit our description to three underlying aspects of a mindset that become manifest in a variety of situational behaviors. These three aspects of a mindset are the topic of subsequent sections:

- The Great Engineers
- Entrepreneurial Mindset
- The KEEN Framework
- Entrepreneurially Minded Learning.

Only over the past decade, the development of an entrepreneurial mindset has been recognized for its tremendous potential when coupled with engineering thought and action. Around the globe, the fortuitous pairing of an entrepreneurial mindset and engineering skills has been recognized by industry, universities and their students, foundations, and government.[3] Organizations have dedicated resources to developing an entrepreneurial mindset through educational programs. These educational programs adopt a variety of approaches and pedagogies. The approaches frequently rely upon the development of specific classroom curricula, co-curricular activities, entrepreneurial-oriented competitions, problem- and project-based learning, and targeted experiential learning. In particular, the Kern Family Foundation has developed a network of institutions that aim to foster an entrepreneurial mindset in undergraduate engineering students. As a result, the foundation and collection of institutions within the share-group, the Kern Entrepreneurship Education Network (KEEN), have developed a framework for developing an entrepreneurial mindset in an engineering context. The description of entrepreneurial mindset, its applicability, begins with some examples.

II. AN EXAMPLE OF THE ENTREPRENEURIAL MINDSET: GETTING OUT OF THE GARAGE

When the electrical engineer and on-line retail magnate Jeff Bezos was building Amazon.com, Inc. in 1994, he chose to rent a house in the Seattle suburbs instead of a conventional office space. Why? According to reports, he wanted to say that he'd started out in a garage, an attractive notion that might have been borrowed from the collective lore around startups celebrating secluded inventors.[4] Obviously, Bezos and Amazon are out of the garage. It makes a great story for corporate culture, but it is inconceivable that massive retail innovation could remain in a garage for long. At least for an on-line business, the garage would have to be very well connected to the Internet!

In a very literal sense, innovations within a market must be *connected* with customers to see any benefit. Bezos has noted: "Start with customers, and work backwards ... Listen to customers, but don't just listen to customers – also invent on their behalf ... Obsess over customers." Bezos conveys the need for a broader perspective, greater than simply meeting the needs of today's customer. He recognizes that Amazon's connection to society is essential to the process of discovery, invention, and implementation needed for business success. And while the romantic idea of the secluded "garage inventor" might have been attractive, Bezos recognized that customer-focus first, followed by invention later, would be essential in pivoting when needed, continuously transforming one of the most ambitious and creative on-line retailers today. This might seem obvious for an on-line retailer. But the concept applies to everyday work in all areas, including Bezos's original field of engineering. In order to make a positive impact on society – whether through users, customers, patrons, taxpayers, or other stakeholders – one must begin with a connectedness to the world around you, an essential component of an entrepreneurial mindset.

III. THE GREAT ENGINEERS

The greatest engineers in history exemplify the need for an entrepreneurial mindset. Name ten great engineers. What do they hold in common? It's the type of question that has been asked in on-line polls. Familiar names percolate to the top of the lists: Nikolaus Otto, James Watt, Karl Benz, Nikola Tesla, Alexander Graham Bell, Wilbur and Orville Wright, among others. The lists of recognizable names can be quite long. Even given the short list above, the daily lives of billions of people have been profoundly impacted through their inventions, engineering, and commercialization. It might be presumptuous to suppose that these engineers could predict the enormity of impact on transportation, electrification, and communications – they have proved world changing. But an investigation of the stories associated with these names reveals their understanding of the value of an entrepreneurial mindset.

From the curiosity and investigations of the Wrights, who created a bicycle-powered wind tunnel, to the showy marketing campaigns of Tesla, the financial collaborations of Watt, and the patent races of Bell, these engineers employed an entrepreneurial mindset to achieve their ambitions. They demonstrated their developments to the public and potential customers while still in the early stages. Sometimes the intent was to get early feedback. And in many cases, their demonstrations stimulated an unfolding market interest. Understanding their market value, they raced to protect intellectual property by patenting key developments. And their patents only marked the beginning of seeing their ambitions realized or changed with the times. Based upon their pace of pursuit and the indelible legacy of their work, these engineers are models of an entrepreneurial mindset.

(a) Dolby: Business Strategy and Domain Investigation

There are, of course, many notable and contemporary engineers that have similar stories, bettering our lives through their work. Ray Dolby, 1933–2013, was an electrical engineer originally from Portland, Oregon, who changed the way we listened to music and movies for nearly fifty years through noise reduction systems. In "A Profile of Dolby Laboratories," the authors write:[5]

> The story of Dolby Laboratories, Inc. is in many ways the story of Ray Dolby. By all accounts, Ray Dolby is the consummate engineer and inventor who created and sustained a thirty-seven year dynasty in an industry characterized by rapid development. Ray Dolby, an electrical engineer and physicist, helped develop the first consumer VCR while still a college student working part-time at Ampex Corporation. Although founded in London, Dolby Labs was established as a New York corporation and then relocated its headquarters to San Francisco, California in 1976. For the next twenty-five years, almost every innovation in analog tape noise reduction would originate from the company's San Francisco and London locations. Through his mastery of leveraging intellectual property, Ray Dolby built alliances with the recording industry, reproduction manufacturers, and consumer electronics manufacturers that arguably exceeded Microsoft Windows dominance in the computer industry.

In a 2000 interview with Ray Dolby, he described how he gathered information through his own personal agency when developing what would later become an industry standard known as Dolby Noise Reduction (DNR).[6] One year after founding Dolby Laboratories, he aimed to demonstrate the merit of his solutions to Elstree Film Studios in England. But through an extended visit to this potential customer, he discovered alarming issues in the practice of recording and sound reproduction that might limit his success. "I was shocked during the couple of days at Elstree to see the appalling state of design, manufacture, and maintenance of the recording equipment. I realized that a lot of work had to be done cleaning up [their] existing practices before applying noise reduction." He began to investigate the limitations of the equipment that would have made his own cleverly engineered solutions for noise control inconsequential. As a result, he developed a deep understanding of the supporting equipment and how to make improvements necessary to make DNR valuable. As Dolby recognized, this type of information is only obtainable through direct engagement with practitioners. The ability to gather information that leads to decision-making insights would be a hallmark of his career and the success of Dolby Labs. Another hallmark of the company was the licensing of the Dolby(R) trademark for recording and playback equipment and media. Contrary to conventional wisdom at the time, Dolby licensed his technology to equipment manufacturers, making the Dolby symbol an element of the value proposition. The decision came from a deep understanding of the motivations of each stakeholder – the equipment manufacturer, the record labels, and the consumer. Innovations from Dolby Labs have impacted movie audio, surround sound, gaming, and digital broadcast television. Ray Dolby's entrepreneurial mindset enabled his industry innovations, both technological and strategic.

(b)   Heilmeier: Intrapreneur in Industry and Government

George Heilmeier, 1936–2014, was a Pennsylvanian engineer responsible for discovering liquid crystal displays, the basis for the device that you may be using to read this text.[7] Through his combined work at RCA, Texas Instruments, Bellcore, the Department of Defense, and the Defense Advanced Research Projects Agency (DARPA), he honed his ability to quickly assess the value of proposed engineering projects and take calculated risks when needed. He was not a typical bureaucrat. Rather, he was an intrapreneur who understood the importance of developing ideas into value.

As the newly appointed director of DARPA, Heilmeier was dissatisfied with the accountability within DARPA, which was recognized as the most risk-taking governmental research agency. His approach required individual accountability combined with a shrewd engineering mind. In an interview long after his appointment at DARPA, he stated that you weren't going to get a couple of million dollars from DARPA just by saying, "We're going to go off and do good things with x-number of graduate students and y-number of professors for a year."[8] That era was over. You would get your money based on articulating what you were trying to do and how it was done today and the limitations of current practice, and so on. Those were the questions that became known as "Heilmeier's Catechism."[9]

Heilmeier's Catechism is a set of nine incisive questions that should be answerable for any engineering proposal. The questions focus on understanding the created value. Demanding there was no jargon, Heilmeier would ask questions such as "If you are successful, what difference will it make?" To him, identifying opportunities for a larger organization meant there were expectations, understood risks, and accountability. Heilmeier worked for the agency as an intrapreneur with an entrepreneurial mindset.

(c) Kranz: Exploration with Determination

Gene Kranz, 1933–, is the engineering graduate of Parks College, now part of St. Louis University, who served as the Flight Director for NASA's Gemini and Apollo space programs. Kranz's determination has been characterized by the phrase, "Failure is not an option."[10] However, the risks associated with rocketry and space exploration were all too familiar. His long service included the tragic Apollo 1 mission and also the Apollo 13 mission that experienced in-flight mechanical failures. His mantra of "tough and competent" was demonstrated through his resourcefulness and persistence in the safe return of a manned spacecraft. Though he may have been on the ground in a characteristic white vest, his entrepreneurial mindset was evident in the way he approached the mission: *exploration with determination*. Today, the legacy of services, products, and accomplishments of engineering can seem commonplace and therefore ordinary, but they are far from it.

The work of the highlighted engineers, like many others, has produced extraordinary results. And while their innovations alone are remarkable, there's always much more needed to introduce and cultivate an innovation toward its fullest potential. What do these engineers listed above share besides ingenuity, a passion for technical development, and engineering skills?

IV. ENTREPRENEURIALLY MINDED ENGINEERS CREATE VALUE

Engineering is the application of science and mathematics by which the properties of matter and the sources of energy in nature are made useful to people. Engineering as a profession facilitates a career aimed at creating useful products, services, systems, and infrastructure. Within a modern society, engineering is a linchpin to providing a high quality of life. Engineering often builds a bridge between scientific discovery and utility – making scientific discovery viable, valuable, and available.

Fundamentally, engineers use their skills in science, mathematics, systems, and processes to create *value*. Value is determined by stakeholders and through forces such as markets, micro and macroeconomics, political will and legal processes, and societal needs and cultural views. Value is intrinsically connected to these forces and to the motivations of the stakeholders. The question "Why?" always elicits underlying relationships, whether technical or those related to the forces of value. In most occupations, satisfaction and effectiveness are highest when you know "why," in addition to knowing "what" and "how." As such, it is imperative that engineers, as fundamental value creators, understand their engagement with these forces in a highly connected world and competitive global economy. Undergraduate engineering programs provide the first opportunity to educationally engender an "engineering *know-why*" in addition to an "engineering *know-how*."

Higher education has an obligation to develop leaders. Answering the call, even the earliest western versions of higher education expressed this aim. Today, it would be difficult to find a mission statement that doesn't include leadership as a goal. Moreover, higher education toward professional degrees is connected to the development of *societal leaders that will pursue the well-being of society*. Accordingly, any particular profession will claim a specific type of leadership. For example, within the medical professions, higher education is developing leaders for physical and mental health; for legal, leaders for building a civil and just society; for sciences and mathematics, leaders for investigation, exploring, and discovery; and for business, leaders of exchange and enterprise. Fortunately, over the past twenty years, institutions of higher learning have reaffirmed that engineering education creates leaders that are not only technical but are leaders of *value creation*. As evidence, a growing number of entrepreneurship programs are now connected to non-business majors, most often engineering. The result has been a four-fold general increase in the number of entrepreneurship programs from 1975 to 2006.[11]

Higher education has the privilege and obligation of developing a student's mindset in a manner apropos to the area of study. In general, a mindset is the collection of mental attitudes and ideas with which a person approaches a situation. In the best educational environments, the mindset and specific skills are developed simultaneously. Because many professions have been developed over the span of centuries, there are examples of writings regarding mindset – some of which are incredibly enduring. For example, a medical professional may be required to take the Hippocratic Oath. While the Hippocratic Oath is an ethical code, it inherently expresses an overarching concern for the human condition, a key element in a medical mindset.

For engineering, various creeds, oaths, and codes of conduct have been recorded. The National Society of Professional Engineers publishes a code of ethics that originated in 1935 and is in use today for state credentialing.[12] In 1974, the National Academy of Engineers adopted the *Engineer's Creed,* a pledge regarding high technical performance and honesty. In 1966, a group of engineers in the U.S. Midwest established the *Order of the Engineer* which focuses on ethical obligations. All of these examples emphasize technical accuracy, ethical behaviors, and public service.

No one would argue with an oath toward ethical behavior or technical acuity. But these engineering oaths are not the way forward. The *creation of value* is the engineering leader's motivator. Value creation is consistent with the definition of the engineering profession at the top of this section. At present, mindset development within engineering education is woefully inadequate. The solution is to develop an entrepreneurial mindset within engineers. Entrepreneurially minded individuals have a keen sense of opportunity identification and value creation. Engineers who have an entrepreneurial mindset are leaders in their profession and their communities.

An entrepreneurial mindset is applicable to any context, for example in an established for-profit corporate environment, or within a new venture, or within a non-profit, government or non-governmental organization. An entrepreneurial mindset is applicable to any situation. It is an entire outlook on life. And when coupled to engineering, an *entrepreneurially minded engineer* leads society and the profession as the intermediary between science and application. Entrepreneurially minded engineers use their technical skills in an artful way, focusing on identifying opportunities to create value.

V. ENTREPRENEURIAL MINDSET

An entrepreneurial mindset is applicable in any context, but is particularly potent when coupled with engineering thinking and skills. Successful stories of engineering may be punctuated with technical developments, but they are facilitated through an entrepreneurial mindset. The stories and actions of each great engineer (Otto, Watt, Benz, Tesla, Bell, Wrights', Dolby, Heilmeier, Kranz) all illustrate aspects of an entrepreneurial mindset.

This section begins with a working definition for an entrepreneurial mindset. The three-C's characterize key behaviors of the entrepreneurially minded individual. The three-C's are: Curiosity, Connections, and Creating Value. There is a nuance to each behavior:

1. *Curiosity*: Demonstrates a constant curiosity about our changing world.
2. *Connections*: Habitually gathers information from many sources to gain insights.
3. *Creating Value*: Identifies unexpected opportunities to create extraordinary value.

(a)   Constant Curiosity about the Changing World

Curiosity is the desire to know, to see, or to experience that motivates exploratory behavior directed toward the acquisition of new information.[13] More succinctly, "Curiosity is the engine of achievement," comments educator and author Sir Ken Robinson in a 2013 TED Talk. While neuroscientific and psychological models describe why humans exercise curiosity, the result is learning, whether formal or informal.[14] Curiosity is both a driver and a behavior, an approach to a situation and therefore a candidate for a mindset. Seminal literature constructed a theory of human curiosity based upon an individual's motivation and behavior:[15]

*   Epistemic curiosity: The desire for information induced by conceptual conflict.
*   Perceptual curiosity: A drive aroused by mentally assembled stimuli, reduced by continued exposure.
*   Specific curiosity: Increasing knowledge through openness to ideas, future orientation and enjoyment of problem solving.
*   Diversive curiosity: Novelty seeking related to courage and sociability and negatively related to boredom.

The type of curiosity that is most aligned with the description of an entrepreneurial mindset is Berlyne's *Specific Curiosity*. The future-oriented individual is curious about the changing world. The broad term "changing world" refers to cultural, socioeconomic, demographic, technological, political, and environmental changes and trends with emphasis on the inherent connectedness.

(b) Gathering Information from Many Sources to Gain Insights

Insight is a deep and intuitive understanding of a person or topic and is largely individual rather than collective. This is particularly true of creative insight. You can't have someone else's "aha-moment." While an environment and culture may enhance creativity, a key concept to gaining insight is personal agency. Some engineering educators require their students to begin projects with a discovery phase. Students discuss their proposed project with 50 people before designing anything, digesting their results into a few key insights. Because of the dynamic nature of an evolving proposal, personally performing the interviews is critical.

In a study of the process to gain insight and avoid fixation, Jennifer Rudolph and her colleagues[16] presented a "garden-path" problem to a group of anesthesiologists. Each anesthetist was asked to diagnose a medical situation over a period of time. The subjects played an active role and could alter the process or request more information. Information was progressively disclosed which would first suggest one condition, followed by information that would likely lead to an alternate diagnosis. The study was to determine what type of behavior led to the quickest correct diagnosis. The expectation was that the subjects would form two groups: one that quickly arrived at a diagnosis by "exploiting old certainties" and another that would defer judgment and work toward a diagnosis by "exploring new possibilities." The hypothesis was that the open-minded group would fare better when, in fact, both of these groups performed the same. However, a third group emerged that performed significantly better. When surprised by inconsistencies, this group altered the process, requesting more and different information. The personal agency of the subjects was key.

Since the early 1900s, authors have written prolifically about gaining creative insight. In 1926, social psychologist and London School of Economics co-founder Graham Wallas wrote *The Art of Thought*.[17] It records his theory outlining the four stages of the creative process: preparation, incubation, illumination, and verification. The book was based upon his own observations and on the accounts of famous inventors and polymaths. Later, James Webb Young wrote *A Technique for Producing Ideas*.[18] Decades later, Arthur Koestler produced his seminal theory of "bisociation," which posits that insights emanate from two interacting "matrices of thought."[19] Bisociation has become an area of educational research. And with typical aplomb, Steve Jobs stated, "Creativity is just connecting things." He goes on, "When you ask creative people how they did something, they feel a little guilty because they didn't really do it, they just saw something. It seemed obvious to them after a while." Jobs's notion may not be very helpful to an educator who desires their students to be more creative and more insightful.

Contemporary author Gary Klein conducted some qualitative research about insight.[20] When he categorized 120 cases of insights, that is "aha!" moments, they fell into five categories of thinking with various frequencies:

- 82 percent   Making associations and connections
- 38 percent   Resolving contradictions
- 25 percent   Resorting to creative desperation
- 10 percent   Noticing coincidences
- 7.5 percent   Investigating curiosities.

Klein's methods and results are certainly subject to interpretation. An educator might conclude that a focus on pedagogies that develop associative behaviors would be most effective. However, associative thinking is largely dependent upon domain knowledge. For example, an expert in a given area will be able to perform more mental associations. With fewer dependencies on domain knowledge, educators focused on stimulating curiosity might yield the greatest gains in developing more insightful students. Klein's study provides a snapshot of insight.

(c)   Identifying Unexpected Opportunities to Create Value

Creating value requires action and practice. Engineering faculty members develop the muscle of value creation within students primarily through projects. In an educational environment it can be challenging to continually engage students in activities with a reasonable degree of authenticity. Many universities currently use external validators of value. The voices of local business operators and alumni in student projects add an element of authenticity that cannot be achieved without an external customer.

Opportunity identification has been the subject of numerous researchers of entrepreneurship. Of note, in his book *Entrepreneurship: From Opportunity to Action*, author David Rae[21] lists types of opportunities:

- A "gap in the market" for a product or service
- A mismatch between supply and demand
- A future possibility which can be recognized or created
- A problem that can be solved, for example by applying a solution to a need
- A more effective or efficient business process, system, or model

- A new or existing technology or approach which has not yet been applied
- The transfer of something that works in one situation to another, such as a product, process or business concept
- A commodity or experience people would desire or find useful if they knew about it.

It might be valuable to note that creating value differs from capturing value, as noted by numerous authors. The ability to capture value is often determined by ownership – and is the fundamental difference between an entrepreneur and an intrapreneur. Together, the intertwined three-C's are the basis for the entrepreneurial mindset.

VI. THE KEEN FRAMEWORK

The Kern Family Foundation is continuously refining a framework for fostering an entrepreneurial mindset in engineering undergraduates. The original work began in 2005 when KEEN was formed. Over the past decade, more than 30 universities have implemented aspects of entrepreneurial engineering, acting as a share-group. They share teaching resources, exchange tools, and relate best practices. With feedback from the members of KEEN, the foundation has modified the framework over the years while remaining true to the original charter. The most recent revision to the KEEN Framework for Entrepreneurial Engineering is shown in Figure 2.1.

(a) KEEN Student Outcomes with Example Behaviors

At each member institution, faculty and administration use the framework as a guide to developing course modules, the curriculum and co-curriculum, extracurricular activities, and even program sequences. The framework is not prescriptive as a specific curriculum or implementation. Rather, the framework is helpful in eliciting the distinction between a mindset and a set of complementary skills. Figure 2.1 shows a sample section of the framework with additional example behaviors associated with the entrepreneurial mindset. The framework is also useful as a guide for program assessment and the development of related instruments.

Figure 2.2 shows an expanded view of the KEEN Student Outcomes. Example behaviors are categorized into the definitional elements of entrepreneurial mindset.

KEEN
STUDENT OUTCOMES
EXAMPLE
BEHAVIORS
ENTREPRENEURIAL MINDSET
CURIOSITY
DEMONSTRATE constant curiosity about our changing world
EXPLORE a contrarian view of accepted solutions
CONNECTIONS
INTEGRATE information from many sources to gain insight
ASSESS and MANAGE risk
CREATING VALUE
IDENTIFY unexpected opportunities to create extraordinary value
PERSIST through and learn from failure
COUPLED WITH
ENGINEERING THOUGHT AND ACTION
APPLY creative thinking to ambiguous problems
APPLY systems thinking to complex problems
EVALUATE technical feasibility and economic drivers
EXAMINE societal and individual needs
EXPRESSED THROUGH
COLLABORATION
FORM and WORK in teams
UNDERSTAND the motivations and perspectives of others
AND
COMMUNICATION
CONVEY engineering solutions in economic terms
SUBSTANTIATE claims with data and facts
AND FOUNDED ON
CHARACTER
IDENTIFY personal passions and a plan for professional development
FULFILL commitments in a timely manner
DISCERN and PURSUE ethical practices
CONTRIBUTE to society as an active citizen

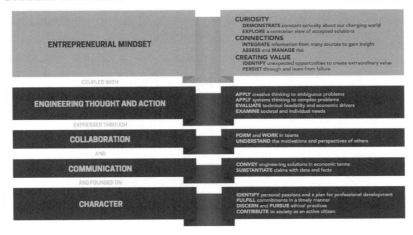

Figure 2.1 *Program outcomes for KEEN member institutions*

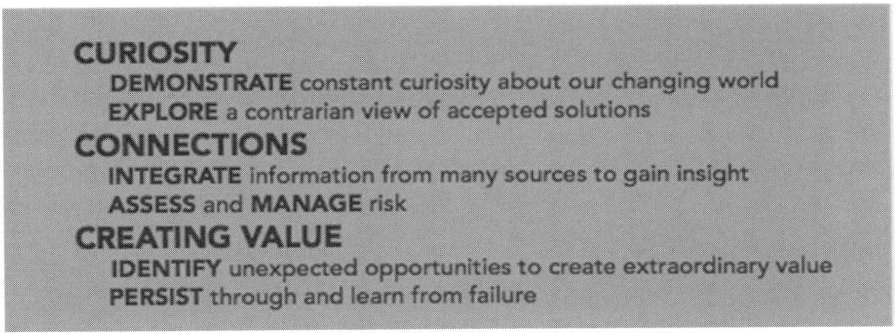

CURIOSITY
DEMONSTRATE constant curiosity about our changing world
EXPLORE a contrarian view of accepted solutions
CONNECTIONS
INTEGRATE information from many sources to gain insight
ASSESS and MANAGE risk
CREATING VALUE
IDENTIFY unexpected opportunities to create extraordinary value
PERSIST through and learn from failure

Figure 2.2 *Example behaviors associated with the Entrepreneurial Mindset program outcome*

(b) Complementary Skills

Skills are complementary and enabling in the development of a mindset. Hopefully, a surgeon has a collection of skills that complement a care for the human condition. A police officer has law enforcement skills that complement a mindset toward civic safety and rule of law. An engineer needs a collection of skills that complement an entrepreneurial mindset.

Some skills are listed as example behaviors alongside the KEEN Student Outcomes (Figure 2.1). In order to connect to specific domain knowledge, KEEN has identified a set of complementary skills shown in Figure 2.3. These skills are typically mapped to specific courses, modules, or supplementary curricular materials.

Figure 2.3 Complementary skills

VII. ENTREPRENEURIALLY MINDED LEARNING

Colleges of engineering within KEEN are redefining engineering education as the creation of value through the artful application of science and technology. These schools are fostering an entrepreneurial mindset in their engineering undergraduates. An emphasis on value creation is intrinsically connected to the *"why"* part of any engineering equation. Faculty members in KEEN now teach the *"know-why"* alongside the *"know-how."* Their work is creating lasting change through Entrepreneurially Minded Learning (EML).

EML is an emergent pedagogy. It can be found increasingly on campus and in literature. In an introduction to a thematic journal issue on the topic, Karim Moustaghfir and Nada Trunk Širca[22] wrote the following regarding entrepreneurial learning:

> Entrepreneurial Learning has recently emerged as a new practice involving both entrepreneurship and higher education processes. … Building on an educational case study, Rae (2009) defines entrepreneurial learning as learning to recognize and act on opportunities, and interactive socially to initiate, organize and manage ventures. … [Entrepreneurial learning] is a dynamic process of awareness, reflection, association, and application that involves transforming experience and knowledge into functional learning outcomes (Rae 2006). … Entrepreneurial learning is hence complex and interconnected with a somewhat ad hoc approach to formal learning and a heavy reliance on experiential learning (Warren 2004). … This learning cannot and should not be divorced from the specific context, including organizational context, within which it takes place.

EML is a student-centered pedagogy in which students learn about a subject through the experience of identifying opportunities to create value. Students learn both thinking strategies and domain knowledge. The EML format originates from a school of thought where engineering, business, and societal interests converge. EML encompasses all modes of opportunity identification including gap analysis, recognition of a mismatch between supply and demand, creative use of new or existing technologies, and newly created opportunities arising from societal and economic trends. One learning mode of EML redefines problems as opportunities to create solutions valuable for a new or existing market. In this way, EML may incorporate problem-based learning (PBL) as well as other pedagogies including project-based learning, experiential learning, and active and collaborative learning (see Table 2.1).

Table 2.1   Entrepreneurially Minded Learning

Pedagogy	Emphasis
Subject-Based Learning	Students learn in a variety of settings, but the focus is mastery of domain knowledge
Experiential Learning	Students learn through direct experience in a domain (learn by doing)
Project-Based Learning	Students learn domain and contextual knowledge from an instructional approach utilizing multifaceted projects as a central organizing strategy
Active/Collaborative Learning	Students learn through peer interaction
Case-Based Learning	Students learn domain knowledge and decision-making processes employed by experienced professionals in a historical case
Problem-Based Learning	Students determine the information, strategies, and domain knowledge required to solve the problem
Entrepreneurially Minded Learning	**Students learn to create value, gathering and assimilating information to discover opportunities or insights for further action**

The goals of EML are to help students develop methods of integrating knowledge, effectively identify opportunities, perform self-directed and continuous learning, and develop effective skills that support enterprising behavior. EML is a style of constructivist and active learning, and the constructs differ markedly from traditional classroom teaching.

Few literature surveys exist which describe EML. Further, most references relate specific practices and results rather than concrete connections to learning models. This is to be expected from an emergent pedagogy. One pedagogical model for EML begins by identifying a broad area of opportunity. It need not be stated as a problem. For example, the broad topic might simply be "human weight." In this case, one might imagine issues associated with health, whether obesity or malnutrition. Students work either individually or within groups. They first investigate the broad topic and, driven by their curiosity, narrow their attention to a *channel*. A channel includes a societal and economic context, including present-day status and anticipated trends. A channel may be as narrow as a particular market, industry, or customer. Conversely, a channel might represent a broad societal context. The topic and channel serve only as a starting point for an investigation that will lead to an opportunity.

Similar to following a vein of gold when mining, the investigation of the selected channel requires students to demonstrate resourcefulness in uncovering and combining information from many sources to gain insight into the next direction in which to invest their efforts. For example, students might gather information from family members and peers, potential customers, experts, current events, and repositories of research data. Continuing with the example above, an investigation of human weight might be simultaneously informed by both personal experiences and information available from the World Health Organization. In this way, students of EML learn to fluidly transition between 5-foot and 50,000-foot views of a selected topic.

Like PBL, EML students relate what they know, what they would like to know, and how and where to access new information. But distinct from PBL, students of EML aim to discover a new opportunity in the channel (e.g. market). Further, EML emphasizes the personal agency and social emergence of students. A student's sense of ownership is an important element of successful EML. When compared to other constructivist pedagogies, it is also important to note that EML is not a pure form of inquiry learning. The efficacy of pure inquiry learning has been a subject of debate.[23] Sole reliance upon students to recognize patterns and underlying principles from inquiries can leave educational holes and does not take advantage of a broader set of experiences or history. A skilled and experienced instructor is essential to EML.

The role of the instructor (known as the *guide* in EML) is to facilitate learning by supporting, guiding, and monitoring the learning process. The guide must stimulate a student's curiosity, assist students in developing solution strategies, and encourage the students to be constantly dissatisfied with their own solutions. The guide must stretch their understanding of all dimensions of the solution – and its role within the societal and economic context. That responsibility means that "lack of instruction" is sometimes as important as teaching. This mentorship role of a guide requires high-functioning social skills as well as domain knowledge. The guide may also be responsible for developing the necessary expertise, thinking models, and even network contacts necessary to explore the channel and arrive at the ultimate outcome of the process: a validated opportunity to create value. The learning process must include options for the students to *pivot*, pursuing a new direction when a channel is exhausted or a better opportunity becomes evident.

A word about the application of EML to the sciences and also to engineering: EML is unlike traditional educational pedagogies, particularly those designed for scientific education, for example chemistry, physics, and biology. Sir Karl Popper, professor and preeminent philosopher of science, wrote, "The search for truth is one of the strongest motives for scientific discovery." This is a well-understood characterization of scientists. The same idea was in *Roving Mars*, by Steven Squyres,[24] in which he provided insight on the differences between scientists and engineers working together on a Mars exploratory rover mission.

Science education naturally follows a model in which students "search for truth"; consequently, educational programs for the sciences traditionally emphasize elemental understanding of relationships and fundamental principles. The creation of value is not a grounding motivation for a student of science. Even so, it must be added that scientists are often naturally motivated to find opportunities to create value from their work, as demonstrated by innumerable historical examples. But the grounding motivation for learning and the educational process in the sciences is the search for truth.

Engineering differs from science in that it is the art of the application of mathematics and science to create value. Authors on both sides of the fence have appropriately highlighted the distinction between engineering and science. Isaac Asimov, prolific writer and professor of biochemistry, is quoted, "Science can amuse and fascinate us all, but it is engineering that changes the world." Within some engineering disciplines, the distinction between engineering and service receives additional emphasis. In a friendly "Survival Guide for Chemical Engineering" aimed at incoming students at North Carolina State University, Prof. Lisa Bullard writes:

> Engineering is different from purely scientific fields. Where chemists and physicists futilely search for truth, engineers realize and accept limitations and concentrate on what is practical. Upcoming students should be ready to be trained in this way of solving problems. An engineering education seems to be more of a way of looking at the world and putting it to use than looking at the world and trying to explain it.

Accordingly, educational models for engineering should be distinct from science. But at present, they are not. Within undergraduate engineering programs, the traditional model of education is through lecture-based courses that promote fundamental analysis, with a comparatively light treatment of design, much less an emphasis on value. This traditional approach is devoid of the intrinsic grounding motivation to create value. Exacerbating the problem, the process of engineering education esteems and rewards students who are predisposed to the educational approach used in the sciences. And the most scientific of these students become faculty members – creating a circular system with a predictable emphasis on the scientific method. How many introductory circuits labs are focused on verifying Kirchhoff's laws? How does a student who becomes expert in the analysis of free-body diagrams through traditional methods understand the creation of value? Within a statics course, how does a word problem about the analysis of the maximum bridge load promote a habit of mind around creating value? The dominant pedagogy is mismatched to the underlying motivation for engineering.

Why is EML needed? EML offers a paradigm shift from traditional teaching and learning philosophy. It further extends the PBL pedagogy that originated in the medical school of thought and successfully adapted to engineering. When engineering educators recognized a void, PBL was the quick and available answer. PBL has already impacted engineering education, by bringing more emphasis to solving problems. And within the field of engineering education, EML supersedes PBL by focusing on opportunities to create value.

Is there really a need for another pedagogical approach? Definitely. EML fills an important gap in the suite of tools available to engineering instructors. Emphasizing the creation of value in an engineering student's educational experience provides a much-needed bridge to a bright future, both for them and for the society they will inhabit.

NOTES

1. J. A. Timmons. 1989. *The Entrepreneurial Mind*. ERIC; B. Bird. 1988. "Implementing entrepreneurial ideas: The case for intention," *Acad. Manage. Rev.*, 13(3), 442–453; J. Autere and A. Autio. 2000. "Is entrepreneurship learned? Influence of mental models on growth motivation, strategy, and growth," in *Academy of Management Conference*, 2000; W. Gartner. 1989. "'Who is an entrepreneur?' is the wrong question," *Entrep. Theory Pract.*, 13(4), 47–68.
2. H. Zhao, S. E. Seibert, and G. T. Lumpkin. 2010. "The relationship of personality to entrepreneurial intentions and performance: A meta-analytic review," *J. Manage.*, 36(2), 381–404.
3. T. J. Kriewall and K. Mekemson. 2010. "Instilling the entrepreneurial mindset into engineering undergraduates," *J. Eng. Entrep.*, 1(1), 5–19; C. Lüthje and N. Franke. 2003. "The 'making' of an entrepreneur: Testing a model of entrepreneurial intent among engineering students at MIT," *R&D Management*, 33(2), 135–147; M. H. Polczynski and S. V. Jaskolski. 2005. "Entrepreneurial engineering education," in *Proceedings of the NCIIA Ninth Annual Meeting*, 17–19; V. Souitaris, S. Zerbinati, and A. Al-Laham. 2007. "Do entrepreneurship programmes raise entrepreneurial intention of science and engineering students? The effect of learning, inspiration and resources," *J. Bus. Venturing*, 22(4), 566–591.
4. "Jeffrey Preston Bezos (2014)" *The Biography.com website*. 11-Oct-2014.

30 *Embracing entrepreneurship across disciplines*

5. P. H. Williams, D. Isom III, and T. D. Smith-Peaches. 2003. "Profile of Dolby Laboratories: An effective model for leveraging intellectual property," *Nw J Tech Intell Prop.*, 2(1), 81–98.
6. I. Allen. 1975. "The production of wide-range, low-distortion optical soundtracks utilizing the Dolby noise reduction system," *J. SMPTE*, 84(9), 720–729.
7. G. H. Heilmeier, L. A. Zanoni, and L. A. Barton. 1968. "Dynamic scattering: A new electrooptic effect in certain classes of nematic liquid crystals," *Proc. IEEE*, 56(7), 1162–1171.
8. G. H. Heilmeier and A. Norberg 1991. "Oral history interview with George H. Heilmeier," Charles Babbage Institute, Center for the History of Information Processing, University of Minnesota, Minneapolis.
9. G. Heilmeier. 1992. "Some reflections on innovation and invention," *Found. Award Lect. Natl. Acad. Eng.*, Washington DC.
10. G. Kranz. 2001. *Failure Is Not an Option: Mission Control from Mercury to Apollo 13 and Beyond.* Simon and Schuster, New York.
11. R. Brooks. 2006. "Entrepreneurship in American higher education: A report from the Kauffman Panel on entrepreneurship curriculum in higher education," Kauffman Foundation of Entrepreneurship.
12. M. J. Holliday. 1994. "Ethical responsibilities of engineering profession," *J. Prof. Issues Eng. Educ. Pract.*, 120(3), 270–272.
13. J. A. Litman and C. D. Spielberger. 2003. "Measuring epistemic curiosity and its diversive and specific components," *J. Personality Assessment*, 80(1), 75–86.
14. J. Litman. 2005. "Curiosity and the pleasures of learning: Wanting and liking new information," *Cogn. Emot.*, 19(6), 793–814.
15. D. E. Berlyne. 1954. "A theory of human curiosity," *Br. J. Psychol. Gen. Sect.*, 45(3), 180–191; D. E. Berlyne. 1964. "Curiosity and exploration," *Science*, 153(3731), 25–33.
16. J. W. Rudolph, J. B. Morrison, and J. S. Carroll. 2007. "Confidence, error, and ingenuity in diagnostic problem solving: Clarifying the role of exploration and exploitation," in *Academy of Management Proceedings*, 1–6.
17. G. Wallas. 1926. *The Art of Thought.* Harcourt Brace, New York.
18. W. Y. James. 1965. *A Technique for Producing Ideas.* McGraw Hill, New York.
19. A. Koestler. 1964. *The Act of Creation.* Hutchinson & Co., London.
20. G. Klein. 2013. *Seeing What Others Don't: The Remarkable Ways We Gain Insights.* PublicAffairs, New York.
21. D. Rae. 2007. *Entrepreneurship: From Opportunity to Action.* Palgrave Macmillan, New York.
22. K. Moustaghfir and N. T. Širca. 2010. "Entrepreneurial learning in higher education: Introduction to the thematic issue," *Int. J. Euro-Mediterr. Studies*, 3(1), 3–26.
23. P. A. Kirschner, J. Sweller, and R. E. Clark. 2006. "Why minimal guidance during instruction does not work: An analysis of the failure of constructivist, discovery, problem-based, experiential, and inquiry-based teaching," *Educ. Psychol.*, 41(2), 75–86; C. E. Hmelo-Silver, R. G. Duncan, and C. A. Chinn. 2007. "Scaffolding and achievement in problem-based and inquiry learning: A response to Kirschner, Sweller, and Clark (2006)," *Educ. Psychol.*, 42(2), 99–107.
24. S. Squyres. 2005. *Roving Mars: Spirit, Opportunity, and the Exploration of the Red Planet.* Hachette Digital, Inc., New York.

3. Challenges in faculty entrepreneurship in the sciences: becoming an entrepreneur but staying at the university

Robert W. Brown

I. INTRODUCTION

Starting a company is a 100-hours-a-week endeavor and occupies your mind 24 hours a day, but a full-time faculty in today's university is … very much full-time, too! I want to describe one possible path one might take to have the satisfaction of doing both. In a sentence, this path requires a team effort but maintains individual pride and ownership! As a faculty professor spearheading a pioneering entrepreneurial master's program and an applied physics PhD program, I have advised or co-advised more than 50 master's theses, doctoral theses, and postdoctoral traineeships in industrial work, been closely involved with five successful startup manufacturing companies, and spent 33 years collaborating with industry. Based on this experience I would like to propose a viable path to becoming an entrepreneur without leaving the university and without an initial invention or discovery. The way along the path is facilitated by the training we have, the teaching we do, and the two most important words may very well be "former students."

In the present chapter, I develop a series of steps for the pathway of the faculty entrepreneurship anchored at a university, the "partnered faculty entrepreneur." My background history is introduced in the next section and the definition of entrepreneurship is given in Section III. The importance of an entrepreneurship education (Section IV) is followed by the example of our own master's degree program in entrepreneurship (Section V). I discuss ideas for teaching creativity and innovation in sections VI and VII, respectively. Section VIII contains the details of the foundation for our faculty model. Finally, the take-home (or stay-at-work) message in the form of steps proposed to establish a faculty entrepreneurship staying at the university is in Section IX.

II. BACKGROUND: TWO SCORE AND FOUR YEARS AGO

This section briefly describes my faculty experience over the past 44 years, which will provide a setting for the entrepreneurship model of the present chapter. It will show both the historical growth of the model and the seeds of its germination. We will revisit this history in Section VIII for details to help examine the generality of the approach.

It all started with a Big Bang. I received my PhD with a thesis in theoretical elementary particle physics, which we now regard as the underpinnings of cosmology, the science of the beginning and evolvement of the universe. Hence I could understand Sheldon's whiteboard pictures and formulas on the popular TV serial, *The Big Bang Theory*. These days the fields of cosmology and high-energy particle physics are subsumed under the general area of astroparticle physics. I strengthened my analytical, numerical, and programming muscles in quantum field theory calculations during the decade that followed graduate school and postdoctoral work. My teaching of advanced physics courses comprised equally important exercise machinery. Classical and quantum electro-dynamics classes were certainly critical lecturing drills. Such research and teaching technical training set the stage for my later and analogous computational efforts in industry.

I came to an industrial fork in the road at about the ten-year mark in my faculty life. Two of my former students, postdoctoral and graduate, were working at a medical imaging company, Picker International. Picker was an American pioneer in X-ray equipment manufacturing and was turning its attention in the 70s and 80s to the beginning of the magnetic resonance imaging (MRI) revolution. Electronic coils needed to be designed for the new MRI systems under development, for which performance analysis was required. My former students asked me to collaborate with them in the mathematical simulation of the coils, since my computational background put me in a good position to help out.

It was gratifying to put my theoretical basic research skills to work in improving commercial products, especially in the world of medical care. Imagining this would just be a part-time job, a small perturbation of a regular teaching and scholarship routine, I failed to take into account the MRI revolution, which was just beginning – and continues to this day.

Yearly changes in the products for Picker and other original equipment manufacturers (OEMs) required the regular repeating of physical modeling and mathematically optimizing the performance of the various magnetic field coils. As far as human resources were concerned, many more technically trained people were needed in all facets of the growing imaging world than were available at that time. So not only was there a lot of work to be done by our team, but we began to train new students at the university. We initiated an imaging graduate school course, especially for industrial personnel, and created a PhD track in industrial applications. The class has had a successful 30-year run with an annually healthy enrollment by students coming from engineering and science departments as well as industry. (They also come from our entrepreneurial master's program, which is described in the next paragraph.) More than two-dozen industrial PhDs have graduated, with various entrepreneurial bents to many of their careers.

Once we began collaborating with industry on research and development of products, opportunities multiplied: the number of companies interested in our modeling and optimizing approach grew and so did an interest in entrepreneurship. Various ideas for startups arose, especially in view of the needs of the companies that could not be met by their in-house resources. With encouragement and financial support of our alumni, we pioneered an award-winning two-year professional MS entrepreneurship program at Case Western Reserve University (CWRU). It is now in its fifteenth year of operation, with dozens of its own alumni (I have co-advised most of its 40 graduates to date). Students in this program have a capstone activity involving either an internship in industry or their own startup company. Section V is devoted to its role in our faculty entrepreneurship model.

In the 30 years of industrial collaboration and entrepreneurial activity, patenting has been a regular activity. One of my former students has estimated that our two dozen PhDs have their names on more than 150 patents, a number that increases monthly. Most of these patents are co-held by the different companies, including startups (see the next paragraph) with which we are involved, and eight patents have been co-held by myself. We discuss the role of intellectual property (IP) in our entrepreneurship model in Section VIII.

Our entrepreneurship history comprises six startup companies, where five are manufacturing firms. All five are successful in that each has lived longer than nine years and remains in a growth period. Three of the five have over a hundred employees and the other two employ more than fifty people: all five are successfully following business plans that predict

significantly larger companies within ten years. Each of these manufacturers is working on products early in its life cycle that have the potential
for order-of-magnitude growth. The influence of the startups on the
development of our entrepreneurship model is included in the discussion
of Section VIII. The take-home lessons of the case made for the faculty
entrepreneurship are laid out in Section IX.

III. ENTREPRENEURSHIP DEFINITIVELY DEFINED

If we are going to talk incessantly about entrepreneurship, we really
ought to define it. The idea of having your own business does not say
enough. Indeed, one dictionary entry[1] tells us that an entrepreneur is "a
person who starts a business and is willing to risk loss in order to make
money." The notions of risk and profit make sense, but how should we
reference them in our definition?

The first indication we may need to further analyze is simply the
problem of what we mean by "risk." One reads about all kinds of risk.[2]
There is "demand risk," which is connected to whether there is a market
for your service or product. Will customers really want it? There is
"technology risk." Can you do what you set out to do, or do you need a
new technical breakthrough? There is "execution risk," which references
your ability to recruit talent. And there is a "financing risk." Is money
available on acceptable terms? Besides expanding our definition to
include more details about risk, we know entrepreneurship is not just a
startup activity. The concept should describe some period of time from
the initial imagining all the way, we hope, to a thriving business. Should,
and can, all of this be explained in our own dictionary entry? On the
other hand, the entry ought to only be a sentence or two and not a long
paragraph!

Well, people in high academic places have thought about all this and
come up with a rather different definition, and one that's quite succinct.
A Harvard quotation[3] has been characterized as "the best answer ever." It
reads, "Entrepreneurship is the pursuit of opportunity beyond resources
controlled." An entrepreneur is someone who can take an invention to
commercialization, or can fully address some underserved marketplace,
only by obtaining the building and equipment, the product or service
distributional network, and the capital beyond what she personally owns
(frankly, I think she may very well finance herself completely and still be
entrepreneurial, but certainly it is usually the case that outside help is
needed). All of this has to happen before the available cash is all gone.

The statement about "controlled resources" distinguishes this new enterprise from established businesses in which resources are readily available.

The faculty entrepreneur exemplified in this chapter is a special case of the above definition. The faculty person who stays tethered to the university, but wishes to be an important part of a business, must be part of a team. Former students, former colleagues, or other people are integral to starting out. As we have emphasized, it is not possible to have a part-time stand-alone faculty entrepreneur. Thus a "partnered faculty entrepreneurship" as we have envisioned is *the pursuit of opportunity beyond the resources controlled and as part of a team effort.*

While the faculty entrepreneur works only part-time on the business, she sustains the effort. She may be spending time on the day-to-day nitty-gritty activities, raising money through grant proposals, meeting with all levels of customers or users, recruiting university students, advertising, and so forth. But this time would not be more than what a full-time faculty person spends on consulting as allowed by employment contracts of a university.

IV.   ARE ENTREPRENEURS MADE, NOT BORN?

Universities find themselves in two inextricably intertwined education revolutions, the online web-based course offerings and the education initiatives for active learning. Who among us has not heard of MOOCs (massive open online courses) or flipped classes? The MOOCs are attracting considerable media attention, but the flipped or blended courses are probably the model most favored by university faculty in order that the on-campus student population may still have live contact with faculty. In flipped classes, the roles of the traditional lecture and the homework exercises are switched. Students are asked to prepare at "home" ahead of time for class by watching a short video, or doing reading, on concepts, principles, and the like. The class then can use active learning with interactions among students and discussion leaders as they apply the new concepts. There is then the opportunity to begin homework immediately during class time. Follow-up work at "home" continues, of course. We see in this emerging world online tools being utilized (not just before class but also in class, too) to facilitate the transition from a passive lecture to an active classroom. Traditional lecturing is not wholly replaced: besides its role in the video-taping, it can share the class time with active learning.

We bring up new teaching initiatives because it has been suggested that entrepreneurship should be part of our children's education, even starting in kindergarten. At the heart of trying to improve learning is the goal of developing critical thinking skills (in place of a footnote, we may here define critical thinking as: (1) understanding the justification, connections, and relative importance of ideas; (2) constructing and evaluating arguments; and (3) learning how to address problems beyond what you have already studied). In science, technology, engineering, and mathematics (STEM) – to which we should add "art" (STEAM) – we observe much attention has been paid to how we can teach creative and critical design thinking. Nowadays, increasing attention is being paid to teaching entrepreneurial thinking. You can readily find entrepreneurial curricula, and faculty concentrating in entrepreneurship, in economics departments and business schools. As we have said, we ourselves founded a pioneering master's program in entrepreneurship, which is the subject of the next section, more than a decade ago.

This program fits into the "ESTEAM" panoply components envisioned by Nambisan[4] for a comprehensive kindergarten through master's degree ("K-18") approach to making entrepreneurship a part of all education. From the entrepreneurship definition in the previous section, ESTEAM should teach us how to discover and pursue solutions to problems (i.e., find and address opportunities or needs). Despite the inability to predict the future and the limits on our resources, we want to learn how to grow a new business. And we want our children to learn simple aspects of this as early as possible. Wonderful examples can be found in asking young students to ponder energy and climate issues and their solutions, which inevitably brings forth questions about how the solutions might be carried out with new businesses. Even in these elementary school years, it will be evident that art and technology and mathematics and, well, STEAM, will often be intertwined. As has been our own experience – see all the networking described in Section VIII – interdisciplinary work cutting across many different subjects rather naturally arises in entrepreneurship. With all these thoughts in our collective mind, a pervasive curriculum and a variety of internships and summer camps are contemplated over the entire school experience. We turn our attention next to our own "17–18" portion of the K-18 vision.

V. OUR ENTREPRENEURSHIP PROGRAM

Think of an MBA program with a high-tech entrepreneurial bent. Fourteen years ago we began a Physics Entrepreneurship Program (PEP) that had such a bent and went on to win a number of recognitions and awards. Like the startups we mentioned in Section II (and will expand upon in Section VIII), its longevity and evolution into a Science and Technology Entrepreneurship Program (STEP) serving physics, mathematics, biology and chemistry departments of CWRU speak to its success.[5] It is a robust ESTEAM contributor.

This two-year professional MS curriculum is flexible and includes a real-world project in innovation with an existing company or the student's own startup. Core courses cover state-of-the-art science and technology, practical business, and the how-to of creativity and technology innovation. The program connects the student with mentors, advisors, partners, funding sources, and job opportunities.

What are these core courses? Two year-long courses that are themselves innovative are Modern Science and Technology for Innovation and Feasibility and Technology Analysis. The first course strives for scientific literacy in a given track (biology, chemistry, etc.) and spends time on analyzing the IP behind major developments. We look at the latest and greatest in technology, try to understand new products and their components, and delve into the creativity behind the inventions. Because creativity and invention are such interesting and vital subjects, we devote the next section (IV) to the description of new initiatives and how-to-invent formulas discussed in the first year-long course. Whether or not a new proposal is feasible is a core topic in the second course. Crudely, students learn to be a lie or (expletive-deleted) detector. More positively, we look at the increasingly popular notion that innovation can be taught, another topic central to our entrepreneurship education and the subject of Section VII. A definition of innovation that could be summarized[6] as "something different that creates value for buyer and seller" is expanded upon and starts off that section.

Accounting and finance courses from the business school are also part of the STEP curriculum. Understanding how most companies fail by running out of money between the stages of incubation and commercialization – the "valley of death" – is an important lesson. Valuation is another one, where a primary concern of all entrepreneurs is studied: "How to charge!" We have our own examples of this question in Section VIII. Marketing and the need to be an effective salesman in every business, not just startups, are also scrutinized.

Students are asked to take a technical course or two in the STEP curriculum. We come full circle here because a popular course is the imaging class created in our own faculty entrepreneurship saga. The incorporation of our imaging course into STEP has had major repercussions, which are reflected in Section VIII.

Finally, there is the student capstone experience complete with thesis. She either partakes in an internship (90 percent do this) or starts a company (the other 10 percent). The internships are mentored by experienced people from the business world, and the corresponding thesis topic also comes from the business world. Much help is available in starting a company, including full marketing solutions comprising advertising, graphic design, public relations, multimedia services, and so forth. At graduation, the student has a firm idea of what it takes to be a CEO (Chief Executive Officer) of an early stage enterprise. When a startup grows up, it is often necessary to recruit a new CEO for later stages, but in our experience the original CEO has often had the street-smarts to remain in that position – see Section VIII.

VI. TEACHING CREATIVITY

We continue to develop the concept of a stay-at-home faculty entrepreneur who takes advantage of opportunities that may present themselves through industrial collaboration, often leading to an idea for a business without going "outside the box." But independent of whether or not we remain a full-time university faculty member, a separate question is how do we come up with the idea itself? It may simply be mothered by the necessity of solving a problem or by observing an unmet or underserved market. It may simply arise from the desire of an existing company to outsource or seek an outside source for a need.

But perhaps we want to create a new product or service more spontaneously? In the CWRU STEP program we are turning more attention to teaching students to be creative. In doing so we like the approach found in the book, *Systematic Inventive Thinking* (SIT) by Boyd and Goldenberg.[7] It is particularly emphasized that creativity "inside the box" can be taught; we resonate with having this phrase come up again, but here it refers to a formulaic approach to invention, not to our position inside the university, which is different from what we mean now.

SIT starts with defining the system or service you are trying to improve or take to a new level. To help us think about this, consider a desktop computer with a monitor, keyboard, mouse, microprocessor (CPU), RAM, internal hard drive, and so forth. These are the components of the system. To improve it we shall stay with these components and not consider any outside, unconnected components. What has been learned[7] by studying a large data set is that most and most effective inventions derive from the components we already have. This is staying "inside the box," where the solutions are really the creative ones; we do not go "outside the box." The outside world of components is "anarchy" so it is not clever and generally not helpful to just combine unrelated, separate systems.

Boyd and Goldenberg have fun with the famous metaphor for thinking outside the box, which is the usual mantra for coming up with novel ideas. Their argument is that it is actually thinking inside the box, and hence consistent with SIT.

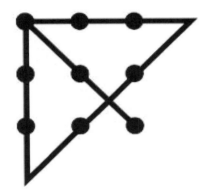

Figure 3.1   The nine-dot puzzle

Consider the square of nine dots shown (Figure 3.1) and the puzzle that asks how one can intersect all dots with only four straight lines that must be connected along one path. The fact that the solution requires the lines to intersect outside the box is usually regarded as a metaphor for the necessity to think outside the box. The authors point out an inconsistency with this interpretation. In comparison with one study, where only 20 percent of a group solved the riddle, another group was given further instructions: "In order to solve the riddle intersections of lines outside of the imaginary square should be created." Even with this help, still only 20 percent solved it. The lesson suggested is that it is not thinking outside the box that is needed but instead just using the original straight-line components in a novel way is the key. The famous outside-the-box example is actually an inside job! (By the way, the reader might have fun seeing how, if the dots have finite size and are not infinitesimal the nine dots can all be touched by three connected straight lines. The standard solution and this one are examples of the SIT formula coming up.)

In the remainder of this section, we will lay out the SIT formula for creativity and give examples of its usage. In SIT, we first make a careful and complete list of the components of a system we want to improve. We then use one (or perhaps go through them all) of the following techniques: (1) SUBTRACT a component; (2) DIVIDE (i.e., rearrange) the components; (3) MULTIPLY (i.e., add a copy of a component but with a new role for it); (4) UNIFY (i.e., make a new task for a component); and/or (5) CORRELATE (i.e., find new relationships or dependences among the components). (The reader should not worry, we will give examples to help understand all of this.) After applying these techniques, we are to imagine the benefits of the new system. And then ask, "Is it possible?"

The following real-life examples show the five techniques in action:

- SUBTRACT a component: The components of a detergent are an active detergent ingredient plus perfume plus a binding agent. Now subtract the detergent and you have a "clothes freshener" of value for people who want to freshen their clothes even if they are not dirty. This has become a $1 billion market!
- DIVISION/REARRANGEMENT: Move the AC motor component of an air conditioning system outside of the house to alleviate noise and to sequester its own heating. This is now commonly done.
- MULTIPLY a component: Start with a razor as the system and add another blade with a different role. Thus create multi-track razors where the first blade pulls up the hair and the second blade at a slightly different angle cuts it off. Note that adding more blades is not so creative (this is because they are not very different in their roles).
- UNIFY a component (i.e., consider a new task for it): "Captcha" is the familiar system to protect websites from computer-generated spam or viruses. It takes a human to visualize the word or string of distorted symbols. Now invent "reCaptcha," which recruits many human web surfers to help decipher difficult-to-read words from old books and thus transcribe hundreds of thousands of volumes every year. This is quite a nice new role! As an additional, quick example, think of hooking up generators to all the exercise machines in the gyms. We should assign this new role!
- CORRELATE a component (i.e., find new relationships; this is also called "attribute dependency"): Remember when Domino's Pizza related its price to the time taken for home delivery? Even though we know about the problems they had with accidents, even today Domino's stands out in branding because of that old campaign where they chose to relate the two components (which are functions here rather than physical parts).

For our purposes, the SIT methodology has not been necessary for starting a business. In our experience, a new commercialization direction has often happened spontaneously from the needs and underserved markets we have discovered in our industrial partnerships. Nonetheless, SIT is really interesting, most of our efforts can be understood in terms of its rules, and, we believe, it will be valuable in our and the reader's future entrepreneurial efforts.

VII. TEACHING INNOVATION

We actually organize our STEP teaching around the more general concept of innovation, which includes inventiveness. However, as defined, Edison and Tesla were innovators who were also system inventors, but Steve Jobs was an innovator who did not invent the physical systems at the heart of his commercialization. How do we define innovation? The hierarchy of idea, invention, and innovation is evident in the definition:[8]

> Innovation: A subset of creativity that involves the creation of a new idea, but also involves its implementation, adoption and transfer. Innovation and discovery transform insight and technology into novel products, processes, and services that create value for stakeholders and society. Innovations and discoveries are the tangible outcomes.

As an aside, it is interesting to notice the time delay between the idea or discovery and the production line. Consider a (very) few examples. Giant MagnetoResistance (GMR) was discovered in 1988, but it was ten years later when IBM rolled out products utilizing this mechanism. The E-Ink proof of concept took place in 1997: the Sony E-Reader and Kindle appeared in 2004 and 2007, respectively. In the art world, Beethoven gave an extensive motif development in his Eroica symphony, but the world had to wait for Symphony No. 9 to hear this development applied to the timpani and chorus. (In the SIT language, we unify the orchestral system to create a new task for the existing timpani and chorus components.)

The premise of our entrepreneurial MS program, as an actor in the ESTEAM theater, is that innovation can be taught (at various times, innovation and entrepreneurship are rather interchangeable in our discourse). Our mission is to impart fundamental knowledge needed to advance and analyze new STEAM technology, to provide mentorship outside (and inside) the core courses, but not to disregard the "10,000 hour" rule[9] (examples include the time put in by professional athletes, the

Beatles in the early Hamburg years, or any college graduate who worked an average of 50 hours a week for four years).

We may borrow an acronym[10] to describe the critical thinking about innovation in STEP. It is NABC, referring to Needs, Approach, Benefits per costs, and Competition. Needs are the problems that need to be solved. Approach includes the solution and the way we will establish proof of principle for the new product. The implementation of technology and networking is included in the approach. Benefits of the new commercialization – which eventually must be in the form of income, versus your costs in bringing it about – represent a significant part of the business planning. Is there competition already out there or quickly assembled to match the new "disruption" you bring to the market table? Are there alternatives, like hybrid cars competing with all-electric cars?

To NABC, an additional ingredient is posited, constituting part of the STEP educational text. One speaks of NABC plus Champion. The champion is an outsider – not an investor or partner –who will very much benefit from your endeavor or at the very least be very enthusiastic about it. An OEM to whom you will sell your product can be a champion. A government representative may see the value of the enterprise for her constituency – and lubricate the path to government funding or (increasingly decreasing!) earmarks. For STEP, NABC + Champion succinctly illustrates the way innovation is taught.

VIII. CASE STUDY: FOUNDATION FOR FULL-TIME FACULTY MODEL

I have now laid the groundwork – the entrepreneurship definition, the entrepreneurship education, and our own master's program in which inventiveness and innovation are studied – for us to explain what I believe is a viable life of entrepreneurship: a faculty person who remains full-time at a university but justifiably can be called an entrepreneur. My own experience over four decades will serve as details for the explanation. We divide the discussion below in ten parts: (1) the relevance of any professor's expertise; (2) the key roles of former students and colleagues in partnering with industry; (3) the "automatic" emergence of business ideas from industry; (4) connections to the formulas for creativity in SIT; (5) growing the population of former students and colleagues; (6) a role in startups; (7) patenting, publishing, and proposals; (8) working with the university administration; (9) tenure tracks; and (10) risk versus benefits.

1. Any Expertise is Relevant: Much as we tell beginning students, we should not make ourselves ill with worry as to whether a particular line of employment is best for us. If we follow our passion and thoroughly master any trade or art, it will most assuredly put us in position to be an entrepreneur somewhere sometime. In my case, I began as a theoretical elementary particle theorist with prideful accomplishment. In recent years, experiments conceived by my particle physics team have been successfully carried out in major Fermilab efforts involving more than 500 researchers from approximately 100 institutions and are presently also being worked on at the Large Hadron Collider in Geneva, Switzerland. Such basic research seems far afield from the practical world, but the relevance is the computer programming, numerical analyses, and analytical methodologies I learned that were important for my subsequent industrial work. Building up a reputation for accomplishment whatever the area was quite significant, too (writing a successful text in areas relevant to industry was also an effective reputation builder in my case – and with former students as co-authors). My teaching and mentoring activities were also relevant, and not only because of the additional analytical skills and expertise a teacher develops (in a class, a teacher may very well learn the most!), as I will indicate next.

2. Former Students and Colleagues as Partners in Industry: Probably the key ingredients for the stay-at-home faculty entrepreneur are the undergraduate, graduate, and postgraduate students mentored by her. In teaching the introductory, upper-class, and graduate courses, and in advising the undergraduate capstone as well as graduate master's and doctor's theses, the faculty person is making solid contact with future working partners. Indeed, while I was building a research expertise, I was growing a set of "former students." Two former students at work in industry recruited me to work with them on the improvement of an MRI coil. The skills I had developed in my previous work were well suited for the modeling and optimizing of this product's performance. Thus emerged a general pattern by which to this day my former students act as co-advisors and co-mentors of my present students. Rather than consulting, these collaborations are more properly called sponsored and regular research partnerships. Like the original basic research and teaching, the partnerships lead to more expertise, mastery, and internships for present students, to more networking among more companies, especially those in which more former students are employed.

3.   Automatic Business Ideas: Working with outside companies gener-
      ates all kinds of opportunities for faculty entrepreneurship. An
      initial university–company contract is usually addressed to solving
      a problem that has come up. Often the company has learned of new
      developments for which the faculty collaborator may bring to the
      table an additional, missing skill set. Improving existing products
      (or service), or analyzing a company's ideas for a new product, is
      another typical target. (We will consider the IP questions in such
      collaborations later in this section.) In hitting those targets, the
      approaches are regularly seen to be applicable for other products. In
      my own early experience, I was able to apply the optimization
      techniques I learned in basic research. One was a so-called inverse
      method where in functional analysis we start with the desired
      output (some quality like low coil inductance) and ask what input –
      what coil winding pattern – would give this output. (If you saw how
      complicated these patterns can be, you would appreciate how
      difficult it is to posit such patterns as an input!) I immediately saw
      many different industrial applications of the techniques leading to a
      variety of products. Our faculty–postdoc–student team has gone on
      to model products for a dozen companies. When you can build a
      good model of a product, you can then optimize its performance
      over the model parameters. A simulation of a product saves you
      much time. Instead of physically rebuilding a product many times
      to find better performance by trial and error, computer simulations
      can be run hundreds of times faster to find the best product. A
      simulation tool, however, is just one of many ways a faculty person
      can almost automatically see new business ideas emerge in apply-
      ing her independently based skills to a different set of problems.

4.   Connections to SIT: It is enjoyable to see how the combination of
      skills and products from different worlds fit nicely into the SIT
      algorithms. Recall SIT studies lead to the argument that true
      inventions fall into the subtract–divide–multiply–unify–correlate
      categories. SIT is a relatively new proposal, so our creative
      industrial work over the past 30 years has not been the result of
      starting with SIT rules and then coming up with products. But upon
      reexamination, we do fairly pervasively see connections between
      our approaches and SIT. For example, the optimization techniques
      fall into the "correlating components" rule in which the function
      (e.g., the inductance of a coil) is related to another function (e.g.,
      the magnetic field of the coil). The SIT pioneers rest their rules on
      two central principles. The first is what they call a "closed world"
      principle, which is the "inside-the-box" notion we mentioned

before. The true invention is the one manipulating the set of components you already have. The second is "function follows form" rather than "form follows function." That is, rather than beginning with a problem and trying to solve it, start with the desired solution and ask what problem it solves. This is just our "inverse problem" approach. In the future, we anticipate creating new industrial products by systematically following SIT rules.

5. More Former Students: As we expanded our involvement in commercial projects over the years, dozens of undergraduate interns, senior-year capstone theses, master's and doctor's students – and postdoctoral people who came to us for retraining – were aligned with our industrial partnerships. Many of the undergraduates who entered the job market immediately upon getting their bachelor's degrees and almost all the entrepreneurial master's and doctor's degrees went to work at the same companies with which we were partnering. Hence we were growing our valuable "former student" population. This led to a positive feedback circuit because companies began to see us as a valuable training ground for future employees. Everything fed on itself as other former students out in industry established ties to our university group to partner in research and generated new jobs for later generations of students. Abetted by a 900-page imaging textbook we wrote, and called the "green bible" of the field,[11] our research and teaching reputation continued to grow.

6. Startups: We now come to a description of our principal entrepreneurial efforts:
    *   A former student came back to team up with me to start a Cleveland MRI radiofrequency-coil manufacturing company about nine years ago. He had spent a half-dozen years with one industrial partner and initially came back to CWRU to direct our MRI research. However, an underserved market, our rich electrodynamics expertise, a deep understanding of quality assurance (hence the name Quality Electrodynamics or QED), and novel hardware development (e.g., miniaturization that falls under the "subtraction" and "unify" creativity rules in SIT) propelled us to build an MRI company with 120 employees (20 of whom came from CWRU) and many awards (Forbes, Inc. 500, etc.). I was an early interim president, but my former student was and continues to be the brains and brawn behind this entrepreneurship.
    *   Another mentee was the brains and brawn behind starting an American company to make the whole MRI system with

operations in Cleveland and in Chengdu, China. Besides my original role as a co-founder and recruiter of a half-dozen technical persons (all former students!), AllTech Medical Systems (AMS) referenced my faculty reputation and business history in raising substantial funding from investors. It has received more than $100 million in financing. AMS is also an ongoing sponsor of CWRU research.

- Investors came to me as a faculty expert for detailed reference and recommendations for building a new image-guided radio-therapy company, ViewRay, Inc. (VRI). After an extensive discussion (I was a "champion" for VRI in the parlance of Section VII), VRI moved from Florida to Cleveland, so that it could then hire the necessary MRI experts (including more of my former students), and now nine years later has successfully begun to treat cancer patients at several sites across the country. VRI has also partnered with CWRU in a major research grant to improve its hardware designs.

- The global market problems in obtaining helium have stimulated a new application of our modeling methods in designing high-temperature superconducting magnets that require little liquid helium (a forced subtraction in the SIT language!). We now have a partnership with another new company, Hyper Tech Research, which makes high temperature superconductor (HTS) wires. This has blossomed into new sponsored research and exhibits the potential for another new manufacturing company.

- We have designed and prototyped a low-cost portable malaria detector with four successive undergraduate senior capstone theses representing various steps in the development. This has led to a company that has won five entrepreneurial business contests in a row, where a former CWRU student provided the charisma, salesmanship, and time needed for an incipient business.

- By now we are working with a dozen companies and have a platform for business creation: "OPTIMISE," the Ohio Platform for Tomorrow's Industrial Medical Imaging Systems and Equipment.[12] And all of this started because of former students!

7. Patenting, Publishing, Proposals: What is the role of IP in all of this? In the past, sharing IP was the single biggest problem for university faculty working with industry. Universities are looking at this more broadly now, however, recognizing the value in nurturing successful businesses is on par with any need to have controlling interests in patents. Of course, faculty entrepreneurs should share IP

with the university depending on what facilities and funding have been utilized in starting a business. Startups need IP as they grow to protect products and buttress their financial valuation, but interestingly they may sometimes delay patent applications to avoid divulging trade secrets. This reminds us to note that, in the past, more data, details, and prototyping were needed to construct a successful patent application, but now? Well, it appears that the patent offices in 2014 are now looking for more general, vague, "blue-sky" (i.e., unproven) submissions. I also note, in passing, an entrepreneur may have to undergo a legal deposition (i.e., get mercilessly grilled by an aggressive patent lawyer) in defending her IP. I have gone through this and it is really painful, another entrepreneurial price to pay. But if you prepare for it like a final exam you can survive and learn to manage it.

We publish, eventually, all of our industrial work. "Eventually" means a small delay may be needed to give our industrial partner time for an invention disclosure or marketing advantages, but industry often does desire publications as a reputation-builder. As an example, radiologists who have input in buying medical equipment read the journals on clinical research in which the marketed equipment may be used and highlighted. Publications are also critical for successful grant writing and funding proposals. Grants were critical for my faculty entrepreneurship, coming from a forest of federal acronyms (SBIR/STTR/NIH/NSF/DOE) and state programs with my startups as partners. In several instances, I used my summer salary to pay for expenses for incubations, which was consistent with the grant targets. Funding agencies are generally quite enthusiastic about supporting new business and job creation.

8. University Administrative Challenges and Support: The entrepreneurial path is strewn with continuing systemic obstacles. Although the university faculty engaged in business faces many challenges, she can get help in many ways. There will be a potential conflict of interest between your faculty position and your company whenever you or your students do university research in partnership with the company. But a conflict management plan can and should be created by the university administration (typically, the faculty person must recuse herself from any purchase decisions involving her company, acknowledge her ownership in any publication pertaining to the company's products, and so forth). While a professor may very well forsake any salary and settle for a share of the company, it is possible to use the fairly widespread rule of one day

a week to consult outside the university to justify some remuneration. The ownership and compensation do have to be declared in the conflict of interest management.

For help with IP, apportioning shares in the company, writing a business plan, getting financing, and how to charge for a company's services or products, there are many business advocates inside and outside of the university available. A chronic sore point for faculty everywhere is the inability to get help in writing grant proposals, let alone starting up a company. University administrations generally are trying to put tech-transfer and entrepreneurial assistance in place to address these systemic issues.

9. Tenure Tracks: One more challenge for our faculty entrepreneur is – will we get tenure? Our model has rested on the idea that the faculty member first would build up her muscles and her network via traditional research and teaching. Only then is she in a position to identify an idea and partner(s) on which to build a business. This is consistent with the usual tenure schedule and historical subjects (e.g., condensed matter and astroparticle physics in my own department). Entrepreneurship will generally wait until after tenure is earned, as mine did. But there is no rule against assistant professors having successful business ideas, and we envision a day where entrepreneurship will be a standard tenure-track area in which to work!

10. Risks versus Benefits: Although we started with risk avoidance when we chose not to leave the university, an entrepreneurship may represent a career change (as well as the possible financial investment noted previously). We may no longer have time to keep on top of what is happening to the seeds and plants from our original career garden; faculty are likely reluctant to try any new career direction for precisely this reason. But the hope of the partnered faculty entrepreneur is that she will not be prevented from some continuing investment in her earlier work, and the venture will show benefits of a new kind. Learning of my experiences described in this section can serve to encourage faculty to pursue entrepreneurship, overcome the fear of career shifts, and leverage their skills to good effect. Partnered faculty entrepreneurship will encourage the business colleagues (my former students) and offer a unique perspective to inspire present students. I certainly observe a more positive orientation on their part towards this way of thinking as a result of these stories.

IX. TAKE HOME – OR TAKE TO WORK – MESSAGES

I summarize in this last section a career path along which, I believe, a faculty member can be richly entrepreneurial, yet remain at a full-time research or non-research university. Although there may be valuable training available earlier in your life, we confine our journey to the path taken during the faculty years. We go more or less chronologically, remembering the key ingredient needed for a faculty person to stay at home (i.e., at the university) is one or more partners. So here is a career path for you, the faculty entrepreneur.

- Obtain a tenure-track position. At present this corresponds in general to your having received a PhD in traditional STEAM disciplines and not in entrepreneurship – the university of tomorrow may have a very different faculty composition necessitating a corresponding change in this first step.
- Master a discipline anywhere in STEAM, noting that social science and art are just as valuable, training and graduating students as you go.
- Establish and support a network of former students, colleagues, and collaborators in scholarship/research, especially those out in industry.
- Promote ESTEAM through internships, business schools, master's programs, and so forth.
- Choose a commercialization venture from connections with industry, network, SIT, and so forth.
- Choose a business partner from your network (or have them choose you) who will lead.
- Get help from business people inside or outside the university, or online, to write a business plan, determine shares, manage IP, get financing … , and learn how to charge for your product or service.
- Establish a conflict of interest management plan with the university.
- You may be an interim president, recruiter, researcher, grant writer, advisory board member, for your company, but representing a sufficiently limited participation consistent with a full-time faculty position.

It is evident from my own career that one can be involved with a number of entrepreneurial efforts, but the more efforts there are, the less you yourself will be involved in any one of them. In any case, you will have the pride of promoting entrepreneurship and society, and helping to create new jobs! And if you do leave your old home (i.e., university) or retire, you have a new home to live in!

ACKNOWLEDGMENT

I am grateful to Ed Caner and Bruce Terry of CWRU STEP for their advice and sharing their business wisdom. I am likewise indebted to Satish Nambisan for his leadership, support, and ideas concerning ESTEAM. A summary preview of the ideas presented here appeared as "Starting Up But Staying Put," in *American Physical Society (APS) News*, January 2015, Vol. 24, No. 1, p. 8.

NOTES

1. http://www.merriam-webster.com/dictionary/entrepreneur (accessed on 1 Oct. 2014).
2. Eisenman, T. R. 2013. "Entrepreneurship: A working definition" available at http://blogs.hbr.org/2013/01/what-is-entrepreneurship (accessed on 1 Oct. 2014).
3. http://www.inc.com/eric-schurenberg/the-best-definition-of-entepreneurship.html (accessed on 1 Oct. 2014).
4. Nambisan, S. 2014. "Make entrepreneurship a part of education," *Milwaukee Journal Sentinel*, available at http://www.jsonline.com/news/opinion/make-entrepreneurship-a-part-of-education-b99214666z1-247680431.html (accessed on 1 Oct. 2014).
5. http://step.case.edu/.
6. Bruce Terry, private communication.
7. Boyd, D. and J. Goldenberg. 2013. *Inside the Box: A Proven System of Creativity for Breakthrough Results*. New York, NY: Simon and Schuster.
8. Carlson, C. and W. Wilmot. 2006. *Innovation: The Five Disciplines for Creating What Customers Want*. New York, NY: Crown Business.
9. Gladwell, M. 2008. *Outliers: The Story of Success*. New York, NY: Little, Brown.
10. Carlson and Wilmot, 2006, op. cit.
11. We have just published a second edition: Brown, R. W. et al. 2014. *Magnetic Resonance Imaging*. New York, NY: Wiley-Blackwell.
12. http://optimise.case.edu/.

4. Physics entrepreneurship: an evolution from technology push to market pull

Orville R. Butler and R. Joseph Anderson

I. INTRODUCTION

Physicists are not natural born entrepreneurs. Yet physics-based entrepreneurship plays an important role in innovation and the transformation of American industry in just about every sector of business. We derive those conclusions from our eight-year study of physicists in large-scale industry and our five-year study of physicist entrepreneurs. The History Program at the American Institute of Physics spent nearly eight years studying physicists in large high-tech companies, interviewing physicists and R&D managers at 15 of the top 25 employers of PhD physicists in an attempt to understand physicists' roles in industry. Our report documented the shifting role and nature of R&D in major high-tech corporations during a time when the premier industrial R&D centers appeared to be in decline, if not on the verge of disappearing.[1] Among other things we tracked the shift in corporate R&D from knowledge creation to knowledge acquisition. As it became evident that in-house longer-term research no longer drove innovation in the corporate world, we wondered where that new research was being done and how the corporate world acquired innovative knowledge. Of course some of the research came from research institutions – government laboratories and university research centers – but more frequently interviewees told us that university and government research, broadly speaking, was not ready for prime time industrial innovation. It still needed to be "de-risked" before it could enter the marketplace. Instead, our corporate interviewees told us that they most often acquired innovation from startups that had de-risked the new technologies. They said that only 10 to 20 percent of corporate R&D projects resulted in new products and that it was far cheaper to buy the de-risked innovations than it was to create them.[2]

Since the corporate world is now frequently relying on scientist entrepreneurs to create and de-risk innovations, we applied for and won a grant to study physicist entrepreneurs who were bringing physics innovations to the marketplace. We interviewed 136 PhD physicists who had started more than 160 companies over their careers and, when we interviewed them, were operating or had recently operated 91 startups. Thirty-five of those startups had received nearly $1.2 billion in venture capital funding, and 24 included some angel funding. Although we were generally not given angel-funding amounts, those who told us received about $19 million in angel funds. We think it's reasonable to assume that the total angel funding to all of the companies we interviewed could range between $25 and $35 million. Forty-five of the startups in the study had received a little over $150 million in Small Business Innovative Research (SBIR)/Small Business Technology Transfer (STTR) grants and 35 had received some other form of government grant. Fifty-three of the startups included substantial out of pocket funding by the founders. Again, most founders declined to reveal the amounts. Only ten of the startups we interviewed had received no outside funding. Forty of the 91 startups had been spun out of universities. Another six had obtained critical technology or been spun out of national laboratories.[3]

II. A QUESTION OF ENTREPRENEURSHIP

Who is a physicist entrepreneur? Is it a physicist who founds a company? One who manages the risk of that company? One who increases the company's value before selling it to the highest bidder? Why do they take on entrepreneurial activity? To achieve wealth? Bring new technologies to the market? Fulfill some innate inner drive? These were critical questions in our study of physicist entrepreneurs. We presumed that having a PhD in a physics-related field and having started a company were necessary conditions, but many of our interviewees told us that these were not sufficient for them to be called entrepreneurs. Whatever else might be said about them, the physicist entrepreneurs in our study do not fit many of the traditional notions of entrepreneurship, which have been recently summed up in Walter Isaacson's biography of Steve Jobs and include high risk tolerance, competitiveness, independence, creativity, and rebelliousness.[4] Many of the physicists questioned whether the term was even appropriate for them.

Less than 16 percent of our interviewees described themselves as entrepreneurs, although many who did not use that self-description talked about their entrepreneurial activity. Instead of entrepreneurs, they saw themselves as businessmen, scientists, academics, or scholars, but entrepreneurship was not the core of their existence. Occasionally some of them would admit that they had an entrepreneurial interest or sideline. Forty-four percent used the term businessman while nearly 32 percent viewed themselves as "academics" or "scholars" in spite of the fact that only 18 percent held academic positions when they founded their companies. Twenty percent saw themselves as physicists or scientists and 22 percent used the term "researcher" as a self-descriptor. Nearly 11 percent saw themselves as technical managers, while 9 percent described themselves as "engineers," an identity physicists are frequently given in industry.[5] Seven percent used terms we interpreted as meaning commercializers of technology, emphasizing that they were bringing technology from its scientific roots into the commercial realm. Three percent saw themselves as primarily inventors. Many were almost surprised to find themselves taking on entrepreneurial roles.

University technical transfer officials that we interviewed told us that physics departments were typically among the weakest science departments for spinning out new high-tech companies. Medicine and engineering typically led in entrepreneurial activity, but biology and chemistry also appeared to generate far more entrepreneurial activity than physics departments. Their physics departments made, at most, minor contributions to the entrepreneurial activity at the respective universities. Carol Mimura of Berkeley told us the physics department contributed "very little" to entrepreneurial activity there. "We haven't had a lot of inventions disclosed by physicists. I don't know if it is because the nature of the research is very far from being a commercial product, and/or physicists don't usually think about the commercial application of what they're doing." UCLA's Katheryn Atchison asserted that they had "about five active entrepreneurs out of physics." Other universities told us that the physics department's contribution was "none currently," "darn little," "very small percentage," "only a very small amount." Even at Stanford, considered a hot bed of entrepreneurial activity, a physicist entrepreneur told us, "This type of entrepreneurship is well established at Stanford. It is not so well established in the physics community, especially at SLAC, but it is very well established in engineering and computer science at Stanford."[6]

Those who used the "business" self-description frequently modified it. "I'd say I'm a bit of both [academic type and business type]," Shankari Mylvaganam of Sapient Discovery asserted. But she concluded, "I would be more of a scientist than a businessperson, if that's what the question is." Chris Myatt, co-founder of Precision Photonics and of MBio Diagnostics, decided he thought of himself "mainly as a businessman now, but I'll tell you I'm one of the most technically sharp businessmen out there."[7]

Some actively resisted the notion that they were entrepreneurs. "I don't really perceive myself as an entrepreneur," Dana Anderson, a founder of ColdQuanta, told us. "What I perceive myself is as somebody very interested in the welfare of this nation, and trying to evolve a technology that I think can play an important role in society, in the welfare of this country, have an economic impact in the very long term."[8]

Others found entrepreneurial activity to be the result of a change in themselves or their environment. One theoretical physicist starting his first company told us, "I just like the theoretical non-applied physics, and so I never saw myself as an entrepreneur. This was sort of a midlife crisis, so I just stumbled upon it." Another asserted, "I started out as an academic type ... and drifted into business."[9]

Many expressed surprise that they had ended up participating in entrepreneurial activities. "When I was growing up, I was going to be a professor or a scientist," Nathan Myhrvold of Intellectual Ventures told us. "I would have been very adamant about it." "It's not something I ever pictured myself doing as I entered college, and then graduate school," Robert Black of Civatech Oncology confirmed. "I imagined a life in academia," Philip "Flip" Kromer of InfoChimps put it even more bluntly. "This was kind of the last thing that anybody ... thought I would be. Nobody, least of all me, would have ever said that I would start a business." Ron Ruth of Lyncean Technologies asserted, "There was certainly nothing I had learned in my coursework that would have drawn me or connected me with industrial applications in physics, or how to do it even. I didn't have any sense of how to do it. I was pretty naïve about that sort of thing." Gang Chen, co-founder of GMZ Energy and a professor at MIT, asserted, "I never really thought of having a company until probably after I came to MIT." Many, if not most, of the entre-preneurs we interviewed, including some who by definition could be described as serial entrepreneurs, affirmed that entrepreneurship was not an essential component of their identity.[10]

Others, while adopting an entrepreneur identity, gave very specific definitions that many in the business and venture capital communities would find limiting. Philip Wyatt of Wyatt Technology Corporation echoed Dana Anderson's concerns about transforming society, revitaliz-ing the economy, and creating secure American jobs.

> [In] the old days, you come out of high school, you go to work for Sears & Roebuck as a salesman and you were there for the rest of your life. Not anymore. So I think it's important that we build companies for the long term

that have a security. It's the security, and also an environment that continually is exciting and challenging. You want people to be very excited with the work they do.[11]

For Wyatt, entrepreneurship was not, and never would be, creating a new company, rapidly increasing its value, and then selling it to the highest bidder. Instead, he argued that "a physicist as an entrepreneur must have established a successful company of at least a decade old and that was still going." Focusing on any exit strategy would, he claimed, "decimate an entrepreneurial venture very quickly." Adding value to a company rapidly to sell it and get rich was fine, but it was not entrepreneurship. Entrepreneurship was creating and establishing institutions, providing employee job security and protecting the long term economic interests of the community.[12]

Others saw little difference between being an academic physicist today and being an entrepreneurial physicist. Academic physics is no longer merely spending time in the laboratory and teaching classes. Professors often spend more time seeking research funding than they spend uncovering the physical secrets of the universe. William Bertozzi, of MIT and Passport Systems, asserted, "Applying for funds to do the research, that in a way is probably being entrepreneurial. Because nobody ever told me what to do. I was always deciding for myself what would be best in terms of science, and so on. So, it's a different kind of entrepreneurship."[13]

Others saw changes in academic physics, the decline in tenure track professorships, and the restructuring of industrial R&D driving physics graduates towards entrepreneurial activity. Max Lagally, of the University of Wisconsin, Madison, told us that with a 5 percent return on proposal writing, the traditional academic route, even if you could obtain a tenure track position, was "very hard and it's getting harder all the time. ... Then the opposite extreme is places like Intel and AMD and Applied Materials ... where you're just pigeonholed in some job that you do over and over and over again. ... A lot of people are saying, 'Hey, is there anything else?'" What else is possible except to join a small company with high risk or form your own, right?

No matter what their reasons for starting a company, only a few physicist entrepreneurs that we interviewed saw entrepreneurial activity as a calling. Physicists, it seems, are not naturally entrepreneurial in the business sense. Instead something happens to them before they engage in entrepreneur activities.[14]

III. ENTREPRENEURIAL GENE? OR LEARNED BEHAVIOR?

Scott Shane, in *Born Entrepreneurs, Born Leaders: How Your Genes Affect Your Worklife*, suggested that there may be entrepreneurial genes or inherited characteristics that influence entrepreneurial activity. While he subsequently admitted that it was extraordinarily difficult to determine which characteristics of entrepreneurship might be inherited and which might result from growing up in an entrepreneurial environment, he found in studies of identical twins and fraternal twins a higher rate of shared entrepreneurial activity among the identical twins and calculated that between 30 and 40 percent of entrepreneurial skill is innate.[15] Given that tech transfer officers and our other interviewees portray a comparatively low level of entrepreneurial activity in physics departments, we conclude that there is perhaps something different between the genetic or personality traits of physicists and those of classic "Steve Jobs" type entrepreneurs.

Max Lagally noted that the closer academicians are to pure physics, the less likely they are to take on entrepreneurial activities. "The guys who lie closest to physics are the ones who want to do fundamental research, and the guys that sort of weave away into little related disciplines are much more ready to do some of these other things." For most physicists entrepreneurship and business activity were not a natural calling.[16]

Given what appears to be physicists' reluctance to join in entrepreneurial activity, one might think that those that do would be driven by a genetic influence countering most physicists' preference for pure research and that physicist entrepreneurs would have strong family histories of entrepreneurial activity. But we did not find that. To the contrary, just over 27 percent of the physicist entrepreneurs we interviewed could identify any other entrepreneur in their family history and only a little under 6 percent identified strong family histories of entrepreneurial activity. Even more surprisingly, only a little over 12 percent noted a strong entrepreneurial environment growing up. Since most physicist entrepreneurs expressed some level of surprise that they had become entrepreneurial, it seems unlikely that they had a genetic predisposition to entrepreneurship.

Our interviews with 136 physicist entrepreneurs plus a few of their co-founders suggests that entrepreneurship, for them, was more like a learned habit rather than something that genetically drove them. Their interest in entrepreneurship was as much a mechanism to fulfill their role as a physicist as it was to build companies. If physicists are not naturally entrepreneurial, perhaps those that turn to entrepreneurship do so because they have become socialized in ways that change their attitudes and skill sets.

How then do physicists become entrepreneurial? Association with entrepreneurs appears, for many, to be critical. In many respects the descriptions physicists in the study gave for the process of beginning entrepreneurial activity appeared to require proximity to entrepreneurial activity so that they could become infected, so to speak. John Pacanovsky, of Triangle Polymer Technologies, recalled,

> I started thinking about it watching my colleague who was starting his company. I've kind of watched the infancy of his project and his business grow and kind of followed him through it and watched his progress, and learned to do by doing. I really didn't work with him; I just kind of absorbed a lot of the information he had to offer.

Pacanovsky wrote a proposal for a project with the Navy that was accepted. "At that point, things kind of fell into place to start working on an initial project. At that time it was when I really kind of broke off and started doing it on my own."[17]

Since only about 27 percent could identify any family member involved in entrepreneurial activity and less than 6 percent described an extensive family entrepreneurial history, we found most described their foray into entrepreneurial activity as the result of earlier association with entrepreneurship. As Qi-De Qian of IC Scope Research put it, "It's an acquired taste."[18] Nearly 37 percent of the entrepreneurs we interviewed had previously worked at startups founded by others. Thirty-eight percent had previously begun companies. Forty-seven percent of the entrepreneurs we interviewed had either worked at a startup or previously founded one. More significantly, nearly 63 percent of the companies where we interviewed – 57 of the 91 – had at least one founding physicist member who had either previously worked at a startup or started a company. Presumably many of those who had previously started companies had done so in partnership with someone who had entrepreneurial experience. Since we did not interview most of the non-physicist co-founders, we presume that an even greater percentage contained founders who had infected them with entrepreneurial excitement and at least some of the requisite knowledge. If this is so, then it does appear that for physicists entrepreneurship is an acquired taste spread through close association with other entrepreneurs.

IV. ENTREPRENEURIAL PUSH AND PULL

We broadly classified the 91 companies in the study into "technology-push," "market-pull," and "service" companies. Forty-nine of the 91 startups were founded to bring new technologies, often based on the scientific research of one of the founders, to the marketplace. The 35 market-pull companies typically applied well-known principles of physics to create a solution to a market bottle-neck or to increase technological performance. They were created in response to perceived market demands. Seven service companies provided services – either research or consulting – that emphasized the skills and talents of the founders. While they might help with product development, their product was their knowledge and research capabilities. A few companies claimed to be pushing new technologies but their track record and dependence on SBIR funding suggested they might actually be service companies. Entrepreneurial motivation and the skills of the physicist entrepreneurs varied depending on the type of company they founded.

The physicist entrepreneurs we interviewed tended to enter the market enamored with the ability of technology to impact and change society for the better. Through extended engagement with their particular market, they evolve to a better understanding of the needs of the market and slowly shift from a view that physicist entrepreneurs can change the world to one in which they serve some set of customers providing technological answers to at least some customer needs. Early physicist entrepreneurs tend to enter the market driven by their technology, but they thrive in that market by responding to customer desires and insights. As a result, physicist entrepreneurs either shift towards playing a scientist/technologist in their company and delegating broader entrepreneurial activity to associates or they evolve away from physics and become more business oriented. First time entrepreneurs tend to be what we call technology-push entrepreneurs. Those with more extended entrepreneurial activity are increasingly likely to found market-pull companies.

V. TECHNOLOGY-PUSH ENTREPRENEURS

Entrepreneurial activity for most physicists appears to be a means to another end, rather than an end in itself. Mary Fuka, then of TriplePoint Physics, and now founder of Enphysica, who had previously co-founded three other companies, asserted that most physicists did not go into business because they wanted to or that they "love to make a lot of money." Rather they went into it because, as she put it, "This is the way that I can make this thing happen." Henrique Tono of Ingrain agreed:

My heart really lies in designing instrumentation and things of that order, but my career has taken me into a business focus that I'm not particularly proud of, I have to admit, and I'm not particularly pleased with. It has become a means to getting somewhere and doing something that otherwise I couldn't do.

What "this thing" was often depended on how the physicists viewed themselves. Motives for establishing companies varied wildly, but few, if any, started companies merely to be starting business ventures.[19]

Like a virus which fundamentally changes its host, many physicists described fundamental changes in their perspectives and outlooks as they evolved as entrepreneurs. Many physicists described their entrepreneurial experience as transformative. "I changed," Nicholas Economou told us. "I started out as a technical person sort of with academic interests, but sort of evolved into more of a business focus." As Economou described the process, he said that as he became more associated with startups while doing basic research at Bell Labs and later at Lincoln Laboratory: "I saw a lot of interesting technology. Just the idea of starting a company sounded like fun."[20]

Technology-push entrepreneurs' identity was frequently tied to their research and the technology derived from it. They often lacked a financial motive, focusing on increasing the impact that their technological innovation might have on business or society instead of focusing on the establishment and increased value of the company they founded to commercialize their technology and make money. Ron Ruth asserted that none of the founders of Lyncean Technologies "would have done something that was just oriented towards making money." Instead "we'd had this idea that making an impact, a broad impact on science and society was really, you know, fundamentally important and that that sort of meshed with our, with our career goals." His co-founder Rod Loewen agreed: "It's not about turning a company over and getting it sold and then going on to the next project. That's not my motivation." Tom Lee, whose SA Ignite was the fourth company he founded, asserted, "For me the financial side alone is not enough. I like to create something from nothing."[21]

Some physicists took on the entrepreneurial mantel because they wanted their research and the technologies they had developed to make a real-world difference. John Criscione, for example, asserted: "It really never occurred to me that I'd want to do entrepreneurship ever. It just was never on my list of things to do." But his perspective changed when his university's technology transfer office told him that the odds of his technology successfully transitioning to the market were minimal unless he started a company. He concluded,

> I consider myself certainly an academic ... I would never call myself a businessman. ... [but] I guess entrepreneur is the best word for it because what I want to do is change people's lives. I want to get the technology used. I don't want it to be [just] a nice article in a publication somewhere.[22]

What really moves technology-push physicist entrepreneurs is the technology or the science behind that technology and a belief that it can greatly impact the world, changing people's lives. The focus of technology-push physicist entrepreneurs differs from entrepreneurs generally. For these physicist entrepreneurs the focus is on building and commercializing their technology – frequently a technology derived from their own scientific research. Mary Fuka, of TriplePoint Physics, asserted: "I've known a lot of business people who are really motivated by business and money, and they don't really care what their product is. They might have a specialty, but what really moves them is the business end." Jason Cleveland, of Asylum Research, contrasted his own view: "I'm definitely still a scientist and building instruments is what I enjoy doing. But for me the business part is something that has to be done to sort of accomplish the other goals that I have."[23]

More frequently than for the market-pull entrepreneurs, technology-push entrepreneurs began their companies with the core founders being primarily scientists and technicians who understood their technology. Some regretted this early emphasis on scientific co-founders and failure to include co-founders with complementary skills. One told us that in an earlier startup he had "made the mistake partnering with some other physicists who were equally interested in trying something new, and that didn't go anywhere."[24]

Technology-push entrepreneurs also placed far less emphasis on the business and market aspects of the company. If this was their first startup they might assume a "if we build it, they will come" attitude, something several physicist entrepreneurs recalled in their lessons learned from earlier startups. Tom Lee, of SA Ignite, asserted of one of his earlier companies, "You build it and they will not come." In his later companies he shifted more to a market-pull perspective. As he put it, "You sell it first, they will come, and then you build ... what you sold." Richard Selinfreund of Companion Diagnostics recalled:

A lot of times in physics what you're doing is looking for the huge commercial fit for your product, and you're never smart enough, you're never trained to go look for it. You have to go find it. And a lot of times when you find that commercial fit, it's an accident.

Some even regretted having to "sell out" when business success came in applications that had social impacts they did not value highly. They struggled to justify their involvement. Selinfreund asserted,

I lied to myself and said it was okay to just stuff our pockets with cash and go with things that the world really wanted instead of what a physicist really wants to do, which is to do things that the world really doesn't want. I'll have to tell you, I'm struggling with it today.[25]

Unlike market-pull companies responding to a market need with a well-established technology, technology-push companies had to find or create the markets for their product. Yet because of their focus on developing the technology they often delayed the marketing aspect of the company. Without well-defined markets the notion of customers with whom they could interact was equally ill defined. Many relied on SBIR programs and other government research programs to fund the development of their technologies. Too frequently the government contractor became the "customer" in the technology-push companies' minds and research replaced product development and a search for markets as the driving force of business. Others marketed to a limited niche market that sustained the company but provided relatively little room for growth. Many had to evolve in ways that would strengthen the business component of the startup or limit their market to customers they already understood. As a result many physicist-founded startups have relatively slow growth patterns. Several physicist entrepreneurs told us that they expected their companies would never grow beyond $20 to $40 million a year. They had no problems with that but realized that it also barred them from venture capital resources to start or sustain their companies. For many that, too, was a good thing. Matt Kim of QuantTera told us, "I wanted to build a company where I could really do something, make some contributions. ... With venture capital, sometimes you don't do that. You do what makes money in terms of cash return instead of what makes a good product."[26]

Because their devotion to the technology took precedence over a concern for markets, technology-push startups would devote extended time to perfecting their product. Rod Loewen of Lyncean Technologies told us Lyncean's plan was to have a product "ready to be commercialized so we could just turn out another one." But because of recent scientific and technological advances, "It took a couple years we'd say commissioning, which is actually getting everything to work the way we want. But now we've spent still another couple more years really enhancing, trying to get the performance up to the values that we think it can have." Co-founder Ron Ruth concluded: "I think that, actually, industry could benefit from physicists, but physicists probably could benefit just as much from understanding what it is that happens in the marketplace."[27]

Despite their focus on the technology, many physicist entrepreneurs talked about a shift towards a more business orientation. Michael Naughton, of Boston College and Solasta, told us that he had "morphed into some combination" of academic and businessman. "I have absolutely zero training in business or entrepreneurship, but I think those are largely driven by common sense." He declared that it was important "not to be like the traditional scientist, which is basically what we've started as, meaning completely oblivious to all matters of money. It doesn't pay to be completely oblivious. It pays to just use common sense and smarten up about it."[28]

Many, if not most, of the technology-push entrepreneurs, who devoted full time to their startup, remained focused on developing their technology and either downplayed the business aspects or sought a business partner to manage that aspect of the startup. Robert Black of Civatech Oncology relied on his spouse to handle important business aspects of the company. Even so, he told us: "You can't just go out on a wing and a prayer hoping to avail society of your great work. It's a serious enterprise and you have to use the skills that you've learned to address all these aspects."[29] Physicists who wanted to remain "physicists" increasingly turned their business functions over to others. Robert Fischell, who over his career had begun 14 companies, declared that his role had changed in the last 7 companies. "When I start a new company I'm CEO, and I replace myself as soon as possible so I can go back to the inventing mode, and sometimes the application of physics principles to what we are doing."

Other technology-push entrepreneurs tried to limit their role to the early startup stages of their companies. Once the technology had been established as marketable they, like Robert Fischell, turned the operation of their companies over to others. Henrique Tono, who when we interviewed him was with his fourth startup, told us that a critical part of it was the creative process often associated with academia rather than business. He loved starting companies. "Starting a company is all about having a vision about putting together different pieces of the puzzle to make that happen," he asserted. But once he made that vision a reality and put together a team that could accomplish that he told us, "The day-to-day running of the operation bores me to tears – talking to investors, going out there and running the P&Ls and the balance sheets and that kind of a thing is total drudgery."[30]

The driving force and focus of the business for the technology-push companies was their innovative technology, and, at least initially, they presumed the market would find them. Customers tended to be viewed as a natural outgrowth of a society in awe of the new technology. Eventually technology-push companies had to address the market and customers if they were to survive. Sometimes they succeeded in creating a new market, but the technology rather than the market or customer remained the driving motivation for the business. As their technologies entered the market, customers took on greater importance, but for most technology-push entrepreneurs, adaptation to the market and refocusing on the customer was a painful process.

VI. MARKET-PULL ENTREPRENEURS

Unlike technology-push entrepreneurs, who form companies to bring a new technology to an ill-defined market, market-pull entrepreneurs engage the market prior to the founding of the company. Market-pull startups can be subdivided into true market-pull companies that develop a product as a response to an existing market need, service companies that provide skilled consulting services or R&D/product development services as a niche specialty, and lifestyle companies that focus on customers and market needs but are primarily vehicles to provide the founders with the ability to live in a location and have a lifestyle that they prefer. In contrast to their technology-push counterparts, market-pull entrepreneurs begin by engaging their potential customers and drive the technological innovations to customer demand. Frequently, market-pull entrepreneurs begin their companies because potential customers want products they have made in a non-business capacity. A few professors in the study founded market-pull startups in response to requests by other researchers for them to make equipment they had constructed for their own research. Henry Kapteyn, for example, told us Kapteyn-Murnane labs began manufacturing femtosecond lasers because:

> Enough people asked us how to duplicate it, and we wrote something up with even shop diagrams to make the thing. But then we started getting a lot of people asking us, "Well, [are] you going to start a company so that we can just buy this stuff instead of having to build it ourselves?"[31]

Those outside of academia generally had been employed in industry, sometimes at startups where they found ways to improve on existing technologies. Unlike technology-push entrepreneurs seeking markets for their creations, market-pull entrepreneurs create products in response to the market. Because market-pull entrepreneurs are actively engaged in the marketplace, they are even more likely to have been involved in the entrepreneurial community prior to the founding of their company. Two critical characteristics make up the market-pull physicist entrepreneurs. Unlike most technology-push entrepreneurs, they are less emotionally tied to the technology they are creating. Frequently they are applying an off-the-shelf technology in a new way.

Market-pull founders also tend to have longer histories of entrepreneurial activity during which they have evolved from researcher to businessman. Ningyi Luo recalled that during his work for a startup in 1994 the founder always urged him to pay less attention to the "scientific things that have no direct impact" and to focus instead on "something that has more direct benefit of the user and the company." Over time, he asserted this influenced himself and "started realizing we have to be more practical ... we have to have more specific deliverable goals." His co-founder of Pavilion Integration, Lindsay Austin, recalled a similar transformation. "At some point I realized that I was more interested in the business side than I was in being a researcher." The beginning of Pavilion Integration, Austin told us, "was a convergence of what could technology do, what's the market need? ... There was no research ever done."[32]

Frank Levinson, a co-founder of Finisar and now a venture capitalist, recalled: "It's easy to get entranced by the science, but starting companies is about starting a business. It's about making a profit. It's about having customers." For market-pull companies, creating the business takes priority, and the customer takes precedence over the technology. For most the business was created either in direct response to a market demand, or as a solution to a niche problem recognized by the founders. Dhruv Bansel of InfoChimps told us: "We didn't start out really as a business; we started out as a nonprofit service that we would build so that scientists could share data, and it just kind of really grew from there and became what it is today." Shortly after founding the company the InfoChimps founders entered an entrepreneurial contest where the winners would become part of a seed-stage incubator in Austin, Texas. While they did not win, they had extensive interaction with the entrepreneurs running that program, which helped them to transform from a solution to a data-sharing problem to a successful big data entrepreneurial venture. Whether they are first time entrepreneurs or seasoned professionals, market-pull entrepreneurs are driven by the market demand to establish their company.[33]

We defined a subset of market-pull entrepreneurs as "lifestyle" entre-preneurs. Lifestyle entrepreneurs may provide customers with either a service or a product. Like other market-pull entrepreneurs, their business is more likely to be driven by customers and market demand than by some unique technological contribution. However, they did not start their business to fill a market need. Instead they, at least initially, entered business for the freedoms it provided them. They are customer and market focused, but their motive for entering the marketplace was not the customer; nor did they, like the technology-push entrepreneurs, envision changing the world. Rather they engaged in entrepreneurship because it provided them with the ability to live where they wanted to live with a lifestyle with which they felt comfortable. They entered business to provide them with greater control over their life. They found a market which their business could accommodate in ways that satisfied them personally. Bill O'Brien of Mad City Labs told us:

> Our philosophy has always been we're here to create a lifestyle for ourselves, to be in control of our own destiny, to do what we love to do, and that's about it. Maybe someday there will be the big cash-out, but I'm not holding my breath for it, and if it doesn't happen I'm perfectly happy.[34]

Similar to the lifestyle entrepreneurs, service entrepreneurs rarely brought a new technology to the market. Instead they frequently provided a service – a job shop, research service, or similar function – that depended greatly on skills they had learned as physicists – their product remained their skills and specialized knowledge rather than a tangible technology or knowledge. Several readily admitted that they were life-style companies with little concern for the perpetuation of the company beyond the work life of the founders. As such they might introduce and develop new technologies to the marketplace while doing contract research or consulting, but those technologies did not typically derive from fundamental scientific research of one or more of the founders. Frequently service entrepreneurs provided consulting services either to the government or to industry. Their product was their skills and their customers were those needing to use their skills.

In many respects service and lifestyle entrepreneurs are perhaps both the least and the most entrepreneurial of physicist entrepreneurs. Their reasons for going into business were defined by self-interest: to secure themselves employment or to provide skilled R&D for a broad range of corporate and government entities. Quartek, founded by Reyad Sawafta, found a business niche in providing product development for corporations and startups – a niche once filled by corporate labs. "Our philosophy," Sawafta told us, "is to develop technology and find partners who are leaders in that field and team up with them. ... We present to them the idea of the technology. If they like it, then they come and share and provide some funding to take this technology further." Sawafta told us that his firm took product development to "within months to a year of commercialization by a partner. We get, in exchange for that research, support." Unlike a stand-alone product developer, he never manufactured or marketed the final product and so could specialize in his R&D skills. Others such as G. Gordon MaClay, of Quantum Fields, and Darrell Conway, of Thinking Systems, formed their companies in order to support their consulting activities with NASA, other government organizations, and industry.[35]

A few of the companies that we classified as technology-push companies appeared to approximate service companies over time. Initially they entered the marketplace to change the world with their particular technology. They often depended on SBIR grants to fund their research and technology development. Over time, however, some technology-push companies either were unable to move their technology to the marketplace or at least had not yet found a sustainable market. As a result they continued to fund their operations through contract research and continued SBIR grant proposals that increasingly diverged from the technology they originally sought to introduce. Instead of product development focused on their research skills, to survive long after reliance on a product based on their original reason for entrepreneurial activity would have forced them out of business. Technically they were still in a development stage, but one wondered if those companies would ever transition to a product/manufacturing stage or raise their technology to a level that a manufacturer would want to acquire.

VII. PREPARING PHYSICISTS FOR ENTREPRENEURSHIP

Since most physicists in the study did not plan to become entrepreneurs it is perhaps not surprising that only one of our interviewees had taken an entrepreneurship course that led to their entrepreneurial activity. The physicist, Rod Loewen, took a course called Evaluating Entrepreneurial Opportunities at Stanford while he was working on his doctorate at SLAC. He told us that the course opened a new world to him "that most people will never even see at SLAC. I mean you would never even go there, this whole entrepreneurial business school idea. SLAC is this island of its own funding, its own mission statements, and its own mentality. It's a very closed environment." More than anything else, he asserted, the course taught him the importance of "collaboration with people who are outside your normal sphere of influence." He would, he declared, never have started his business had he not taken the course.[36] One other person whom we interviewed had taken a number of business courses as an undergraduate, and a couple of entrepreneurs obtained MBA degrees after successful venture exits.

Entrepreneurship courses might serve as a catalyst infecting physicists with entrepreneurial notions, but getting physicists to take such courses might prove difficult. Max Lagally, who occasionally gave seminar lectures on entrepreneurship at the University of Wisconsin, told us that while physics students, or at least students with physics backgrounds, would attend his lectures, they typically were already at the edge of physics saying, "'Is there anything else besides just pure fundamental physics?' So there's a group of people that chafe a little bit at the sort of idea that it has to be truly fundamental to be called physics."[37]

Changes in the work environment – reduction in opportunities both within academia and the corporate sphere – have led many in the literature, and one of our interviewees, Max Lagally, to call for entrepreneurship courses, to encourage entrepreneurship as a "third way" to fill a gap in employment opportunities for physics graduates. Traditionally trained physicists who start their own company are ill prepared to run them. As we have noted earlier, their interests trend towards developing and improving their technologies, and they often only vaguely understand the market end of their business or the complex issues involved in starting a company. Some brought in associates who had business skills. Richard Selinfreund of Companion Diagnostics recalled his first startup, "I'd got along two years ... , being a brilliant neuroscientist going out of business" before bringing in a partner to focus on the business end of the startup. He told us "the first thing for an entrepreneur to do is to go find the best business guy on the planet to be your partner."[38]

Others turned to entrepreneurs and entrepreneurial networks to learn about business issues that did not come naturally to them. Matt Kim of QuantTera told us, "I didn't make a lot of mistakes because of the goodness of heart of seasoned business people just being nice to me. There's a guy I can call any time." Robert Black of Civatech Oncology called North Carolina's Council for Entrepreneurial Development a "watering hole for entrepreneurs." He asserted, "it's great because you go there and you see people. You know, it's almost like a preparatory company for a stage production. 'Oh, you know, what play are you in now?'" Many turned to a university technical transfer office to utilize their networks. John Criscione asserted that Texas A&M's Center for New Ventures in Entrepreneurship and the Office of Technology Commercialization played critical roles in helping him address issues. "They really have been involved in small businesses throughout and they're well familiar with financing issues, with staffing issues, as well as with lab space and stuff like that. They know what's involved, and they want to see us succeed." Whether they utilized informal networks of entrepreneurs they built themselves or formal institutional networks that they relied upon to learn about specific issues, entrepreneurial networks played a far greater role than entrepreneurship courses or formal training in the education of the physicist entrepreneurs we studied.[39]

VIII. CONCLUSION

Entrepreneurship for physicists appears to be an evolutionary process. Most enter entrepreneurial activity devoted to a concept or technology that they think will transform at least one small sector of the world. Their entrepreneurial vision focuses on the impact that technology will have. Over time they evolve towards increasing interaction with the marketplace or they turn to others to handle the business functions of their startup. Many focus on building their institution rather than obtaining a rapid return on investment. This focus on technology impact and institution building runs counter to many notions of entrepreneurship, but remain essential to bringing physicists to the marketplace. The marketplace in turn slowly influences them as they evolve from a focus on technology impact towards one of response to the market.

In the process of beginning or working for other startups, they engage new communities with different values to the "research for knowledge's sake" that is typical of research physicists. Frequently their initial engagement with an entrepreneurial community results because they are already on the border of the pure physics community. By being on that border they are less resistant to infection by entrepreneurial values. That infection is more likely to establish itself through frequent collaboration with established entrepreneurs – either by working for a high-tech startup, partnering with an entrepreneur in a startup, or by serving as a consultant to a startup. That collaboration with the startup community appears to be a critical component. We found very few who came to entrepreneurial activity through an extended corporate experience, and most who did also spent an extended amount of time working in or collaborating with startups.

The degree to which physicist entrepreneurs developed an entrepreneurial spirit varied. Many, at least by the time we interviewed them, remained focused on bringing added technological value to the marketplace, and a few told us that while their entrepreneurial activity had weakened their qualifications as physicists, they would return to physics following a successful exit of their company. More frequently their increased association with the entrepreneurial community transformed them. They came to a better understanding of the business community and realized that they faced many issues – the acceptance of technological change by the customer and the business community, the adaption of technologies in ways acceptable to the customer, and the broadening of technological markets – that business could address in ways that technology could not. The more they interacted with the non-technological members of the entrepreneurial community, the more their entrepreneurial spirit shifted, increasingly responding to the customer and the market.

NOTES

1. See R. J. Anderson and O. R. Butler (2008), *History of Physicists in Industry. Final Report.* American Institute of Physics (http://aip.org/history/pubs/HOPI_Final_report.pdf) (accessed 20 July 2014).
2. R. J. Anderson and O. R. Butler (2008), op. cit.
3. O. R. Butler and R. J. Anderson (2013), *Physics Entrepreneurship and Innovation: You Can't Depend on Large Companies Anymore.* American Institute of Physics (http://aip.org/sites/default/files/history/files/HoPE-Report-2013-web.pdf) (accessed 20 July 2014).
4. Walter Isaacson (2011), *Steve Jobs*, Simon and Schuster, New York.
5. In our study of physicists in industry we found that most physicists' work was called engineering and often they even aspired to be called engineers by their associates..
6. We interviewed managers in technology transfer programs at Harvard; The Massachusetts Institute of Technology (MIT); Boston College; Stanford; University of California, Los Angeles (UCLA); University of California, Berkeley (UC Berkeley); Wisconsin Alumni Research Foundation; Indiana; Purdue; and Georgia Tech. In addition, one entrepreneur we interviewed had been closely connected with developing technology transfer policies at the University of Colorado; Catherine Ives interview by Orville R. Butler, Boston College, Sept. 29, 2010; Carol Mimura interview by R. Joseph Anderson, Berkeley, California, Sept. 2010; Stephen Fleming interview by R. Joseph Anderson, Atlanta Georgia, Apr. 27, 2011; Bill Brizzard interview by Orville R. Butler, Indiana University, Oct. 20, 2010; Isaac Kohlberg interview by Orville R. Butler, Harvard University, Sept. 30, 2010; Ronald Ruth interview by R. Joseph Anderson and Orville R. Butler, Palo Alto, CA, Feb. 3, 2010; Katheryn Atchison interview by Orville R. Butler, Los Angeles, CA, Apr. 9, 2011.
7. Shankari Mylvaganam interview by Orville R. Butler, San Diego, CA, Mar. 8, 2011; Christopher Myatt interview by Orville R. Butler, Boulder, CO, Apr. 29, 2011.
8. Dana Anderson interview by Orville R. Butler, Boulder, CO, Apr. 27, 2011.

9.   David Oakley interview by Orville R. Butler, Boulder, CO, Apr. 26, 2011; Philip Paul interview by Orville R. Butler and R. Joseph Anderson, Dublin, CA, Feb. 3, 2010.
10. Nathan Myhrvold interview by Orville R. Butler, Bellvue, WA, Dec. 2, 2009; Robert Black interview by Orville R. Butler, Research Triangle Park, NC, Jan. 20, 2010; Philip (Flip) Kromer interview by Orville R. Butler, Austin, TX, Apr. 8, 2011; Ron Ruth interview, op. cit.; Gang Chen interview by Orville R. Butler, Cambridge, MA, Aug. 5, 2009.
11. Philip Wyatt interview by R. Joseph Anderson and Orville R. Butler, Santa Barbara, CA, Mar. 10, 2011.
12. Philip Wyatt interview, op. cit.
13. William Bertozzi interview by Orville R. Butler, Billerica, MA, July 29, 2009.
14. Max Lagally interview by R. Joseph Anderson, Madison, WI, Dec. 13, 2010.
15. S. Shane (2010), *Born Entrepreneurs, Born Leaders. How your Genes Affect Your Worklife*, Oxford University Press, New York.
16. Max Lagally interview, op. cit.
17. John Pacanovsky interview by Orville R. Butler, Triangle Research Park, NC, Jan. 21, 2010.
18. Qi-De Qian interview by Orville R. Butler, San Jose, CA, Feb. 1, 2010.
19. Mary Fuka interview by Orville R. Butler, Boulder, CO, Apr. 25, 2011; Henrique Tono interview by Orville R. Butler, Houston, TX, Mar. 25, 2011.
20. Nicholas Economou interview by R. Joseph Anderson and Orville R. Butler, Peabody, MA, July 27, 2009.
21. Ronald Ruth interview, op. cit.; Rod Loewen interview by Orville R. Butler, Palo Alto, CA, Feb. 3, 2010; Tom Lee interview by Orville R. Butler, Chicago, IL, Jan. 12, 2011.
22. John Criscione and William Altman interview by Orville R. Butler, Houston, TX, Mar. 25, 2011.
23. Mary Fuka interview, op. cit.; Jason Cleveland interview by Orville R. Butler, Santa Barbara, CA, Mar. 10, 2011.
24. Gill Travish interview by Orville R. Butler, Los Angeles, CA Mar. 9, 2011.
25. Tom Lee interview, op. cit.; Richard Selinfreund and Dick P. Gill interview by R. Joseph Anderson, Indianapolis, IN, Nov. 9, 2010.
26. Matt Kim interview by Orville R. Butler, Tempe, AZ, Jan. 13, 2010.
27. Rod Loewen interview, op. cit.; Ronald Ruth interview, op. cit.
28. Michael Naughton interview by Orville R. Butler, Newton, MA, Aug. 5, 2009.
29. Robert Black interview, op. cit.
30. Robert Fischell interview by Orville R. Butler, Dayton, MD, Dec. 21, 2009; Henrique Tono interview, op. cit.
31. Henry Kapteyn interview by Orville R. Butler, Boulder, CO, Apr. 25, 2010.
32. Ningyi Luo and Lindsay Austin interview by Orville R. Butler, San Jose, CA, Feb. 2, 2010.
33. Frank Levinson interview by R. Joseph Anderson and Orville R. Butler, Tiburon, CA, Feb. 1, 2010; Dhruv Bansal interview by Orville R. Butler, Austin, TX, Mar. 22, 2011.
34. Bill O'Brien interview by Orville R. Butler, Madison, WI, Dec. 15, 2010.
35. Reyad Sawafta interview by Orville R. Butler, Greensboro, NC, Jan. 18, 2010; G. Jordan Maclay interview by Orville R. Butler, Richland Center, WI, Dec. 15, 2010; Darrell Conway interview by R. Joseph Anderson and Orville R. Butler, Tuscon, AZ, Jan. 11, 2010.
36. Rod Loewen interview, op. cit.
37. Max Lagally interview, op. cit.
38. Max Lagally interview, op. cit.; Richard Selinfreund and Dick P. Gill interview, op. cit.; Douglas Arion, professor of physics at Carthage College has been actively calling for entrepreneurship courses for physicists. See Doug Arion (2013), 'Entrepreneurships Role in Physics Education,' *Astrobetter* (http://www.astrobetter.com/entrepreneurships-role-in-physics-education/) (accessed 20 July 2014). Also see Douglas N. Arion (2013), 'Things Your Advisor Never Told You: Entrepreneurships Role in Physics Education,' *Physics Today* 66(8), 42–47.
39. Matt Kim interview, op. cit.; Robert Black interview op. cit.; John Criscione and William Altman interview, op. cit.

PART II

Healthcare and bioscience entrepreneurship

5. Bioentrepreneurship: opportunities and challenges

Arlen Meyers

I. INTRODUCTION

Global and regional economies thrive on innovation. Entrepreneurship is their single most important competitive advantage. Clusters and eco-systems designed to facilitate innovation and entrepreneurship have emerged around the world, including those that focus on the life sciences. In this chapter, I will present some basic concepts describing entre-preneurship and the entrepreneurial mindset, how those principles apply to the unique environment of bioscience and healthcare, and lessons learned for those in other entrepreneurial domains.

An entrepreneurial mindset[1] refers to a specific state of mind which orientates human conduct towards entrepreneurial activities and out-comes. Individuals with entrepreneurial mindsets are often drawn to opportunities, innovation, and new value creation. Characteristics of such an entrepreneurial mindset include the ability to take calculated risks and accept the realities of change and uncertainty.

Scientists, engineers, and medical practitioners are in a unique position to be entrepreneurs, in that they identify unmet healthcare needs and work together with business partners and investors to develop and commercialize solutions that add value. The result is the creation of new drugs, devices, diagnostics, digital health products and services, health-care delivery innovations, and new healthcare business models. Life science entrepreneurs, also known as bioentrepreneurs, practice the art of bioentrepreneurship.

Entrepreneurship has many definitions with specific application to the biomedical and engineering sciences and health. We define bioentrepre-neurship as the pursuit of opportunity in the life sciences using scarce, uncontrolled resources. The goal is to create customer/user/patient/stakeholder-defined value by researching, developing, and commercializ-ing biomedical and healthcare innovation. This definition includes several key elements including: (1) process; (2) outcomes; (3) deploying innovation; and (4) scarce resources that are, in general, applicable to other kinds of entrepreneurship.

1. Bioentrepreneurship is a process: Similar to all entrepreneurs, bioentrepreneurs mostly act. Indeed, they plan and monitor their activities but the process is proactive and hands on. Innovators are constantly experimenting and rapidly adapting to changing macroeconomic stresses, market shifts, and technological advancements. Seeing opportunity and exploiting it, experimenting, rapidly changing course, and bootstrapping are core bioentrepreneurial competencies.

2. Bioentrepreneurs create customer-defined value: To be successful, the innovative product or service must have tangible and intangible benefits in the mind of the buyer that far exceed the tangible and intangible costs. Moreover, the customer has to define the offering's value, not the bioentrepreneur. Customers vote with their wallets. Bioentrepreneurs are notorious for falling in love with their technologies. However, their opinion of the value of their idea is irrelevant, since the ultimate determination of the value of a product will be whether a customer buys it.

3. Bioentrepreneurs innovate: Bioentrepreneurs innovate by creating things that are new, better, smarter, faster, cheaper, and/or are more attractive than the status quo, the competition, or the alternatives. In some instances, the difference is incremental and minimal. In others, it is disruptive and entirely novel. Moreover, there is a difference between an idea, an invention, an improvement, and an innovation that is both qualitative and quantitative. An idea is something that stays in your mind. An invention is an idea reduced to practice. Improvements are old ways of doing things that add marginal value. Innovations are new ways of doing things, sometimes using old ideas new ways, that add substantial value, usually at least ten times that of the existing offerings.

4. Bioentrepreneurs use uncontrolled, scarce resources: Bioentrepreneurs use resources that are difficult to find and frequently have to bootstrap and scrape together technology, people, power, money, and other resources to move their ideas forward. Intrapreneurs, those who work for someone but act like entrepreneurs within an organization, are faced with specific challenges coping with the structure, processes, and cultures of their employers.

II. BIOENTREPRENEURSHIP IS NOT PRACTICE MANAGEMENT

Some healthcare professionals confuse practice management with bioentrepreneurship. There is a big difference between the two. The goal of practice management is to run a medical practice so that it is efficient, effective, scalable, profitable, and sustainable. Practice management is the operations side of the business, just like any other industry. The goal of bioentrepreneurship, on the other hand, is to create value in the marketplace by exploiting biomedical product or service innovation. Practice management is part of bioentrepreneurship, but a means towards an end, not the end itself. Once an entity is created, it needs to run profitably to be sustainable and grow. Practice management is, by definition, a management exercise. Bioentrepreneurship requires innovation, creativity, and leadership.

Each of these activities requires very different knowledge, skills, and abilities. Few people, not just healthcare professionals, are equipped to do all. Moreover, providing doctors, dentists, nurses, or pharmacists practice management education or all the MBA courses in the world will not necessarily result in more innovation. In addition, entrepreneurship is but one element of innovation. Innovation is only one element of competitiveness, either locally or globally. Competiveness requires several elements in addition to innovation, for example, intellectual property protection, laws that protect private property, and a stimulating macroeconomic environment that rewards risk and provides capital. Bioentrepreneurship is about creating new products and services. Practice management is about running the business. Entrepreneurs create value. Innovators are entrepreneurs who created big value.

III. THE FOUR HORSEMEN OF BIOENTREPRENEURSHIP

Bioentrepreneurs differ depending on their employment situation, their goals, and the roles they play in the biomedical and health innovation development process. Most bio-businesses usually include four different individuals playing different roles to create and develop a startup: technopreneurs (technical professionals like life scientists, healthcare professionals, or engineers), market perceivers (those who work in a given industry with close contact to patients or potential customers), business developers (those who know how to create, deliver, and harvest the value of an enterprise), and investors (those who invest money, time, and expertise to the enterprise).[2]

There are significant differences in how these participants approach the process of life science commercialization. Technopreneurs are primarily solution driven. They typically invent or discover something and then search for an application or market. They adopt a "technology push" approach. Market perceivers, on the other hand, adopt a "market pull" perspective – they typically start by uncovering or sensing a market need, and then seek to develop a product or service that will satisfy those needs. Investors and business developers are primarily interested in seeing a return on their investment. They use a market pull model. Investors provide money to fuel innovation. Business developers are business model experts and excel at creating, scaling, delivering, and harvesting value in a company. Whether a technopreneur, market perceiver, business developer, or investor, one can identify six basic types of bioentrepreneurs.

IV.   THE SIX TYPES OF BIOENTREPRENEURS

Physician entrepreneurs, unlike scientists and engineers, come in six different types depending on how they create value.

1.   Private or independent practice: Most research shows that about 50 percent of US doctors and most dentists are independent medical practitioners who own their own businesses. However, the situation for medical doctors is changing as more and more doctors become employees of healthcare organizations. The reasons for the increasing numbers of employed physicians are many and include practice management hassles, student debt, work-life attitudes, generational attitudes about work, and differences in how the genders practice. Like other non-medical small businesses, the primary goal of the business is to generate enough profit to satisfy the needs of the owners. The scope and scale of the practice is typically limited by the ability of any one doctor to see a certain number of patients per day. In addition, the exit often involves the sale or transfer of the practice once the owner retires or dies. While some private, independent practices generate substantial revenues, they are less than large scalable companies, and the practices are typically funded by retained earnings. The intent of the owner is not to scale the practice to as large as possible, but to maximize revenues given finite time and resources. Independent, private practitioners are

fundamentally small business owners that need to deliver professional services at a profit. However, because of the conflict between the ethics of medicine and the ethics of business, several private practice doctors have a conflict when it comes to "running a practice like a business," with unfortunate results.

2.   Scalable startup entrepreneurs (technopreneurs): Unlike private practices, scalable healthcare and biomedical startup companies attempt to commercialize drugs, devices, diagnostics, healthcare IT products, new business models, and expanded service platforms. These bioentrepreneurs start a company with a vision that could change the world. Their job is to search for a repeatable and scalable business model. The goal of the scalable startup entrepreneurship is to create wealth for shareholders. There is a difference between biomedical and health innovation. Biomedical physician entrepreneurs are interested in commercializing drugs, devices, diagnostics, vaccines, and biologics. Health and healthcare physician entrepreneurs are interested in digital health products and services, care delivery innovations, business process innovation, or systems improvements. Digital health describes the application of information and communications technologies to improve human health. Digital health companies, led by physician entrepreneurs, have exploded, fueled by cheap communications, Internet technologies, and health consumerism driving the demand for information and access to providers using mobile technologies. iTriage, at www.itriage.com, for example, was created by two emergency room doctors. The iPhone app helps patients with deciding where to go for care and is designed to eliminate unnecessary emergency room visits.

3.   Employed physicians acting like entrepreneurs in their organizations (intrapreneurs): Large companies, like multihospital healthcare systems or chains of healthcare service products, have finite life cycles. Most grow through sustaining innovation, offering new products that are variants around their core products. As more healthcare knowledge workers become employees of hospital systems and healthcare delivery organizations, they become "intrapreneurs," meaning they mine new ideas and underutilized value within the organization. While inventions and discoveries can occasionally result in licensing revenue or spin out opportunities for the employer, more typically intrapreneurs contribute to or devise process improvements that eliminate waste and improve outcomes or service line extensions that are designed to offer new diagnostic or therapeutic innovations to patients. Changes in patient tastes,

new technologies, legislation, new competitors, and other factors can create pressure for more disruptive innovations – that is innovations that create entirely new, unheard of products/services sold into new markets or novel, unprecedented ways to sell existing products/services. Endoscopic surgery is an example of a disruptive innovation. It completely transformed the way surgeons performed historically invasive procedures. Device manufacturers capitalized on new products to improve endoscopic techniques, and hospitals had to readjust many of their existing systems, protocols, and medical equipment to fulfill patients' demand of the minimally invasive endoscopic approach. Creating innovation within organizations is not easy and requires systems, processes, and a culture that rewards innovators and provides them with the support and resources they need to change the status quo, often by defying established, vested interests who are resistant to change.

4. Entrepreneurs trying to improve the human condition (social entrepreneurs): Social physician entrepreneurs, fundamentally, try to improve the human condition. They are innovators who focus on creating products and services that solve social needs and problems like eliminating smallpox or malaria or creating non-profit organizations or offering biomedical and health innovation and entrepreneurship educational and training programs. Unlike scalable startups, the social physician entrepreneur's goal is to make the world a better place, not to capture market share or to create to wealth for the company. They may be non-profit, for-profit, or a hybrid. An example of a social entrepreneurial endeavor is the Society of Physician Entrepreneurs (SoPE), at www.sopenet.org. SoPE is a global, non-profit, physician led biomedical and health innovation and entrepreneurship network whose mission is to help members get their ideas to patients. Members are an international, interdisciplinary group of biomedical and non-biomedical entrepreneurs, service providers, industry representatives, investors, academics, and other innovation stakeholders who are interested in building community based innovation networks to advance ideas. SoPE provides its members with education, networks, and resources and delivers content and programs virtually, via social networks and through international chapters that offer regularly scheduled education and network events.

5. Freelancers, consultants, and independent contractors: These are physicians who have pursued alternative, non-clinical career tracks and help other doctors get their ideas to patients by providing consultation and other services like strategic planning, sales and

marketing, financial management, website development, or social media integration.

6. Physician investors: Like all high net worth professionals, doctors invest in things they know best, and physician investors are no exception. They have the added advantage of being on the front lines and understanding the market opportunities and have several ideas on how to address them. Physician investor entrepreneurs participate at every level of investing, from angel networks to participating in hedge funds and venture funds. Many specialize in biotech, medical device, or digital health. Life Science Angels, at www.lifescienceangels.com, is an example of an investment company specializing in biotech and medical device companies and has several physician investor members.

Using this model, most practitioners are private practice entrepreneurs. Some have a need to perfect their practice management skills. Some physician entrepreneurs create new products, services, and/or platforms and seek to scale the business for an eventual profitable exit. Some practitioners, like those who work for large healthcare organizations, seek to improve processes or create new delivery models to drive growth. Finally, some doctors are social entrepreneurs, seeking new ways to solve social needs and problems.

V. HOW IS BIOENTREPRENEURSHIP DIFFERENT FROM ENTREPRENEURSHIP IN OTHER AREAS?

At its core, as mentioned above, entrepreneurship, regardless of the domain, is about pursuing an opportunity to create customer-defined value through the deployment of innovation. However, because of the unique nature of healthcare and healthcare systems, there are several features about biomedical and health innovation and entrepreneurship that differentiate it from that in other industries in several important ways. These features include:

- A highly regulated industry. Bioscience and healthcare, because it involves treating patients, is one of the most highly regulated industries in the United States. The US Food and Drug Administration (FDA) has a primary mission to protect the health and safety of patients, and, in so doing, has imposed stringent rules and regulations that require inventors to demonstrate safety and efficacy before a drug or device can be manufactured or sold in the United

States. The process is often uncertain, subject to constant change, lengthy and expensive and sometimes interferes with the pace of innovation.

- Unique policies and procedures designed to protect human subjects during technology research, development, and commercialization. New drugs and devices often need to be tested in human subjects to demonstrate safety and efficacy. That requires a series of Phase 1, 2, and 3 clinical trials that are often expensive, complex, and not successful. In addition, human subject research is subject to ethical and legal requirements overseen by institutional review boards, regulatory agencies, and administrative bodies charged with protecting the rights of research subjects.
- Complex payment and reimbursement schemes that involve not just the patient, but the government, employers, and other private third party payers. Public and private third party reimbursement schemes create perverse market dynamics for those seeking payment for products and services.
- A high dependency on intellectual property protection. Biotechnology, biopharmaceutical, and medical device ideas are highly subject to intellectual property scrutiny, and few will get to market without appropriate patent protection.
- An industry that is not subject to free market dynamics. Third party reimbursement, employment based insurance, government oversight and regulation, and the politics of healthcare access interfere with traditional consumer driven markets that frequently result in unintended consequences when it comes to cost, access, quality, and the patient experience.
- Difficult financing models that require large amounts of capital over extended periods of time. It is estimated that it takes about $1 billion and 10–15 years for a new drug to get to market.
- Healthcare offers an extremely high risk environment where few products make it to market from the scientific bench to the patient. Only about 10 percent of bioscience products get to market because of the clinical trial, regulatory, and financing risks.
- A complicated conflict of interest landscape, particularly as it applies to physician–industry interaction and collaboration.
- A process that requires handing off the research, development, and commercialization of ideas to multiple team members with various skill sets. Bioscience and life science technology commercialization has been called the most difficult relay race in business. It requires complicated, interdisciplinary business development and scientific teams to collaborate around the world.

● An extremely turbulent and unpredictable healthcare system with unforeseeable insurance, financing, delivery, payment, and access threats and opportunities. The US Affordable Care Act is but the latest attempt to increase access, reduce costs, and improve quality. Like other major healthcare reform and financing efforts, including Medicare and Medicaid passed in 1965, the landscape will continue to evolve and the laws will undergo substantial modification and revision based on political power and the popular will.

VI. WHY IS ADOPTING AN ENTREPRENEURIAL MINDSET IMPORTANT NOW?

The US healthcare system (as well as healthcare systems around the world) is faced with problems that will require innovative solutions and an entrepreneurial mindset to solve them. First, there is an almost infinite demand for care with a limited supply of providers and resources. The aging population of most industrialized countries, and chronic diseases attributable to poor life style choices, requiring the use of new and expensive technologies, is stressing most healthcare systems and, in many cases, attributing to social upheavals. Second, macroeconomic trends, national debt, and scarce financial resources are all resulting in a reassessment of resource allocation and real or de facto rationing of care. Third, societal and technological trends, particularly global consumerism, the Internet, and mobile communications are changing how healthcare is perceived and delivered.

Finally, physicians are beginning to realize that the practice of medicine, like every other professional service, is a business and requires that the practitioner make a profit if they are to continue to practice. In the United States, healthcare reform embodied in the Affordable Care Act is forcing practitioners to reassess the care they give and how they deliver it. They are adopting an innovative and entrepreneurial mindset to adapt to a very turbulent, changing environment and using innovative business models, systems, products, services, and platforms to do so.

VII. BIOENTREPRENEURSHIP EDUCATION AND TRAINING

To address this growing need for an innovative and entrepreneurial mindset among physicians and life sciences professionals, global bioentrepreneurship education and training programs are appearing, though many are still in the early stages of development. The programs are designed to appeal to students at various levels, from community colleges to graduate and professional schools. Some offer courses, others certificates, and others are graduate degree programs. Several offer combined degrees, like MD/MBA or PhD/MBA. In addition, Professional Science Master's programs offer students the opportunity to get a Masters in a STEM discipline (science, technology, engineering, and mathematics) supplemented with business courses.

The objective of all of these programs is to provide students with the knowledge, skills, and abilities necessary to work for industry, or with industry, in research or consulting roles, or start a new company. In addition, some programs are domain specific within the life sciences, specializing in medical device design and development (Biodesign), digital health design and development, or drug/biologics/vaccine discovery and development.

Education, however, is but one of many things that a life science entrepreneur needs to succeed. In addition, they need mentors, networks, experiential learning, a supervised safe place to fail early and often, and money. Regional bioclusters and ecosystems typically provide those resources, like accelerators, generators, technology transfer offices, and angel networks, and, in optimal cases, are integrated into the educational programs.

An example of such a program is the Program in Bioinnovation and Entrepreneurship at the University of Colorado.[3] The program, started in 2011, involves collaboration between the Anschutz Medical Campus and the University of Colorado School of Business Jake Jabs Center for Entrepreneurship. Students are offered an online course, *Building Biotechnology*, that is designed for those in business, science, engineering, law, and the health professions interested in getting ideas to patients. A certificate is awarded to students who take two additional courses in entrepreneurship designed to supplement *Building Biotechnology.*

Bioentrepreneurship education and training programs are in the early stages of development, and there are several barriers to their creation and growth.

- They engage participants in endeavors that get short shrift on campuses – teaching and innovation. Generating clinical and grant revenue often takes priority. Few campuses reward faculty or students for developing or commercializing an idea or pay them extra to teach the courses.
- Money and resources are tight in most campuses and little is available to support these programs. They run on a shoestring, are

expected to be self-funded, and require uncompensated time from faculty being paid by other disciplines.

● Biomedical entrepreneurship rests on a four legged stool that includes education, networks, experience, and money. The last three are difficult to create, scale, and sustain.

● Bioentrepreneurship educators have no home. It is not yet a recognized academic domain, there are limited places to publish peer reviewed research and manuscripts (the *Journal of Commercial Biotechnology* is an exception), and promotion and tenure committees attribute little or no value to the enterprise.

● By its very nature, bioentrepreneurship education is an interdisciplinary, multicampus effort with all of the bureaucratic and systems issues that engenders. There is frequently a lack of alignment among the academic entities involved, and driving growth and short term money issues trump long term investments in entrepreneurship education.

Despite these obstacles, passionate international educational entrepreneurs are creating new programs at the community college, undergraduate, and graduate level, granting course credit, certificates, and specialized degrees. The challenges are many: the programs need to validate their value to multiple stakeholders and leaders need to create sustainable revenue models in collaboration with their local bioscience ecosystems. Success, however, will create more jobs, a higher standard of living, more innovation getting to patients faster, and a way for students to display their talents not just at the bench or bedside, but the boardroom as well.

VIII. WHAT ARE THE KEY CHALLENGES AHEAD FOR BIOENTREPRENEURS?

As noted, the principles and practices of entrepreneurship are, at a high level, domain agnostic. While life science entrepreneurship has unique features and peculiarities, the fundamental goal is the same as other businesses – to create customer-defined value through the deployment of innovation. However, there are several challenges and barriers for bioentrepreneurs:

● A highly uncertain regulatory environment, particularly as it applies to digital health devices.

- Rapidly changing early stage technology funding and financing models due to crowdfunding, changes in the venture capital business model, the emergence of strategic investment funds and super-angel networks.
- The continuing evolution of healthcare reform and financing mechanisms, particularly in the United States.
- The conflict and tension between public care options and private care options.
- Decreasing reimbursements for biomedical products and health services and a relentless focus on cost cutting.
- Legal and regulatory barriers preventing the full deployment and adoption of eCare and telemedicine.
- Bioentrepreneurship educational and training gaps.
- Lack of integration between the digital health technology community and healthcare providers
- Lack of a robust digital health clinical trial and validation ecosystem
- An extremely high-risk environment with a high cost of failure.

IX. WHAT ARE THE KEY TRENDS IN LIFE SCIENCE ENTREPRENEURSHIP OVER THE NEXT FEW YEARS?

The future of bioentrepreneurship is bright and will be characterized by several trends:

- There will be more international bioentrepreneurship education and training programs designed to provide students at various educational levels with the knowledge, skills, attitudes, networks, experiential learning, and resources they need to succeed.
- Community based innovation initiatives will continue to grow, and physician entrepreneurs and patients will get engaged and contribute earlier in the research and development process.
- New financing mechanisms will emerge to fund early stage ventures in an attempt to close the "valley of death" between invention and the later stages of development.
- Major biopharmaceutical, medical devices and digital health companies will embrace open innovation and create regional innovation hubs to collaborate with major research institutions and clinical centers.

- Scientists, engineers, and health professionals will increasingly adopt an entrepreneurial mindset to thrive in practice and change healthcare delivery systems throughout the world.

X. CONCLUSION

Life science entrepreneurs are growing around the world and contributing significantly to the evolution of health management and care delivery and biomedical and digital health technologies. While they have unique intellectual property, regulatory, reimbursement, market, and business model challenges, bioentrepreneurs have the same goals as other entrepreneurs and the skills required to achieve these goals are similar.

NOTES

1. http://lexicon.ft.com/Term?term=entrepreneurial-mindset (accessed on 1 Oct. 2014)
2. http://www.nature.com/bioent/2004/041001/full/bioent831.html (accessed on 1 Oct. 2014)
3. http://www.ucdenver.edu/academics/colleges/Graduate-School/academic-programs/Pages/bioentr.aspx (accessed on 1 Oct. 2014)

6. Healthcare entrepreneurship: the changing landscape

Cam Patterson and Andrew Kant

I. INTRODUCTION

The healthcare sector has long been dependent on sources of innovation and value creation. Novel therapeutics, medical devices, diagnostics, Healthcare IT innovations and services (i.e. healthcare delivery, contract resource organizations (CROs)) will ultimately improve patient quality of life at a rapid pace. The recent passing of the Patient Protection and Affordable Care Act in 2010 (more commonly ACA) has attempted to realign financial incentives for developing new healthcare innovations, while also aimed to reduce skyrocketing healthcare costs. The ACA has been the focus of a greater national debate regarding cost versus benefit and will likely continue to be challenged on its effectiveness for years to come. Policy aside, innovation and entrepreneurship are clear solutions to many of the problems identified within the current healthcare system (i.e. efficiency of patient care, improved survival and outcomes and more robust safety profiles).

Historically, the notion of a true entrepreneur is one who is fueled by independence, creativity, drive to change the status quo and high risk tolerance. These qualities are central to enriching the healthcare ecosystem, particularly in a time when Big Pharma[1] companies are downsizing internal discovery efforts and moving towards decentralization. The healthcare entrepreneurship landscape is riddled with risk, complicated by an unaligned value chain and tempered with expensive (yet wholly necessary) regulatory oversight. Risks aside, the upside is huge. Improving quality of care for patients and addressing unmet clinical needs is fundamental to our innate drive for innovation.

The future is bright for the healthcare industry at large – innovations in personalized medicine, epigenetics, and nanotechnology and yet to be conceived of disruptive technologies will unavoidably change how we think of healthcare. In this chapter, we'll provide a view of the various subsectors of healthcare entrepreneurship, the nuts-and-bolt consider-ations when undertaking a new venture and an analysis of common pitfalls for healthcare startups.

II. INDUSTRY SECTORS IN HEALTHCARE

Drugs

Drug development has come a long way since 1976 when Herbert Boyer founded Genentech and brought synthetic insulin to diabetic patients. Dr. Boyer, along with venture capitalist Robert Swanson, is considered to be responsible for jumpstarting the biotechnology industry. Many other companies have shaped the entrepreneurial path, and particularly with the advent of recombinant proteins and improved drug libraries, the biotech boom took a rapid pace in the 1990s. The 2000s gave rise to the genomics revolution, one which has still yet to run its course. Dr. Boyer's innovative insulin approach and the completion of the first human genome has drastically disrupted the healthcare sector. We are still feeling the aftershocks of this and other momentous discoveries.

Big Pharma has traditionally been the major source of innovation in developing new therapeutic treatments. The FIPCO (Fully Integrated Pharmaceutical Company) model encompasses in-house research and development for lead identification and optimization, regulatory affairs, reimbursement and marketing efforts. This strategy has yielded many game-changing innovations but also created high transaction costs and a proliferation of "Me Too" drugs. From drug discovery to approval, the average R&D investment is roughly $1.2 billion and can take from 10–15 years to reach patients. Adjusted for inflation, this is compared to $800 million in the late 1990s.[2] As such, established pharmaceutical companies have shifted towards outsourced and in-licensed discovery efforts to more efficiently develop therapies and rapidly shift strategic priorities as the market dictates.

Many startups and medium-sized pharmaceutical companies have, by necessity, turned to the VIPCO (Virtually Integrated Pharmaceutical Company) model in advancing their innovations to market. This model focuses on tight relations with Contract Research Organizations (CROs) and connecting with strategic partners, like Big Pharma firms, to align core competencies. Many startups are implementing this model as illustrated by the following examples. Moderna Therapeutics (Cam-bridge, MA) is developing a method to produce biologic therapies within patients' cells, potentially eliminating many issues associated with protein-based therapies. In 2013, Moderna partnered with AstraZeneca in a preclinical development program that encompasses up to 40 different drug candidates, with AstraZeneca providing an initial $250 million in up-front cash to Moderna. Nimbus Discovery LLC (Cambridge, MA) is another example. Their approach is focused on improved drug discovery through a computational chemistry platform. Nimbus maintains collaborations with Lilly Ventures, SR One (GlaxoSmithKline's venture capital arm) and the Bill and Melinda Gates Foundation. They also employ a unique corporate model that enables cleaner and more streamlined partnership deals.[3]

Therapeutically focused startup companies play an important role in filling the innovation pipeline. On balance, attractive assets embody several key factors: novel compounds with defensible intellectual property (IP) portfolios, strong management teams, unmet clinical need and some level of efficacy and safety data. At the moment, most early-stage assets exist squarely within a buyer's market that constitutes multiple therapeutic methods (i.e. small molecules, biologics, gene therapy, etc.) per biologic target, improved formulations/drug delivery for existing drugs, and stem cell therapy approaches. The solution requires creative funding mechanisms, experienced dealmakers and disciplined validation of key assets.

Medtech

This sector encompasses medical devices such as artificial joints, catheters, insulin pumps, pacemakers and wound healing products, as well as diagnostics such as imaging, In Vitro Diagnostics (IVDs), metabolomics and companion diagnostics (i.e. diagnostic used alongside therapeutic product). Medtech is expected to grow at a compound annual growth rate of 4.5 percent between 2012 and 2018 and reach a total market size of $455 billion.[4] The regulatory threshold, compared to that of therapeutics, is markedly lower and, as a result, it is generally easier to obtain Food and Drug Administration (FDA) approval. In addition, the inherent product development risk for these devices is more easily managed as devices are typically more amenable to iterative testing and re-development. This, and other factors, has increased the investor attractiveness of these assets to angel investors and select venture capitalists. While the overall financial return may be lower, the average time to market (TTM) is much shorter (see below). For example, a 510(k) product[5] from concept to FDA approval requires an average of $31 million and 6–7 years of development.[6] On the horizon, technologies like Proteus Digital Health's ingestible sensors, Given Imaging's smart pill technologies and NeuroSpire's mind-machine interfaces are poised to radically change the medical device landscape.

Diagnostic technologies are generating an enormous amount of interest, particularly in the field of personalized medicine. As idiopathic mechanisms of diseases such as cancer are better understood, diagnostics designed to screen patients for sensitivity to particular therapies, or reveal biological pathway dependencies in recurrence, will become essential in providing customized therapy. Not only does this approach offer the potential to adapt treatment, it will enable well-informed and safer treatments. For example, patients diagnosed with HER2 positive breast cancer are currently treated with Trastuzumab (or Herceptin), which specifically inhibits stimulatory signals revealed by HER2 diagnostic screens. As additional therapeutics and diagnostic tests are developed side by side, clinicians will have more control and information for better treatment. This relatively new field of personalized medicine will likely require entrepreneurs to take a more targeted approach to development and partnering.

Healthcare IT

Also referred to as Digital Health or eHealth, Healthcare IT is defined by a range of services and products including telemedicine, health informatics, gamification (i.e. behavior modification), web-based health services (i.e Electronic Health Records), mobile health applications (mHealth) and others. From 2010 to 2012, Healthcare IT venture capital funding increased by close to a billion dollars and is expected to continue growing.[7] The Health Information Technology for Economic and Clinical Health (HITECH) Act, passed as part of the American Reinvestment and Recovery Act (ARRA) in 2009, set forth guidelines for modernizing health record data and incentivized providers to switch to Electronic Health Record (EHR) standards. This policy shift, alongside development of other enabling technologies (i.e. mobile technologies, telemedicine, Big Data initiatives), created momentum around Healthcare IT innovations. The upside is clear. Innovations in this subsector are capital efficient, have low regulatory hurdles and have enormous potential by enabling real-time monitoring and reduced administrative costs, and can provide greater transparency to patients. However, there are clear challenges in this new and unproven market. Regulatory guidelines are in flux, barriers to entry are low for competitors, and market adoption, either by providers or consumers, is hindered by unclear value propositions.

III. OPPORTUNITY ASSESSMENT, INNOVATION AND BUSINESS MODELS

(a) Evaluating the Idea or Opportunity

Not every technology or idea is well positioned to become a startup company. This is especially true within the healthcare domain due to relatively long development timelines requiring sustained capital investment. Healthcare startups often face a plethora of unknowns. Will a given therapy work, as intended, in humans? Preclinical animal models are never 100 percent predictive for efficacy and safety. Will the product infringe upon existing IP (i.e. freedom-to-operate)? Is the management team well equipped to sustain development of the business? The strategy for many early-stage companies takes a page from software engineering – Fail Fast. In other words, the key is to identify and carry out studies that yield the quickest answer to whether the product is unsafe and/or ineffective.

Aside from Class I and II medical devices and Healthcare IT technologies, many risks are focused on technical unknowns that require large amounts of capital to derisk. Safety and efficacy profiles in human patients, scale-up/economic considerations and healthcare reimbursement strategy are all big landmines that present themselves five or ten years after company inception. An entrepreneur is also faced with predicting the competitive landscape in the next ten years. Not an easy task. The difficulty at this stage is gathering enough information to forge a direction that will not limit future research and development efforts. Steve Blank, as part of his Lean LaunchPad class for life sciences states,

> What we found is that during the class almost all of them pivoted – making substantive changes to one or more of their business model canvas components. In the real world a big pivot in life sciences far down the road of development is a very bad sign due to huge sunk costs.[8]

This highlights the need for early validation of the idea and a degree of vigilance and openness to new product development opportunities.

Shane provides a thoughtful breakdown of technology considerations for a startup versus an established company (see Table 6.1).[9] Radical, or disruptive, technologies are generally better suited (although carry the most risk) for startups. When successful, these types of technologies create new market opportunities and often displace existing products from established companies. Incremental technologies are better suited for established firms, as they carry lower risk and focus mainly on resources well established in larger companies (e.g. marketing, product development).

Table 6.1   Technology suited for startups vs. established companies

Startup company	Established company
Radical	Incremental
Tacit	Codified
Early-stage	Late-stage
General purpose	Specific purpose
Significant customer value	Moderate customer value
Major technical advance	Minor technical advance
Strong IP protection	Weak IP protection

Source: Adapted from *Academic Entrepreneurship: University Spinoffs and Wealth Creation* (p. 103), by S. A. Shane, 2004, Edward Elgar Publishing. Copyright 2004 by Scott Shane.

(b) Competitive Intelligence

Understanding competition in the healthcare space can be challenging and requires a solid understanding of potential pivots for competitors. Transparency through regulatory requirements (i.e. clinicaltrials.gov, FDA advisory meeting notes) can help reveal information otherwise difficult to find. Startups at an earlier stage can often find it difficult to obtain information in preclinical stages. The longer development time-lines may aid a startup to identify and pivot to potential competitors coming down the road. As always, timing is key, alongside vigilance using market research databases and scientific conferences. Databases like MedTrack, Frost & Sullivan, Adis R&D Insight and others should be used early on in the process. Not only does this empower management, but it also can create leverage for partnership discussions, given strategic alignment. Perspective is everything: competitors can also be viewed as partners.

Another use for competitive intelligence is to identify drugs, device or diagnostics that may not have a lead indication aligned with a startup's product, but may have a similar mechanism of action or amenable platform. To clarify this point, many companies employ a Go-To-Market strategy through the FDA approval process by targeting an orphan disease. This comes with reduced costs and decreased time to market.

Often the drug may have a similar mechanism of action to a larger market opportunity (i.e. heart disease, cancer). This is common in oncology therapeutic development as many genetic diseases, some classified as orphan or ultra-orphan, could be used as a personalized medicine therapy as improved diagnostic platforms are developed.

(c)   Market Research and Assessment

Both primary and market research is important but not critical for early-stage startups. Oftentimes, the most critical question revolves around technical risk. It's quite possible that a product, proven effective through clinical trials, may be marginalized by competitors or disruptive technologies. However, it should not be the primary concern of early-stage companies. In parallel, it is prudent to perform informal primary market research with key opinion leaders (KOLs) and decision makers to help solidify a case for further development. This can be done more formally through consulting firms, with high costs, or through informal means with an existing peer network. Providing this qualitative feedback to potential investors or grant agencies is important to avoiding funding gaps that hinder the all-important development timeline.

Intellectual Property (IP)

IP covers a broad range of protections such as copyright, trademarks and trade secrets. Healthcare startups often employ patenting as a default ingredient at company inception. For therapeutics and diagnostics, engaging in any level of partnering discussions will be dead on arrival if IP is inadequately protected. In practical terms, patents serve as a robust barrier to entry for competitors, reinforced by decades of case law and careful review by US Patent and Trademark Office Examiners. Issued patents also serve as means of validating novelty and strengthening credibility for investors and strategic partners. An experienced patent attorney is crucial in helping assess patentability and freedom-to-operate, while also enabling an attractive, defensible patent portfolio.

Startups must take great care to file patents strategically as the financial burden can quickly mount, particularly at national phase entry (i.e. filing foreign applications). Costs often range from several thousand dollars to up to $15,000 per country. While filing fees themselves may be nominal, translation fees often inflate costs dramatically. Within 30 months of filing a patent application, a decision must be made regarding which countries to target. It's imperative that entrepreneurs plan for this milestone and commit to those countries deemed necessary to fully commercialize the product and/or avoid hindering business development (BD) efforts. Consideration should be given to those countries in which the therapy, medical devices or diagnostic is well suited: markets likely to produce significant sales or anticipated interests of licensees or strategic partners. This underscores the importance of practicing a Fail Fast strategy.

(d) Business Development (BD)

Beginning with the end in mind is important: exit opportunities are few and the means to achieve them vary greatly. BD efforts can help healthcare startups in several ways: positioning lead products early on for acquisition or licensing, leveraging value from alternative fields of use which the startup is unlikely to commercialize and as a tool for gathering competitive intelligence. An established, high-value network is paramount for a successful BD operation. Startups can employ various tools to target effort including various paid databases (e.g. Medtrack, Thomson Reuters), outsourcing to consulting firms operating under an "eat what you kill" model and face-to-face meetings with third parties. A well-developed in-house BD is crucial for enabling sustainable growth and is evident when reviewing case studies of successful life science startups.

The Campbell Alliance Dealmakers' Intentions, presented at the annual Biotechnology Industry Organization (BIO) convention, publishes current data on the interests of strategic partners and metrics on dealmaking.[10] In 2012, cumulative conversion rates (from Confidential Disclosure Agreement (CDA) stage to deals with upfront payments) are roughly one percent, taking on average six months to complete. This highlights the difficultly and inefficiencies that exist when undertaking business development. BD deals require patience and solid relationship management.

For a startup, attracting a BD manager with experience in Big Pharma (or any given partner) will give the company better insight and connections to smooth a potential deal. BD is often dictated by interpersonal relationships and building trust. While the introductions or initial connections may be facilitated by established relationships, they are normally kicked up to higher-level personnel. Having a combination of an in-house champion and follow-through are the necessary ingredients for successful deals.

IV. UNIVERSITY HEALTHCARE ENTREPRENEURSHIP

Universities have become an additional source for innovation through the translational efforts of basic science discoveries. Holden Thorp and Buck

Goldstein discuss the greater role universities will play, given the deep talent pool and research capabilities, long regarded as focusing solely on basic science.[11] The role of academic institutions in forming the basis for startup companies has existed even before the passing of the Bayh–Dole Act in 1980. This legislation permitted universities to protect inventions, whereas previously, the federal government retained exclusive rights that often severely limited options for commercial development. In recent years, entrepreneurship has become a strong focus of public and private universities in the hope of translating meaningful discoveries into the marketplace.

Startups born from academic research are of particular importance for companies seeking new areas of research and development. Academic institutions have a wellspring of research on novel drug targets and cutting-edge research from thought leaders. This type of innovation is unique to universities but does come at a price. It is very costly and ridden with failed experiments and limited commercialization support. This presents many challenges for startups and potential partners. University startups, due to their undeveloped nature, have difficulty in recruiting experienced talent, securing proof-of-concept funding and, more specifically, divesting academic and for-profit interests. Many universities have begun developing entrepreneurial support programs, either as an extension of technology transfer or in partnership with business or medical schools. These aim to support the issues addressed above and foster internal entrepreneurial know-how, long since separated from academia.

There are unique ingredients for creating a successful university spin-out that can have a dramatic effect on success. First, the prominence and "star" power of a faculty founder highly correlates with successful commercial outcomes.[12] This speaks to the credibility and innovation that such faculty brings to a newly formed startup. The second is that the amount of university support, both financial and programmatic, significantly increases startup activity.[13] This fact seems clear from meta-analysis studies performed on university technology transfer activity throughout the US. It is interesting to note those factors which do not correlate with entrepreneurial or commercial outcomes, namely number of faculty and postdocs, endowment size and incubator presence. To date, many universities are investing more resources in technology transfer and entrepreneurship programs with the hope of addressing the need for translational medicine. Underlying this shift is a greater focus on impacting the public good and fully leveraging government grant sources.

Biotechnology hubs like Boston, San Diego, San Francisco and Raleigh–Durham are all natural hotbeds for university-based startup activity. These regions all have the necessary ingredients to create and sustain startup activity, namely robust venture capital funding and experienced talent networks. The Massachusetts Institute of Technology (MIT) is an exceptional example of a university entrepreneurial eco-system. MIT boasts an extraordinary amount of prominent faculty, dedicated university resources and an active regional economic develop-ment atmosphere to support startup growth. Dr. Robert Langer, one of the most prolific faculty entrepreneurs, is a David H. Koch Institute Profes-sor at MIT. Dr. Langer has launched close to 30 startup companies and holds over 800 patents. While Dr. Langer is unique, it's certain that MIT and the entrepreneurial Boston region has significantly helped facilitate this type of faculty entrepreneurship. Success for a university often will breed more success within the university ecosystem, paving the way for the next generation of faculty entrepreneurs and attracting investment opportunities.

V. REGULATORY AFFAIRS AND CLINICAL TRIALS

The regulatory landscape is heavily dominated by the FDA in the US and International Conference on Harmonization (ICH) in Europe, Japan and as guidance in the US. The FDA regulates drugs, medical devices, veterinary products and to a limited extent diagnostics. Regulatory compliance is a costly undertaking, often requiring millions of dollars to recruit and compensate patients, hire qualified clinical staff, pay fees and manage communication between the regulatory oversight bodies. As a matter of principle and policy, clinical trials are staged in such a way as to mitigate safety risk for human subjects. Phase I trials are heavily focused on safety and dose ranging studies, supporting justification for Phase II trial design. Phase II trials are designed to establish efficacy benchmarks and patient screening. Phase III trials are large, usually multi-site studies intended to confirm both safety and efficacy in a more robust fashion. Phase I–III trials are fully transparent to the regulatory oversight body and require effective communication and relationship management. Depending on the product, FDA regulation will be handled by an appropriate division (e.g. Center for Drug Evaluation and Research, Center for Devices and Radiological Health) and, in cases of combination products, reviewed by multiple divisions. Ultimately, a company will submit a New Drug Application following successful completion of a Phase III clinical trial. When approved, this grants the company rights to market the drug, device or diagnostic, direct-to-consumers (DTC).

Diagnostic technologies may be regulated differently depending on the nature of the product. In Vitro Diagnostics (IVD) are governed by the FDA and are generally focused on blood screening, genetic testing and other tissue-based tests. These are distinct from so-called laboratory-developed tests (LDT) that are designed, manufactured and used within an individual laboratory. LDTs have historically been regulated by the Centers for Medicare and Medicaid Services (CMS) under the Clinical Laboratory Improvement Amendments (CLIA). This regulation is controlled at the laboratory level and is generally regarded as a lower bar for commercialization. It should be noted that the FDA is currently implementing tighter controls for LDTs and attempting to reposition them under their jurisdiction.

Working with the FDA, communication is essential to getting final approval for marketing a new drug, device or diagnostic. As a starting point, the FDA provides a comprehensive set of guidelines that provide a non-binding opinion for FDA's current thinking on any given topic.[14] These range from the basics of Good Laboratory Practices to Consumer-Directed Broadcast Advertisements as well as more specialized topics. In addition to these written materials, the FDA hosts several types of formal and informal meetings, all of which have defined response periods for the sponsor. Type A meetings are intended to assist an otherwise stalled product development program. Type B meetings are held at key milestones in development, primarily for review and feedback. Examples include pre-Investigational New Drug (pre-IND) meetings and end of Phase II meetings. Type C meetings are those which do not fit into the A or B category. These are generally seen as less time sensitive but still require feedback from the FDA. Meetings require significant preparation on the part of the clinical trial sponsor to ensure a maximum exchange of information and clarity. For startups, these usually require the resources of a strategic partner or outsourcing to regulatory consultants. Startups commonly license assets to Big Pharma prior to Phase III trials to fully capitalize on their regulatory competencies.

VI. REIMBURSEMENT: HEALTHCARE VALUE CHAIN

The healthcare value chain is distinct and much more complex in comparison to other business models. Depending on the product in development, the startup must be clear in defining the customer(s) and enact a strategy for successful market adoption and revenue generation. While patients are often the beneficiaries of a given product, they often are removed from pricing and buying decisions. Payers (e.g. health maintenance organizations (HMOs), preferred provider organizations (PPOs), Medicaid) are tasked with developing pricing structures after marketing approval is granted. This creates difficulty for startups since pricing strategies are far removed from product development.

Next along in the value chain are providers, namely hospitals and pharmacies. Providers will bear the burden of costs temporarily, at the discretion of the patient's physician. There may be standards put in place which define allowable costs from the payers but otherwise require negotiation between the provider and payer. In fairness, this is only part of the picture. The complete value chain is much more complicated and includes manufacturers, distributors and government regulators. Understanding the value chain as it relates to a given startup's lead product is essential. For example, value propositions must be considered, not only for patients, but for physicians. Developing a healthcare product requires clear understanding of the clinical use case. While a therapy may be predicted to be effective, if decision support or diagnostic framework is not in place, market adoption will likely be non-existent. In addition, if the cost of goods is orders of magnitude higher than a competitor (e.g. biologic therapies are typically more costly to manufacture), market adoption will also be hindered.

This is also a very current topic in the pharmaceutical space, with recent media coverage and policy discussions focused around Gilead Sciences' hepatitis C therapy, Sovaldi. Gilead had strongly lobbied for pricing around $1,000/day, partly to recover development costs. The controversy is fueled by the fact that Sovaldi is curative in a high percentage of patients, garnering accusations of profiteering at the cost of patients' lives. Similar debates were seen with the advent of innovative anti-retroviral drugs for HIV treatment. The issue remains that regulatory compliance is a very costly undertaking; startups and Big Pharma alike must see clear incentives to continue development. This, however, must be tempered with community engagement and aid programs for low-income patients.

VII. FUNDING MODELS: PAST, PRESENT AND FUTURE

(a) Grant Opportunities and Non-Dilutive Capital

Pre-seed capital is oftentimes necessary to support the formation of a new startup company. Healthcare startups, in particular, require specialized labor, expensive equipment and significant product development.

This type of funding can come from several sources: the friends and family round (typically dilutive) or economic development agencies (non-dilutive grants). These usually are below $100,000 and are focused on enabling launch of the company. State agencies or local non-profit economic development groups are the most common sources. These funding sources are relatively easy to obtain and come with little or no strings attached. The downside is that this funding is piecemeal, stuttering development operations and lengthening timelines.

Small Business Innovative Research (SBIR) and Small Business Technology Transfer (STTR) grants are another source of non-dilutive capital, typically ranging from $150,000–$1.5 million for a 6–12 month period. These grants, coordinated by the Small Business Administration, mandate that each government agency (e.g. National Institutes of Health, National Science Foundation, Department of Defense) must reserve a minimum of 2.8 percent (FY2014) for awards to small businesses. These grants are unique in that they focus on high-risk technology development and provide a significant source of early-stage capital to companies that would otherwise not be available. Awards are staged as Phase I ($150,000–$225,000) and Phase II (up to $1.5 million), reviewed by technical experts designated by the government agency. While these grants fulfill a need not provided by other funding sources, there are drawbacks to this approach: long turnaround times for review often result in stalled company development, and funding opportunity announcements (FOAs) may not perfectly align with the needs of the company. Success rates for these awards are typically around 10–15 percent, depending on the funding cycle and funding agency. Using experienced SBIR/STTR consultants or partnering with an experienced company can substantially increase the success rate.

(b)   Strategic Partnering

Partnering at an early-stage, if well positioned, offers several key advantages: much needed seed capital and access to expertise within the strategic partner. As mentioned earlier, Big Pharma companies are continually downsizing internal discovery efforts, and as such there has been a significant uptick in partnering activity around novel technologies. Successful partnering requires an extensive network, experienced deal-makers and a solid relationship between scientific teams. In many cases, opportunities will be identified by scientific staff, which will then be relayed to BD or technology scouts at established firms. From the startups perspective, it's crucial to identify and understand the needs of a potential partner. The product must align with established firm's strategic vision, be positioned at the appropriate development stage and valued at a reasonable and justifiable level. If these conditions are not considered up front, this will likely stall or kill a potential partnering deal.

(c) Crowdfunding

Crowdfunding remains a lesser-known avenue for many healthcare startups. This is largely due to the relatively high levels of capital needed to advance a product. Funding platforms, like MedStartr, are modeled after non-healthcare crowdfunding platforms such as KickStarter or IndieGoGo. While these models are focused on a philanthropic model, legislation signed into law in 2012 titled the Jumpstart Our Business Startups (JOBS) Act, sets forth guidelines for broadening the scope of crowdfunding. In particular, Title III of the JOBS Act enables non-accredited investors to provide $1,000–$5,000 to a given small business. The key difference here is changing restrictions on accreditation for individual investors. This would enable startups to raise no more than $1 million per year but require disclosure and strict accounting records. While the crowdfunding market is still undeveloped within the healthcare sphere, many Healthcare IT startups have begun to take advantage of it. It's clear that this funding model is not a funding panacea for healthcare startups; however, it has enabled more flexible strategies for early-stage companies.

(d) Angel and Venture Capital Fundraising

As noted earlier, moving products from bench to bedside is a costly undertaking. Both angel investors and venture capital (VC) firms provide vital capital to early-stage companies for research and development. Angel investors and venture capitalists invest with similar goals in mind, namely to provide financial return on investment. For an entrepreneur, it is important to fully understand this reality. While many investors are passionate about improving quality of care and displacing subpar health-care products, the first priority is to return investment to accredited investors (angels) or limited partners (venture capitalists).

Angel investors are typically high-net-worth individuals and often consolidate funds within a group (or syndicates) to diversify investment risk. These investors are generally focused on seed investments or opportunities that can generate revenue within a short time frame. Generally speaking, medical devices, Healthcare IT, diagnostics and service startups align well with their investment strategy. Therapeutic startups, which require substantially more investment, tend to dissuade angels as their initial seed investments can be severely diluted before returns are realized.

Venture capitalists are distinct from angel groups in that they are professionally managed and are capable of larger individual investments. Within the healthcare space, many VC firms specifically focus on drug development, diagnostic and medical device products. While most venture capitalists have migrated towards end of Phase II investments, some still get in earlier. The hope is that these selected risks will create a larger upside for the fund when follow-on funding is deployed. While VC firm numbers have been trending down over recent years, overall investment activity is fairly robust.[15] VC firms have shown greater interest in startup investment since 2006, not only by the increasing number of deals done, but also by investing more per deal. The average seed-stage investment has tripled since 1998. This is a good sign for entrepreneurs, and given the current resurgence of healthcare-focused Initial Public Offerings (IPOs), VC activity is expected to increase.

Among the different VC models, one worth noting is Corporate Venture Capital (CVC). These funds are associated with large biotechnology or medical device firms (e.g. Lilly Ventures, SR One, MedImmune Ventures, Sofinnova Ventures). Models vary from complete autonomy to tight strategic alignment with the parent company. Bruce Booth, Partner at Atlas Ventures (Boston, MA), highlights an interesting trend for those investments in which CVCs were involved: significantly higher rates of licensing deals, mergers & acquisitions (M&As) and IPOs.[16] CVC investment certainly won't guarantee an exit but it's likely to increase crosstalk with Pharma talent and provide access to BD networks.

Third Rock Ventures (Cambridge, MA) has historically outperformed many other VC firms and recently closed a $516 million fund in 2013.[17] Their investment strategy focuses on sourcing technologies via their in-house experienced scientists and forming the company from the ground up. Their evaluation criteria are known as Third Rock Ultra Killer Kriteria (TRUKK). In short, the asset must be within three years of clinical trials, preclinical data must be replicable and Big Pharma shouldn't be poised to compete. Third Rock's model has been widely discussed and had some early successes. It will likely be many years before their current investments translate to medical breakthroughs for patients. Regardless, as VC firms consolidate or fade away, it's likely similar multi-asset incubation models will take hold.

(e) Public Markets: The Changing IPO Landscape

Since the JOBS Act was passed, the healthcare/biotech sector has seen a resurgence of IPOs. This has created a new path to IPO and helped companies by enabling confidential filing of IPO documents, giving companies better control over timing (so-called test-the-water approach). In addition, many IPO offerings in 2010–2012 have performed well. This has renewed the appetite for public market investment in a sector plagued by poor returns in the past. As successes mount, more and more companies are considering an IPO exit strategy. In years past, there was common sentiment within the healthcare/biotech space that the only viable exit strategy was via M&A. This is good news for healthcare startups. Companies now have increased leverage when engaging in M&A discussions. Time will tell whether or not this is a sustainable trend or a biotech bubble, but for now, it has created an improved outlook for many startups.

VIII. PEOPLE

(a) Early-Stage and Growth Management

Newly formed startups are typically very high risk and capital deficient: this often leads to difficulty in recruiting high-caliber talent. This poses several problems for new companies – lack of continuity, less experienced Chief Executive Officers (CEOs) – and can lead to credibility concerns for the company. This "starter" CEO phase is common and, after significant investment is secured, can signal a change in leadership and formal management team. Recruitment of early-stage management requires access to a current and broad network. Oftentimes, finding Connectors (i.e. highly networked individuals) helps finding a suitable person with the right technical background, interest and financial security.[18] CEOs at this stage may be engaged in limited fundraising, exploring licensing opportunities, acquiring assets to better valuation and, most importantly, task management. Time is critical at this early stage. It's often a race to reach specific milestones and achieve a defined value inflection point. Managing tasks within the company to minimize delays is central to enabling a successful exit.

Upon significant investment, a more professional and experienced management team may be recruited to help the company fundraise subsequent investment rounds, manage burn rate and keep the company progressing towards milestones, particularly when problems arise.

Growth management, in the sense of startup, is crucially important to graduating to another level of exposure. The role as a growth CEO requires extensive travel and networking, creating lots of collisions and hoping some stick. It's important to note here that skill sets and interests of early-stage management will often diverge as the company develops. Communication, at the outset, is important to avoid unamicable handoffs with incoming management.

(b)   Recruitment and Leveraging a Scientific Advisory Board (SAB)

A Scientific Advisory Board (SAB) can bring lots of value to a growing startup company. In the beginning, an SAB acts a vehicle for credibility to investors and outside interests. They can also act as a means to perform some market/customer validation which one can parlay in strengthening one's investment pitch. After a Series A round, management and the board of directors will likely work to recruit higher-level folks, using equity and other incentives, to help manage the scientific strategy for your company. Bruce Booth of Atlas Ventures provides a very thoughtful take on best practices regarding SABs.[19] In short, a successful SAB should work to engage productive and easily managed advisors, avoiding window dressing Nobel laureates who may not be available or committed and so on. A properly recruited SAB can dramatically impact the prospects for a budding young startup.

Prior to any significant investment, it's wise practice to convene a "pre-SAB." This is a loose, often unpaid, group of experienced folks that can help quickly expand your network, provide feedback and offer new directions around a technology. The idea here is to reduce the barrier for engagement and see who works and who doesn't. This can also be a proving ground for potential management or full-time employees. If managed properly, convening a group of 4–6 experienced business and scientific folks will help produce lots of valuable discussion which is often difficult to generate otherwise.

IX.   INCUBATORS AND ACCELERATORS

By and large, incubators and accelerators have flourished after the 2008 financial crisis. Models such as Y Combinator (in fact, they have recently included biotech startups)[20] and TechStars have helped numerous IT startups gather the tools and exposure needed to fully commercialize their product. The healthcare sector has followed suit with similar incubation models but with some key differences. Successful life science incubators have partnered or been solely funded by Big Pharma firms, in an effort to capture more innovation, earlier. Janssen Labs, part of Johnson and Johnson, has established locations in San Diego, Boston and San Francisco and has reinvigorated the biotech incubator scene. The ultimate goal is to create, or augment, biotech activity in these three major hubs by providing state-of-the-art equipment, access to talent and flexible terms for fledgling startups. There are also many other incubators associated with economic development groups or universities popping up, including the Massachusetts Venture Development Center (Boston, MA), QB3 (San Francisco, CA), Harlem Biospace (New York City, NY) and the Sid Martin Biotechnology Incubator (Alachua, FL).

Rock Health (San Francisco, CA) is a successful and well-known incubator focused squarely on Healthcare IT startups. Founded in 2010, the model includes seed funding, access to their network of partners and access to incubator space. While it's too early to tell if Rock Health or similar Healthcare IT models will spawn big changes within the industry, the amount of startup activity is promising. As noted earlier, the Healthcare IT sector has experienced growing pains as with any new marketplace, but the success of one or two startups will likely catalyze more investment interest and entrepreneurial activity.

X. CONCLUSION

In this chapter we have reviewed the healthcare entrepreneurship land-scape and challenges for drug, medtech and Healthcare IT companies. As more disruptive technologies and provider adoption of innovation continues, the growth rate of the healthcare sector will continue to increase. The "omics" revolution alongside Big Data, still in its infancy, will drive development of improved diagnostics and inform more efficient life science discovery and validation efforts. In addition, Healthcare IT will have a dramatic impact as technology infrastructure becomes more robust. Opportunities for patient decision support, healthcare delivery efficiencies and consumer-based diagnostics will dramatically change the healthcare landscape. These innovations will be fully realized through the unwavering entrepreneurial drive that exists within the US and globally. There are still challenges associated with healthcare startup development. Examples include an unaligned healthcare value chain, costly regulatory approval and an overall lack of seed capital. In the same manner that innovation is the answer for clinical unmet need in healthcare, innovative approaches to thinking about healthcare entrepreneurship challenges are the solution.

NOTES

1. Big Pharma refers to the world's vast and influential pharmaceutical industry.
2. PhRMA (2013). 2013 Biopharmaceutical Research Industry Profile. Washington, DC. Retrieved June, 2013, from http://www.phrma.org/sites/default/files/pdf/PhRMA Profile 2013.pdf.
3. McBride, R. (2013). Nimbus Discovery – 2013 Fierce 15 – FierceBiotech. Retrieved September 06, 2014, from http://www.fiercebiotech.com/special-reports/nimbus-discovery-fiercebiotechs-2013-fierce-15.
4. Lindgren, C. (2013). The Future of Medtech. Evaluate: London, UK.
5. A product approved via the FDA's 510(k) process, typically the most common, allows the company to market the medical device within the US. This process is substantially less expensive than going through the Premarket Approval (PMA) process, which is analogous to the therapeutic New Drug Application.
6. Josh Makower and Aabed Meer, L. D. (2010). FDA Impact on U.S. Medical Technology Innovation (p. 42). Retrieved August 15, 2014, from http://eucomed.org/uploads/Press%20Releases/FDA%20impact%20on%20U.S.%20Medical%20Technology%20Innovation.pdf.
7. EY (2013). Pulse of the Industry: Medical Technology Report. London, UK. Retrieved June, 2013, from http://www.ey.com/US/en/Industries/Life-Sciences/Pulse-of-the-industry – medical-technology-report-2013.
8. Blank, S. (2013). "Reinventing life science startups: evidence-based entrepreneurship." *Forbes*. Retrieved April 08, 2014, from http://www.forbes.com/sites/steveblank/2013/08/20/reinventing-life-science-startups-evidence-based-entrepreneurship/.
9. Shane, S. (2004). *Academic Entrepreneurship: University Spinoffs and Wealth Creation.* Cheltenham, UK and Northampton, MA: Edward Elgar Publishing.
10. Stewart, B. J., Patel, N., Cao, D. and Rieger, R. (2013). Dealmakers' Intentions 2013. Campbell Alliance: New York, NY.
11. Thorp, H. and B. Goldstein (2010). *Engines of Innovation: The Entrepreneurial University in the Twenty-First Century.* University of North Carolina Press.
12. Powers, J. B. and P. P. McDougall (2005). "University start-up formation and technology licensing with firms that go public: a resource-based view of academic entrepreneurship." *Journal of Business Venturing* 20(3): 291–311.
13. O'Shea, R. P., Allen, T. J., Chevalier, A. and Roche, F. (2005). "Entrepreneurial orientation, technology transfer and spinoff performance of U.S. universities." *Research Policy* 34(7): 994–1009.
14. FDA (n.d.). Guidances. Retrieved September 06, 2014, from http://www.fda.gov/regulatory information/guidances/.
15. PWC (2011). MoneyTree Report. PricewaterhouseCoopers, National Venture Capital Association. Retrieved June, 2013, from https://www.pwcmoneytree.com.
16. Booth, B. (2012). Want Better Odds? Get a Pharma Corporate VC to Invest. LifeSciVC. Retrieved September 06, 2014, from http://lifescivc.com/2012/05/want-better-odds-get-a-pharma-corporate-vc-to-invest/.
17. Timmerman, L. (2013). Third Rock Stocks Up With $516M New Fund, Looks to Start 16 Cos. *Xconomy*. Retrieved September 06, 2014, from http://www.xconomy.com/boston/2013/03/25/third-rock-reloads-with-516m-new-fund-looks-to-start-16-new-cos/.
18. Gladwell, M. (2000). *The Tipping Point.* New York, NY: Little, Brown and Company.
19. Booth, B. (2012). Biotech Scientific Advisory Boards: what works, what doesn't. *Forbes.* Retrieved September 09, 2014, from http://www.forbes.com/sites/brucebooth/2012/09/10/biotech-scientific-advisory-boards-what-works-what-doesnt/.
20. Noorden, R. Van. (2014). Start-up investor bets on biotech: Nature News & Comment. *Nature*. Retrieved September 10, 2014, from http://www.nature.com/news/start-up-investor-bets-on-biotech-1.15096.

PART III

Arts, music, and design entrepreneurship

7. The entrepreneurial musician: the Tao of DIY

Angela Myles Beeching

> Music is social. Music is current and ever changing. And most of all, music requires musicians. The winners in the music business of tomorrow are individuals and organizations that create communities, connect people, spread ideas and act as the hub of the wheel ... indispensable and well-compensated.
>
> Seth Godin, marketer/entrepreneur[1]

I. A BRAVE NEW WORLD

Over the past ten years, technological developments along with cultural and demographic changes have led to an upending of the traditional music industry. File-sharing and the proliferation of online tools for recording and distribution have been the key disruptors, eliminating musicians' dependency on traditional production and distribution channels.

The old school music industry relied on a loosely coordinated system of gatekeepers and middlemen: from labels, distributors, and retail record stores, to music publishers, radio station programmers, artist managers, and booking agents. Today's musicians operate in a DIY (do it yourself) digital world that offers them new opportunities to create their own paths to success.

Flutist and MacArthur award winner Claire Chase defines the musician-entrepreneur as an artist who is also "a producer, an organizer, an activist, and an inventor."[2] Claire founded the acclaimed new music group ICE (International Contemporary Ensemble) in 2001, when she was fresh out of Oberlin College, Ohio. Claire sees her work as part of a growing movement, saying that "the 21st century, in many ways, could be the century of the new business model – the new music band in our case – the modular, adaptive, artist-driven performing arts organization."[3]

Although it's easier than ever for musicians to get their music out, what's difficult is building awareness for one's music in a market flooded with product. As referenced in the Seth Godin quote at the start of this chapter, success in music is all about creating and cultivating a fan base: a community of support that will fuel and sustain musicians' creative endeavors.[4]

To build a fan base, it's important to understand what audiences/customers want. With audiences spending increasing amounts of time online, somewhat removed from each other, there's a need and a desire among fans to make authentic, direct, and personal connections with artists.

"I think that social media is really ... the only way for somebody like me to craft my image," says "Avant cellist" Zoë Keating in a 2010 NPR piece. She now has 1.2 million twitter followers and tweets about life on tour accompanied by her son (now age 3) and her husband. She shares all kinds of ideas and enthusiasms with her followers. "That's what fans want now," says Keating. "They want to have your album right [at hand and to] feel like they know you."[5]

Keating's self-released recordings have gone to the top of the iTunes classical charts. She has built a DIY career without a manager, publicist, or record label. Described as a "one woman orchestra," Keating in performance uses a foot-pedal controlled laptop to create layer upon layer of her own intricate music. She releases recordings on her own label, handles all of her own publicity, and licenses her music regularly for film, TV, dance productions, and commercials.

She launched her unconventional career ten years ago when she quit her job as an information architect and began touring with the rock cello group Rasputina. But her solo act and recordings didn't fit what record labels wanted – she had to go DIY. Her twitter bio exemplifies her entrepreneurial approach: "When all the doors are closed sometimes you're better off making your own building."[6]

The disruption of the old model has also created opportunities for new services and products to meet the needs of entrepreneurial musicians and their fans. From music composition software (like Ableton Live and SuperLooper, which Zoë Keating uses) to online booking platforms (such as SonicBids, GigMasters, Rabble) and online distribution platforms (iTunes, CD Baby, Pandora, Spotify, Bandcamp, etc.), the industry continues to morph. Between outmoded copyright and licensing laws, and the technological breakthroughs and experiments in new business models, this is the golden age for entrepreneurs to re-imagine the music industry.

Starting with a discussion of how musicians are re-defining entrepreneurship, this chapter includes case studies of musician entrepreneurs, as well as details of the necessary skills and the intrinsic challenges. Also included are insights for entrepreneurs of all disciplines, implications for entrepreneur educators, and a set of conditions that are ripe for entrepreneurial development in music.

II. ENTREPRENEURSHIP RE-DEFINED

Derived from the verb "to undertake," entrepreneurship at its root is about initiative. Peter Spellman, author of a number of popular music career books, writes about the derivation,

> The French economist, Jean-Baptiste Say, who lived at the time of the French Revolution, invented the term "entrepreneur" to describe someone who unlocks capital tied up in land and redirects it to "change the future." He was one of the first economists, in fact, to introduce the idea of change and uncertainty as something normal and even positive.[7]

Initiative and creating value are at the heart of entrepreneurship.

Entrepreneurship in the arts encompasses a wide range of practices. James Undercofler, the former Dean of the Eastman School of Music, Rochester, New York, is developing (as of this writing) the nation's first master's degree program in arts entrepreneurship for SUNY (State University of New York) at Purchase, New York. Undercofler defines entrepreneurship using four zones. The most basic (Zone 1) definition, is entrepreneurial thinking or self-empowerment (Undercofler terms this "personal entrepreneurship"). Subsequent zones progress from making a career for oneself (and sometimes others) to starting a "new but recognizable" non-profit or commercial entity, to launching a new and *innovative* non-profit or commercial venture.[8]

For the purposes of this chapter, music entrepreneurship will be understood as taking initiative to create something new of value that meets an unmet need. These three key elements, initiative, value creation, and satisfying a need, have specific ramifications for musicians and will be used as lines of inquiry in the examples and discussion that follow.

III. MUSIC ENTREPRENEURSHIP IN ACTION

To help musicians deal with the practical exigencies of the DIY world, a range of services, consulting practices, and tools have been created and promoted – often by and for musicians.

Derek Sivers was a successful songwriter and bandleader who became an "accidental entrepreneur" because he wanted to sell his CDs online. Without a label or a distributor, it was difficult to manage product distribution of any size. In 1997, well before PayPal and iTunes existed, there weren't off-the-shelf solutions, so Derek taught himself computer programming, set up a merchant account, and built his own shopping cart in order to sell his recordings from his own website. Soon his friends were asking him to post their albums, too, and that's how the company CD Baby was born. Sivers grew CD Baby to become what was then the world's largest online distributor of independent music – all the while keeping the original ethos and mission at the forefront: customer-focused and musician-friendly.[9]

"In 2004, after being approached by Steve Jobs, CD Baby became a digital music distributor. Sivers sold the company to Disc Makers in 2008 for $22 million, and placed his interest in a trust for music education."[10]

Not all music entrepreneurs are tech junkies: some musicians focus on creating new and improved analog instruments and gear. Boston-based percussionist Neil Grover is a prime example. At 24, he was living his dream: playing with the Boston Symphony Orchestra (BSO). He "got to play and was intrigued by a very old triangle that was treasured by the BSO percussionists. It resounded with a unique sparkle and spread of overtones."[11] Neil Grover's curiosity led him to explore the why and how of that particular triangle's vibrant sound.

"With the help of students at MIT's Acoustics and Vibrations Lab, [Grover] set out to uncover the secret of creating a triangle with prominent overtone resonance. The result was his producing a 9″ triangle for his personal use." Neil had no intention of starting a percussion manufacturing company because he was already busy and happy with a full schedule of playing and teaching. But when Boston's top percussion-ists heard the "Grover" triangle, they all wanted him to make more. Grover started doing this one at a time, to satisfy his colleagues' requests, and soon he was getting calls from percussionists across the US. Unintentionally, Grover Pro percussion was born and Neil next added mallets, woodblocks, and other percussion products to his line – and he's continued to regularly add instruments, instruction manuals, and accessories over the past 30 years.[12]

Grover Pro is a successful niche company as opposed to CD Baby which has had a much broader market share. But both Neil Grover and Derek Sivers are illustrations of von Hippel's "user innovators"[13] in that as active musicians they originally set out only to meet their own needs. But in the process they each found a ready market and as "accidental entrepreneurs" then took initiative, created value, and satisfied the unmet needs of their customers. If we consider this in light of Undercofler's zones, these musicians started out in Zone 1 – self-empowered to create something useful for themselves, only to discover there's a need and demand that they can meet, which pushed them on to subsequent zones.

IV. MUSICIAN TRAINING GENERATING ENTREPRENEURIAL READINESS

Through their intensive music training, musicians develop many of the foundational skills and habits that are key to entrepreneurial success. Catherine Radbill (former director of the New York University Steinhardt School's Undergraduate Music Business Program) argues that many of the essential traits commonly associated with entrepreneurs apply equally well to musicians, namely "passion, perseverance, enthusiasm, self-confidence, compassion, adaptability, resourcefulness, creativity, inventiveness, optimism, multi-tasking, and persuasiveness."[14]

Beyond these attributes, intensive music study also builds many of the transferable skills required of entrepreneurs. From hours of individual practice, musicians gain self-discipline, problem solving, critical listening skills, as well as the power to concentrate.

From their ensemble training and performance work, musicians also hone their communication, leadership, collaboration, and presentation skills. From working intensively with both the art and craft repertoire, musicians develop analytical and synthesizing skills. Other transferable skills include the capacity to shift one's focus between the forest and the trees, and the ability to appreciate multiple interpretations of the same text.[15]

Interviewed for a piece in *The New York Times* on the connection between music and success, the former World Bank president (and sometimes cellist) James Wolfensohn adds to this list "the ability to connect disparate or even contradictory ideas." And according to Paul Allen, the guitar-playing billionaire co-founder of Microsoft, music "pushes you to look beyond what currently exists and express yourself in a new way."[16] These traits are integral to the vision and critical thinking skills of entrepreneurial leaders.

But while many entrepreneurial traits may be "natural" to trained musicians, there are also typical obstacles.

V. CAUTION: THE MUSICIAN'S MINDSET

For musicians, the term "entrepreneur" often connotes the business world and therefore is seen, paradoxically, as the antithesis of creativity and art. For some musicians, the work done in the recording and rehearsal studios and onstage is experienced as a protected oasis from the world of business, with its focus on money, numbers, and deadlines.

This kind of "anti-business" thinking undermines a musician's entrepreneurial ideas and ventures. It can hinder a musician's ability to connect with those handling the business side of music: a stumbling block to connecting with club managers, promoters, donor prospects, media contacts, and even fans.

This unfortunate "us versus them" attitude has contributed to musicians being uninformed about how their own industry operates. This in turn has led to many performers and composers, out of ignorance, signing away their copyrights and royalty options, preventing them from earning and collecting their share of profits.

Table 7.1 provides an illustration of the Art versus Commerce tension, the stereotypical musicians' black and white thinking that pits art against business.[17] On the "Art" side of the equation is the world that musicians love: the time spent performing, composing, rehearsing, recording, and coaching.

Table 7.1   The two sides of music: Art vs. Commerce

Music as Art	Business of Music
"Good" (clean: pure of integrity)	"Bad" (dirty: opportunistic, commercial)
Realm of the imagination, creative	Tedious, dull
Us (musicians, people who "get it")	Them (the "other")
True calling	"Selling out" (pandering)
Focus on one's own satisfaction	Focus on the market, creating for/ with others

On the opposite side of the equation is "taking care of the business," which musicians generally consider negative – to varying degrees. For some musicians, the business of their profession is seen as tedious and somewhat burdensome (a "necessary evil"). But for others, the business of music is actually repugnant: idealistic musicians sometimes equate any business dealings with "selling out" – with compromising their artistic integrity.

For musicians, who have typically had no training for "taking care of business," the work may involve a steep learning curve and considerable investment of time and money. The "business" side can include the organizing, promoting, and funding of projects, as well as the practical necessities of booking concerts and tours, tracking of finances, taxes. Since these may be daunting tasks for emerging artists, the anxiety or fear may simply reinforce a musician's avoidance of taking control of her/his own career.

As for why this dichotomy is so prevalent among musicians and other "creatives," philosopher and social critic Lewis Hyde offers a key piece of the puzzle.

VI. THE GIFT ECONOMY

Lewis Hyde's modern classic *The Gift*,[18] has been an enduring favorite among artists of every discipline, as it helps explain the dilemma creatives face in how their artistic output is valued in a market economy. Hyde asserts that a work of art is a gift, not a commodity.

The book presents an anthropological tour of gift exchange practices across cultures. Hyde uses examples ranging from Native American potlatch tradition to South Sea tribesmen circulating shells and necklaces among neighboring communities. Through this tradition tribe leaders show respect and honor towards each other, which in turn helps ensure stability within and among communities.

These gift exchange traditions embody an alternative concept of wealth, value, and ownership because the "gifts" are always passed on to others – they are not intended to be kept, sold, or "monetized." Hyde explains that our more familiar sense of "gifts," common in many European cultures, refers to the possession of goods, as in, "something that's given to me becomes mine, and it's as if it's contained in my ego. I have complete control over it." Hyde contrasts this with the gift economy "in which you are the steward of something which is just passing through you."[19]

Further, Hyde connects the gift economy to talent and artistry, which have long been referred to as gifts, with the possessor of such gifts having the responsibility of "giving back." We also regularly speak of "giving" performances.

As for the exchange of value and the idea of keeping gifts in motion, if we examine what happens between a performer and an audience, we see it is a human exchange: emotional, social, and spiritual. This is what the musicologist Christopher Small has described as "musicking," a kind of collaborative act of meaning-making and community-building.[20]

The live performance experience provides – for both musicians and audience – the opportunity to feel something together, to become in effect a temporary community within the performance space, reminding each person that she or he is not alone. Ultimately, as Christopher Small asserted, the real power of music lies in its capacity to build empathy and community, not in its commodification.[21]

There are some cultures in which everyone makes music, where it's as much a part of everyday life as walking, eating, and breathing. In these cultures there's no such thing as a professional musician, because "musicking" is an everyday activity. In such cultures the gift economy operates unimpeded by market forces.

But we do not live in such a culture. In our mainstream lifestyles, musicians live a dual existence. On the one hand, musicians traffic in the gift economy, in which the currency exchanges are emotional, social, and spiritual capital. And on the other, these same musicians are expected to market, promote, and sell their artistic product as though it were a commodity.

The reality is that the arts are transacted in dual economies: the free market and the gift economies. For musicians (as well as other creative artists), straddling the two economies involves balancing two very different motives, and this can lead to unforeseen conflicts and difficulties.

VII. CASE STUDIES

CASE STUDY NO. 1: AMANDA PALMER AND COLLIDING ECONOMIES

The punk cabaret bandleader Amanda Palmer became the crowdfunding poster child in 2012 for exceeded her goal to fund a self-released new album. Instead of the $100,000 she'd aimed for, she raised nearly $1.2 million from close to 25,000 fans, making her the first musician to break the $1 million threshold on a Kickstarter project. But this also resulted in a public relations nightmare with a substantial portion of the musician community.

Palmer's popular 2013 TED talk, "The Art of Asking,"[22] details how she got started as a musician/entrepreneur. At night she was performing with her band

---

the Dresden Dolls, but her "day job" was busking in Boston as a silent street performance artist/mime, complete with a hat set out in front for financial contributions. Palmer explains that she considered this a kind of service exchange. The money offered was in appreciation for the performance and something of value was exchanged in the human interaction between the person putting money in the hat and the wordless eye contact the human connection Palmer provided.

In line with this kind of exchange of value, Palmer details in her talk how she later came to focus on becoming more connected with fans and supporters of her music. She learned to tweet for what she needed during her DIY grassroots tours, whether it was couches to surf (lodging for her and her band), meals, stage props, or even a neti pot. Palmer describes both her performance experience AND her crowdfunding as "falling into the audience and trusting them." She's referring to the emotional vulnerability inherent in any performance and the extending of this trust to the crowdsourcing of her tour logistics can be seen simply as the aligning of the artistic and business sides of her career.

Consistent with her approach to crowdsourcing her touring, Amanda regularly invited local musicians to play backup for parts of her show and later during the show to "pass the hat" and collect funds from the audience for themselves.

After raising over a million dollars to promote her album, Palmer planned her tour as she usually did, crowdsourcing a few backup musicians at each stop. This is where the problem arose. Because her Kickstarter campaign had raised so much money for the album, the fact that she wasn't paying local collaborators was viewed by many within the musician community as unethical. There was quite a lot of cross talk online and, eventually, Palmer did pay the musicians involved, but the episode left many in the musician community soured on Palmer. Her fans saw things differently.

One way to understand this community relations debacle is to see it as a culture clash between the gift economy and the market economy. As long as Palmer was a struggling musician, it was fine to ask colleagues to give their performance and then pass the hat for compensation. But once she had raised considerable capital, she became a stand-in for the commercial music industry, the market economy ("the man" to many of her colleagues), and so her image as a grassroots mission-driven musician was tarnished.[23]

This case underscores the need for entrepreneurs in any sector to articulate where they stand – philosophically, as well as legally and financially – in relation to their fans, donors, collaborators, and colleagues. Much of the success of music entrepreneurs comes from aligning their interests and needs with the right partners, as is evidenced in the next example.

CASE STUDY NO. 2: UNLIKELY PARTNERSHIPS SATISFY UNMET NEEDS

A key tenet of entrepreneurship education is that any new product or service should fill a clearly defined unmet need. After all, there needs to be a prospective customer base and a market for the product.

This can be a tough concept for musicians who may consider their latest album or composition as their entrepreneurial venture. Musicians don't generally consider their work as filling a practical need, other than a need for entertainment and/or artistry – and these may simply be a question of subjective and fleeting taste.

To determine the need that music fills, it helps to think about music's function in community. Music, aside from its value as art, has other valuable attributes, such as its capacity to draw together disparate groups, creating a sense of bonding and celebration. This idea is played out in this second case, an example of a new piece of music creating value for unlikely community partners.

With a keen interest in geology, Boulder-based composer Jeffrey Nytch had the "crazy idea"[24] of writing a symphonic work that would celebrate the Rocky Mountain region's geological history. What prompted the brainstorm was Jeff's attending of a community seminar on geology and learning that the Geological Society of America (GSA), based locally in Boulder, was celebrating an important anniversary in 2013.

Jeff pitched his idea to the GSA, that they would commission him to write a new "Geological Symphony" to be performed by the Boulder Philharmonic as part of their celebratory anniversary. This was an unprecedented project for the GSA – they had no experience working with composers, let alone with Jeff – and an unusual pitch to the Boulder Philharmonic as well, since they had never partnered in commissioning works with geological associations. The GSA was interested – and the timing worked well for the Boulder Philharmonic, too, which had already planned that the upcoming season would focus on music inspired by the natural world. Considering a new work costs tens of thousands of dollars, Nytch's pitch must have been a good one.

As he detailed as a guest blogger for Greg Sandow's "Future of Classical Music" on *ArtsJournal*, Nytch identified a number of unmet needs that his entrepreneurial project would address. First, the GSA was looking for innovative ways to celebrate its anniversary year convention, to gain media attention, and to draw in new members.

As for the Boulder Philharmonic's needs, an important part of the orchestra's mission is to celebrate its community and region, whose residents are generally quite environmentally conscious. So with the orchestra's overarching programming theme that year being "the natural world," the work was meeting even more needs. Like the GSA, the Boulder Philharmonic was also looking to expand its audience, gain media attention, and attract subscribers. Using the "buzz" of a newly commissioned work, especially one with such an unusual connection to the region, certainly helped.[25]

The resulting piece, Nytch's *Symphony No. 1: Formations*, reflects on "the creation of the continental crust; a brief history of humans' interactions with the geology in Colorado; and the revealing of the modern Rocky Mountains."[26] The work was co-commissioned by the Boulder Philharmonic and the GSA – who secured sponsorship from ExxonMobil, with which it had a long-standing relationship. There was additional funding from the Composer Assistance Program of New Music USA.[27]

What was in this for ExxonMobil to invest its corporate sponsorship funding? They were mentioned in all of the promotional materials for the premiere and in all of the Geological Society's convention materials, cultivating their image as being community-minded and environmentally respectful.

But getting the green light to write the work was only part of the job. In the months leading up to the premiere, to help drive interest (and ticket sales) for the concert, and help people feel a connection to the music, Nytch produced a series of 15 short videos de-mystifying his creative process.[28] Some of these included "field trips" to specific natural sites that were inspirational for his writing. The videos were highlighted and promoted on social media. Closer to the event, as additional "teasers" to the premiere, the Boulder Philharmonic partnered with the Boulder County Open Space and Mountain Parks in programming a series of geological/musical talks and naturalist-led hikes up into the foothills, drumming up even more interest in the project.

The audience at the premiere was more than 1500, a near record for a Philharmonic opening season concert, according to Nytch. And many of those who attended were not the regular symphony attendees. But the real test of a new work is whether or not other musicians perform it after the initial premiere. The good news is that *Formations* garnered interest and was booked for subsequent performances with other regional orchestras out west.[29]

At a time when arts organizations (and symphony orchestras in particular) have been charged to rethink their mission and value in their communities, this type of entrepreneurial project is a hopeful sign of a new era.

The lessons learned in this case are about knowing what the value of the proposed new product or service actually is. And the value lies in the eye of the beholder. Because Nytch was attuned to what might make his proposed new piece of interest to the GSA and the Boulder Phil, he was able to rally the investors to launch his new "product."

The fact that all the partners were unlikely bedfellows made the project that much more newsworthy and, therefore, even more attractive. The challenge for entrepreneurs lies in thinking creatively about potential aligned interests of investors. The rule of thumb is to look at everyone who might benefit from the proposed project and try to see it from various perspectives. In this case, it was the orchestra, the Geological Society, ExxonMobil, the composer, and the community who all benefitted: making it a five-way "win."

CASE STUDY NO. 3: COLLECTIVE APPROACH TO SERIAL INTRAPRENEURSHIP

In this final case study, three entrepreneurial composers started a collective that they developed into a far-reaching international organization with multiple sub-brands, including an acclaimed touring ensemble, record label, music festival, and a US State Department funded international project. It's a lesson in how to transform a struggling startup into a successful multi-armed entity without losing sight of the original mission.

After completing graduate degrees in music at Yale, composers Julia Wolfe, Michael Gordon, and David Lang moved to New York and soon realized that their music wasn't a fit with either of the prevailing new music scenes: neither the downtown avant-garde nor the uptown academic crowd. The composers were more interested in offering adventurous programs to audiences unconcerned with boundaries of genre or borders.

The three wanted to reach audiences who weren't coming to traditional classical new music concerts. They figured their more likely target demographic would be people interested in experimental film, dance, and visual art. So they programmed a music marathon of experimental works at a SoHo art gallery and bought mailing lists from modern dance companies and used these to help promote their initial concert.[30]

In the beginning, the group joked about naming this their "first annual marathon concert" – with no idea of whether or not it would work. But the marathon was a hit and, pooling their collective energies and creativity, the three inaugurated the collective they named Bang on a Can (BOAC) and have been the artistic directors of this acclaimed contemporary classical music organization ever since. Over the past nearly 30 years, BOAC has grown in scope and reach and has had a major influence on the new music in New York and beyond.[31]

For the first five years, they did it all, from licking envelopes to raising all the funds and doing the programming, promoting, and grant writing themselves. Eventually, they were able to hire staff and assemble a board of directors.[32]

As for why they did it, the composers describe their mission:

> We started this organization because we believed that making new music is a utopian act – that people needed to hear this music and they needed to hear it presented in the most persuasive way, with the best players, with the best programs, for the best listeners, in the best context.[33]

BOAC has progressively grown its reach, building a portfolio of diverse and ambitious projects from their core marathon offering. Each one of these projects is an "intrapreneurial" venture in itself – each serial venture presents new challenges and opportunities for the organization, allowing the founders to be perpetually in "startup" mode. Each additional project has added new ways to enhance their connection with and relevance to audiences, fulfilling the mission of the organization. Table 7.2 provides an outline and description of seven of BOAC's "sub-brands," along with the for-profit world equivalent in function.

Table 7.2   Bang on a Can sub-brand development timeline

What	When	Essential Function
Founding & initial marathon concert	1987	Initial product launch
BOAC All-Stars touring ensemble	1992	Field Marketing team
People's Commissioning Fund	1998	Innovative customer funded R&D
Cantaloupe Music	2001	In-house product distribution
Summer Institute of Music for young composers and performers	2002	Embedded promotion campaign and market research with a key target market
Asphalt Orchestra	2009	Street team branding and direct community relations
Found Sound Nation (FSN)	2009	Launch of international division
OneBeat	2012	Government contract (endorsement and funding)

The first of these "sub-brands" added was the touring and recording ensemble, the Bang on a Can All-Stars (1992), launched as a vehicle for showcasing the music of the BOAC composers and others.[34] For composers, having a band of topflight performers regularly touring with your music is like winning the lottery. In the business world, this is the equivalent to having a top-notch marketing team.

In 1998, long before Kickstarter, Indie GoGo, or other online crowdfunding platforms, BOAC created an innovative funding mechanism for fans to pay for the writing of new pieces. The People's Commissioning Fund pools contributions (from $5 to $5000) from more than 1000 member-commissioners.[35] From a business standpoint, this corresponds to having customers pre-order not only the product months in advance, but fund the company's R&D division as well.

BOAC created its own house label, Cantaloupe Music, in 2001 to record the works of BOAC members and others' contemporary classical and post-classical music. Cantaloupe releases have regularly appeared on Top Ten of the Year lists in *The New York Times*, *The Washington Post*, and elsewhere.[36] A group with access to a top recording company is tantamount to a company's having an award-winning in-house product distribution division.

The following year, BOAC launched its annual Summer Institute of Music for young composers and performers, partnering with the Massachusetts Museum of Contemporary Art (MASS MoCA).[37] Because the festival focuses on young and emerging next generation artists, this is the business equivalent of having a division for new product development. And because the festival is located at an avant-garde visual art world destination, it's comparable to having an ongoing promotion campaign and market research embedded with a key target market.

Next came the Asphalt Orchestra in 2009, the BOAC's extreme street band, an iconoclastic 12-piece marching band (brass and percussion). Asphalt Orchestra offers mobile performance such as playing the Lincoln Center Out of Doors Festival.[38] This is essentially street team branding and direct community relations.

And also in 2009, BOAC expanded internationally to serve as producer of the independent project Found Sound Nation (FSN). The focus of FSN is to engage at-risk youth and underrepresented communities in creating original audio and video projects. FSN has led site-specific projects both at home and abroad, working with young people in New York City, India, Zimbabwe, Mexico, Italy, Switzerland, and Haiti.[39]

In 2012, FSN received US State Department funding to offer OneBeat, a post-political residency program that uses music to bridge the gulf between American musicians and those from developing countries.[40] FSN and OneBeat are the business world equivalent to a company expanding its brand inter-nationally through its corporate giving program. And the connection to the US State Department is not unlike a company gaining a government contract – an excellent way to support expanding a brand abroad.

The entrepreneurial lessons learned from the BOAC case are:

- Don't wait to be "discovered." As Seth Godin says, "pick yourself."[41]
- Consider the context of the product (in this case, music): where and how it's performed and for whom.
- Entrepreneurs can avoid post-startup stagnation by becoming serial entre-preneurs within their own organization.

- A distinct advantage to having multiple products and services is having multiple income streams to help the organization re-balance in a shifting economy.
- With an initial core "product" and customer base, expanding with additional services or products is fine, provided the organization has the capacity and that the expansion does not compromise the organization's mission.
- Each potential new project should be analyzed for what it will add to the company as well as the opportunity cost it represents. Analyze potential sub-brands for their targeted key functions: sales, R&D, distribution, promotion, market research, community relations, and opportunities to expand the company reach internationally.

VIII. IMPLICATIONS FOR EDUCATING MUSICIAN ENTREPRENEURS

Based on the entrepreneurial activities of these case studies and of musicians in general, how can educators help prepare more musician entrepreneurs to succeed?

Over the past ten years, an increasing number of conservatories and university music programs have added entrepreneurship courses and programming in a range of formats and services. Some music schools partner with business schools to offer certificates and minors in music entrepreneurship. Other music schools have designed their own specialized coursework and programs, some folding in related curricula covering the areas of leadership, community engagement, and career development.

As detailed earlier, because motivation, mission, and mindset are so particular for musicians, these offerings need to be focused and pitched appropriately for the musician demographic. For example, the assignment of creating a business model canvas or writing a business plan may at first seem incomprehensible to a musician who doesn't identify her/his artistry as a product and whose driving mission has nothing to do with money or making a profit.

However, the essential entrepreneurship concepts – from value proposition, return on investment, and opportunity cost, to testing business models, customer discovery, and lean startups – are absolutely applicable for musicians. These concepts, though, need to be discussed with relevant examples and in a context appropriate to musicians' values and priorities.

Essential to successful entrepreneurship programs of all types are guest speakers, role models, and the use of pertinent case studies. But the most crucial piece, as entrepreneur educator Steve Blank advises, is to have students "get out of the building,"[42] interacting with potential donors, collaborators, audience members, and customers. In addition, many music schools are supporting student startups with seed money incentives, course credit, and mentoring programs.

IX. SIX KEY DEVELOPMENT AREAS FOR MUSIC ENTREPRENEURS

In terms of potential areas of opportunity for music entrepreneurship, there are a number of industry and audience factors that point to growth areas.

1. *Connectivity.* Musicians are looking to technology for inventive ways to connect with fans, build alliances and fan bases, partner with organizations and communities, and to bundle their music with other products and experiences. From streaming live concerts to booking and promoting tours, it's about cultivating artist/fan connections. This is an area ripe for further innovation.

2. *Monetization.* File sharing has made recorded music, for a vast majority of potential customers, essentially free. As of this writing, US copyright and licensing regulations are not adequate safeguards to ensure appropriate compensation for performers, composers, and others in the supply chain. Many are predicting that a subscription model will solve these issues, but as of now, this is still in flux. Whatever the model of the solution, there are opportunities for entrepreneurs who create aligned products and services that tap into the ease, access, and value of music on demand.

3. *Performance Context.* Performers and concert promoters are re-designing the concert experience. The goal is to reach new audiences by experimenting with alternative performance environments in order to promote better connection and communication between musicians and their fans. From flash mob chamber orchestra performances in malls to string quartets performing in bars and on subway cars, music entrepreneurs are exploring non-traditional performance spaces. Recent examples include GroupMuse.com,[43] a crowdsourced platform for organizing chamber music house parties. There is room and demand for more models and partnerships between venues, spaces, promoters, and performers.

4. *Audience Participation.* Increasingly, audiences are seeking interactive art-making experiences. The wave of new tools and toys include Guitar Hero and the MIT Media Lab's Hyperinstruments, allowing anyone to play at being a rock star or to actually compose music, respectively.[44] The demand for the experiential is also

evidenced in the recent rash of musician/audience co-created projects. For example, the Icelandic composer Bjork's album "Biophilia" was released with an app and an interactive educational program exploring the intersection of music, nature, and technology. Using touch screens and downloads, the app lets users manipulate the album's songs and concepts to make "touchable, shakeable, pinchable interactive art."[45]

5.   *Online Learning.* There's an unmet need for affordable, accessible, and scalable music education. This includes everything from individual lessons (instrumental and vocal) to ensemble coaching, and music theory, history, and pedagogy classes. MOOCs (Massive Open Online Courses), Skype lessons, and blended learning (mixing online and in-person) are just the beginning. The current challenges include sound quality and delay, cost, and making digital learning experiences more tailored to and meaningful for individuals. Despite these, there are already many musicians reaping the rewards of being part of the online music learning community.

6.   *Relevance.* To recap Seth Godin's quote from the start of the chapter: music is social and current. Many musicians today are focused on how they can be agents of change through social entrepreneurship projects and partnerships that advance their political, environmental, or social views. Musician/activist/entrepreneur Bono and his projects to help fight AIDS, apartheid, and Third World debt is just one very visible example.[46] Music is a powerful tool for advancing messages and rallying forces.

Behind all of these indicators are the very human needs common to both fans and musicians: self-expression and community connection. Music provides a medium for self-identification and builds our capacity for empathy. In the end, music helps us make meaning.

In sum, musicians are re-defining what it means to be an entrepreneur. Mission-driven musicians exemplify a range of ways to be entrepreneurial, from their basic creativity and self-determination, co-creating with fans, to forming hybrid collective organizations and innovative partnerships.

Their music training itself provides for many of the core strengths needed for entrepreneurship. This, however, is complicated by the fact that musicians operate in both the gift and market economies, and consequently their mission and mindset may complicate their entrepreneurial efforts. The good news is that more and more conservatories and university music programs are offering entrepreneurship programming to help prepare musicians for a changing industry. There's never been more interest in making and sharing music, so for music entrepreneurs, the time for thinking creatively and taking action is now.

NOTES

1. Godin, S. (2008, January 7). Music Lessons: Things You Can Learn from the Music Business (As It Falls Apart). http://sethgodin.typepad.com/seths_blog/2008/01/music-lessons.html (accessed on June 22, 2014).
2. Chute, J. (2013, January 4). "Arts Entrepreneur" Claire Chase Blazing a New Trail. *U-T San Diego*. http://www.utsandiego.com/news/2013/Jan/04/ICE-Claire-Chase/2/?#article-copy (accessed on May 20, 2014).
3. Ibid.
4. Godin, S. Music Lessons.
5. Sydell, L. (2010, August 19). Control Your Image: Women Musicians Seize On Social Media. *The Record: Music News from NPR*. http://www.npr.org/blogs/therecord/2010/08/19/129300878/women-musicians-use-social-media-to-craft-their-image (accessed on July 7, 2014).
6. Keating, Z. twitter bio: https://twitter.com/zoecello (accessed on May 21, 2014).
7. Spellman, P. (2011). Music Entrepreneurship Defined? *Music Career Juice*. http://www.mcareerjuice.com/2011/01/entrepreneurship-defined/ (accessed on May 20, 2014).
8. Undercofler, J. (2012). Defining Entrepreneurship in the Arts. *State of the Art*. http://www.artsjournal.com/state/2012/07/defining-entrepreneurship-in-the-arts (accessed on May 22, 2014).
9. Jensen, E. (n.d.). Musicians Are Natural Entrepreneurs. Berklee College of Music website. http://www.berklee.edu/institutional-advancement/musicians-are-natural-entrepreneurs (accessed on May 21, 2014).
10. Ibid.
11. Grover Pro Percussion (n.d.). About. http://groverpro.com/about (accessed on May 20, 2014).
12. Ibid.
13. Reference to the MIT Sloan School of Management Professor Eric von Hippel's research on user innovation, see http://evhippel.mit.edu/papers/section-1/ (accessed May 20, 2014).
14. Radbill, C. (2010). Music Entrepreneurship: Skills to Nourish the Creative Life. *USASBE Proceedings*. p. 0475. http://sbaer.uca.edu/research/USASBE/2010/p56.pdf (accessed on June 20, 2014).
15. VH1 Save the Music Foundation (2014). The Importance of Music Education. http://www.vh1savethemusic.org/why-music/benefits-to-the-brain (accessed on July 3, 2014).
16. Lipman, J. (2013, October 12). Is Music the Key to Success? *The New York Times*. http://www.nytimes.com/2013/10/13/opinion/sunday/is-music-the-key-to-success.html?_r=0 (accessed on May 20, 2014).
17. Adapted from Beeching, A. (2010). *Beyond Talent: Building a Successful Career in Music*. (2nd edition). New York: Oxford University Press, pp. 144–145.
18. Hyde, L. (2007). *The Gift: Creativity and the Artist in the Modern World*. (25th edition). New York: Vintage Books.
19. Solman, P. (Correspondent) (2013, November 28). Exploring the Economics of the First Thanksgiving. *PBS Newshour*. http://www.pbs.org/newshour/bb/business-july-dec13-plantation_11-28/ (accessed on May 21, 2014).
20. Small, C. (1998). *Musicking: The Meanings of Performing and Listening*. Middleton, CT: Wesleyan.
21. Sisario, B. (2012, June 5). Giving Love, Lots of It, To Her Fans. *The New York Times*. http://www.nytimes.com/2012/06/06/arts/music/amanda-palmer-takes-connecting-with-her-fans-to-a-new-level.html?pagewanted=all&_r=0 (accessed on July 12, 2014).

22. Palmer, A. (2013, February) The Art of Asking. TED Conferences, LLC. http://www.ted.com/talks/amanda_palmer_the_art_of_asking (accessed on May 22, 2014).
23. Clover, J. (2012, October 2). Amanda Palmer's Accidental Experiment with Real Communism. *The New Yorker*, p. C1. http://www.newyorker.com/online/blogs/culture/2012/10/amanda-palmers-kickstarter-scandal.html (accessed on July 4, 2014).
24. Witz, A. (2013, August 29). Composer of Deep Time. *Nature*, pp. 500, 528. http://www.boulderphil.org/images/docs/ComposerofDeepTime_Nature_Aug2013.pdf (accessed on July 12, 2014).
25. Nytch, J. (2013, Oct. 29). The Entrepreneurial Symphony. *Greg Sandow on the Future of Classical Music, an ArtsJournal blog*. http://www.artsjournal.com/sandow/2013/10/from-jeffrey-nytch-the-entrepreneurial-symphony.html (accessed on July 4, 2014).
26. Estabrook, R. (2013, December 23). Rock Music: Colorado's Geologic History, Told By a Symphony, *Colorado Public Radio*. http://www.cpr.org/news/story/rock-music-colorado%E2%80%80%99s-geologic-history-told-symphony (accessed on July 10, 2014).
27. Boulder Philharmonic (2013). Jeffrey Nytch Symphony No. 1 ("Formations") World Premiere. http://www.boulderphil.org/formations (accessed on July 10, 2014).
28. Nytch, J. Vimeo page. http://vimeo.com/jeffreynytch/videos (accessed on July 10, 2014).
29. Nytch, J. The Entrepreneurial Symphony.
30. Bang on a Can. (2014). About Us. http://bangonacan.org/about_us (accessed on July 4, 2014).
31. Smith, S. (2012, April 20). Looking Beyond a Milestone, for Some More Cans to Bang. *The New York Times*, p. AR23. http://www.nytimes.com/2012/04/22/arts/music/bang-on-a-can-wraps-up-25th-anniversary-season.html?pagewanted=all&_r=0 (accessed on August 14, 2014).
32. Oteri, F. (1999, May 1). The Who and Why of Bang on a Can. *New Music Box*. http://www.newmusicbox.org/articles/bang-on-a-can/ (accessed on July 4, 2014).
33. Bang on a Can. About Us.
34. Bang on a Can. (2014). All-Stars. http://bangonacan.org/bang_on_a_can_all_stars (accessed on July 4, 2014).
35. Bang on a Can. (2014). Peoples Commissioning Fund. http://bangonacan.org/peoples_commissioning_fund (accessed on July 13, 2014).
36. Bang on a Can (2014). Cantaloupe Music. http://www.cantaloupemusic.com/ (accessed on July 13, 2014).
37. Bang on a Can. (2014). Summer Festival. http://bangonacan.org/summer_festival (accessed on July 13, 2014).
38. Bang on a Can. (2014). Asphalt Orchestra. http://bangonacan.org/asphalt_orchestra (accessed on July 13, 2014).
39. Bang on a Can. (2014). Found Sound Nation. http://foundsoundnation.org/about/ (accessed on July 13, 2014).
40. Ibid.
41. Godin, S. (2011, March 21). Reject the Tyranny of Being Picked: Pick Yourself. http://sethgodin.typepad.com/seths_blog/2011/03/reject-the-tyranny-of-being-picked-pick-yourself.html (accessed on July 13, 2014).
42. Kelly, R. (2013, Winter). Get Out... of the Building; Haas Lecturer Steve Blank Pioneers a New Model for Teaching Entrepreneurship. University of California Berkeley Haas School of Business website. http://haas.berkeley.edu/groups/pubs/berkeleyhaas/winter2013/get-out-of-the-building-steve-blank-lean-launchpad.html (accessed on July 13, 2014).
43. Group Muse (2014). http://www.groupmuse.com/ (accessed on July 13, 2014).
44. Cheshire, T. (2012, November 12). Tod Machover Invents Instruments, Robot Operas – Oh, and Guitar Hero. *Wired*, UK. http://www.wired.co.uk/magazine/archive/2012/11/play/hyper-musician/page/2 (accessed on July 13, 2014).
45. Biophilia (2014). About. http://biophiliaeducational.org/about/ (accessed on July 4, 2014).

46. Olson, P. (2012, October 22). Bono's "Humbling" Realizations about Aid, Capitalism and Nerds. *Forbes*. http://www.forbes.com/sites/parmyolson/2012/10/22/bonos-humbling-realizations-about-aid-capitalism-and-nerds/ (accessed on July 4, 2014).

8. Educating arts entrepreneurs: does, can or should one size fit all?

Gary D. Beckman and James D. Hart

Julia majored in art at her local university. In her freshman year, she enrolled in a new arts entrepreneurship course, more to get an elective out of the way than any real interest in the topic. Over the course of the semester, Julia became inspired by the idea of autonomy and adventure that an entrepreneurial lifestyle promised and decided to declare a minor in arts entrepreneurship early in her sophomore year. In doing so, Julia knew that she could gain access to a wealth of resources that the minor offered: mentoring by expert faculty and the resources that they offer, new friends, new networks and significant practical skills based both in an arts policy methodology and the business school. In the end, it was the merging of both the art and business world that attracted her to the minor; it was antithetical in a traditional "arts classroom" sense, yet leveraged her supporting course work. Julia saw this as "the real world." This kaleidoscope of autonomy through a certain practicality an art student could understand was – in her mind – enthralling and might even pay the bills after she graduated.

Her first sophomore semester was an inspiration. She was in her first "real" studio class and would finish the general education requirements in just a few months. Yet she was noticing a shift in her thinking. Certainly Julia was learning new techniques on the canvas but she was finding herself oddly excited about her arts entrepreneurship courses. Seeing how her entire education folded into an entrepreneurial lifestyle was interesting. Literally everything she had learned – and was learning – was being used in planning and executing arts businesses. Julia was discovering her education.

I. INTRODUCTION

Arts entrepreneurship educators address curriculum development uniquely and, as an emerging field, this is not surprising. Without a consensus on what should be taught, how it should be taught and desired outcomes, the field's educators will naturally approach the classroom largely based on their own experiences, beliefs and training. This is not only understandable; it is crucial in building an academic field. If one considers an arts entrepreneurship classroom as a laboratory on both sides of the instructor's desk, where all parties are trying to find their own way to reach their own unique goals, then perhaps we can assume most students want to make a living with their art and faculty want to provide a platform for them to succeed. Though there is certain nobility in this assumption, the fact of the matter is that the classroom's disciplinary diversity may preclude the curricular consensus suggested above.

Certainly some students seek a "template of success" based on their collegiate arts training: do this, hone that, acquire this skill, invest incredible amounts of time and your goal magically manifests. Others may come to the classroom questioning their own artistic, personal, financial and professional goals. Some may enroll in arts entre-preneurship courses with pre-existing arts (or other) business desires, for example looking to improve financial or professional performance, bringing family business models into the classroom, modernizing existing business approaches or simply "wood shedding" pre-existing venture ideas with faculty mentors.

Educators are in a comparable position as they design curricula. Most possess some entrepreneurial or professional success and tend to recreate these experiences though curricula. Others may feel somewhat un-prepared (yet still driven by their desire to help students) and take a "soft concept" approach. Still others rely on traditional business school cur-ricula (a "hard concept" approach) and present these concepts to arts entrepreneurship students with varying degrees of expertise.

Most arts entrepreneurship classrooms (on both sides of the lectern) are a diverse aggregate of desires, knowledge bases and levels of self-efficacy: complex feeling combinations of conflict, preparedness, confusion, excitement and inspiration permeate the space. Contrastingly, mature disciplines typically employ a codified curriculum, which acts as a gravitational force where instructors and students find their own orbit – some closer, some further away. Perhaps the field's present, corres-ponding force is an understood desire for a student's unique success.

We suggest that without a consensus by arts entrepreneurship educators on the field's desired outcomes and – by extension – core curricula supporting these outcomes, our classrooms will continue to lack a key (and basic) component of a student's success. In an effort to illustrate how a consensus-based set of outcomes and curricula may manifest, the authors use a fictional vignette outlining aspects of their curriculum as fodder for discussion.

II. WHAT ARE WE (AS A FIELD) DOING HERE, ANYWAY?

Nationally, traditional thinking in Fine Arts higher education (music, dance, theatre, 2D and 3D art) focuses on training students in effective art creation and understanding primarily through performance training, historical insight, technique and disciplinary theory. However, with a student's training ending at the art, and without accompanying skills in succeeding as a professional artist (i.e., entrepreneurial or even an introduction to basic business processes), emerging arts professionals are left with what can be thought of as half of an education – if the goal is professional autonomy. This traditional model of "all arts technique and no real business aptitude" has led to a furthering of the "starving artist" and "actors being waiters" stereotype. However, with the advent of the Internet, students are communicating cross-culturally and have access to powerful tools enabling them to both create and distribute art. This democratization, the rise of a younger professoriate and a cultural shift that romanticizes entrepreneurs has fueled – in part – a demand by both students and some faculties for a more responsive arts training construct: hence the demand for entrepreneurship training in the arts.

Arts entrepreneurship is an emerging field whose roots extend into the late 1970s and serves as a response to the issues outlined immediately above. Recognizing that professional outcomes of students in the Fine Arts are less than stellar, a somewhat idiomatic and dispersed (if not organic) movement emerged where educators in these disciplines began offering formal courses in what we might call today "Career Development."[1] These efforts where relatively intermittent from academic year to year and were embraced by most students and some faculty members, yet regarded with suspicion and sometimes active hostility by small groups of faculty peers.

With the establishment of the Eastman School of Music's Arts Leadership Program in 1996, entrepreneurship education in the Fine Arts began to overtake the traditional career development model, especially in collegiate music training.[2] The next decade saw steady (if not explosive) growth as formal academic programs and scholarship mushroomed. Primarily a topic in music training for much of the 2000s, arts administration programs – which train future administrators for employment in non-profit arts organizations – are beginning to integrate entrepreneurship education into their curricular efforts. Today, arts entrepreneurship education possesses all the challenges and hallmarks of an emerging field of study: an academic society, peer-reviewed journals and the axiomatic discussions about curricula, scholarship, educator training, trajectory, etc.[3] What distinguishes the field, however, is a tacit agreement that it possesses a contextual component (insofar as where these efforts are housed), in addition to an ongoing discussion about the "weighting" of the field: should the field privilege a more business-based curriculum or a contextualized arts–cultural–economics-based trajectory?

Though the field has not approached the topic of educational goals/ outcomes (much less how to assess them) in a broad-based manner, it is likely that most arts entrepreneurship educators would subscribe to the idea that they care about their students' professional success or community impact.[4] However, some are concerned about art itself and how entrepreneurial arts students may change the way art is created, distributed or consumed.[5] These desires (regardless of arts discipline) help to drive individual classroom content and are considered primary assumptions in this chapter.

Indeed, this is the hallmark of the field, yet the result of these broad, assumed desires for students are curricula that can vary significantly from institution to institution. For example, the authors' students may find each other's classrooms foreign, replete with their own strengths, weaknesses and boring or exciting content drawn from personal experience, content decisions, presentations and even local community concerns. Notably, one author works in a very well respected liberal arts college and the other at a research-one, land grant institution. One author is housed in an arts administration program possessing a strong and significant arts academic presence, the other in a small music department without a single arts major. Further, one author is trained in theatre and primarily teaches arts students. The other is a trained musicologist teaching students in engineering, business, veterinary medicine and the humanities. Both, however, share "real life" experiences in starting and sustaining a myriad of arts ventures – like any working artist.

As authors of this chapter, we possess many differences: disciplinary backgrounds, the arts (and other) ventures we create, the institutions that employ us, the trajectory and desires of our students, the books we read and even opinions about the field. This diversity of experience forges a set of curricular outcomes reflecting our life experiences, circumstances, employment context and desires for our students. At this point in the field's development, arts entrepreneurship educators typically negotiate a position between personal experience and postulating what they feel students need to be successful in the classrooms instead of the field's consensus on a set of educational outcomes. Thus, the authors' curricula (what the students see) are based on a set of localized outcomes for our students, contextualized for our institutional cultures and missions.

For example, the lead author of this chapter (the one that works at a land grant institution with a weak arts academic presence) sees the outcomes of his students enrolled in an arts entrepreneurship minor far differently than an institution with a stronger arts mission. For this author (again, seeing primarily engineering, business and humanities students), developing an arts entrepreneurship program where the primary outcome is helping emerging artists make a living with their art is antithetical to the mission (and actions) of his university. There are few students who could make a living with their art in a traditional Fine Arts context, as his university does not provide arts training at the level required. What is obvious at this author's university, however, is that: (1) the arts in a popular context rules the day; (2) students want to be involved with the arts as their primary mode of financial sustainability in ways that do not center on producing art; (3) the university produces students whose academic majors can impact the production of art through new inventions, which his students clearly recognize; and, lastly, (4) these students are strong popular arts consumers and producers who want desperately to bring more audiences to art.

There are contextual opportunities found at this (and similar) land grant institutions. For example, there is a broader mission and ethos of entrepreneurialism on this campus as seen through an overarching campus-wide entrepreneurship program (the Entrepreneurship Initiative) designed to nurture and support disciplinary-specific academic efforts on campus such as engineering, textile and arts entrepreneurship. This effort's primary visibility consists of two campus-wide entrepreneurship courses and a yearly "business plan" competition – including an arts-only-based competition where students participate in a standard business plan framework (the only difference is that students articulate arts business ventures through feasibility studies, not business plans).

Collaborative cross-campus opportunities such as this can be indicative of future actions such as dedicated workshops for engineering students interested in bringing their arts-based inventions to the arts markets. Perhaps most obvious is the potential for a more traditional collaboration with the campus' business school. In this author's case, his university offers an arts entrepreneurship minor where one component is an "advised elective." During the development of this degree, the business school provided a small menu of foundational courses that would both complement the minor and deliver a more robust academic experience for students.

Similarly, at the second author's small, private, liberal arts university, there is an emerging campus-wide initiative called "Big iDeas." The steering committee for this organization (at the time of this chapter's writing) represents entrepreneurial interests from several colleges on campus. Engineering, business and arts are all at the table. Though in its infancy as an initiative, this cross-disciplinary collaboration centered on arts entrepreneurship is the beginning of a process that works outside the typical silo mentality. One of the Big iDeas program goals is to generate larger and more profound cross-campus, cross-disciplinary entrepreneurial collaborations.

Staying with this example, the desired outcomes for this cohort are contextually based on the four observations above. Given these inputs, this author has two primary desired outcomes for his students: (1) preparing students to be a part of an entrepreneurial, 21st century workforce; and (2) helping emerging arts entrepreneurs develop for- or non-profit arts ventures. For this author, the first outcome is primary and far more realistic. As the field (at least informally) recognizes, expecting students to start an arts business is an exceptional outcome given the pressures of the college experience, tuition bills after graduation and their desire to complete an academic program in four years. Nevertheless, located in one of the nation's entrepreneurial hubs, startup and entrepreneurial culture permeates this campus. At this institution, undergraduates starting businesses and securing provisional patents – while still in school – is far more common than most universities boasting arts entrepreneurship programs. However, this author has identified as an additional (and far more realistic) outcome, helping to prepare students to successfully participate in an emerging entrepreneurial workforce.[6] Preparing his students to "use entrepreneurial skills to enhance workplace productivity and career options" in their future non-arts profession is an emerging desired skill set identified by over 70 percent of businesses in a recent study of American employers.[7] This same study also identified creativity, innovation, leadership, teamwork, critical thinking and major forms of communication as critical applied skills appropriate for future employees.[8] Anecdotally, this author suggests that many arts entrepreneurship efforts introduce students to, or employ, these skills in the classroom.

Yet the second author of this paper offering the same academic degree at his institution (a private, liberal arts institution with a very strong academic and arts presence offering both undergraduate and graduate degrees housed within an arts management program) sees programmatic outcomes differently. This effort aims to entrepreneurially empower their students through their artistry both in terms of quality and its potential for impact. Given this institution's more artistically traditional and professionally oriented arts training focus, this effort exists to catalyze the artistic training students receive. Thus, this program aims to provide a lens through which students can process the "felt impact" of an entrepreneurial lifestyle despite significant obstacles and competition, in order to increase their chances of making a living in the arts. In short, this program's outcomes center on teaching students how to create "work."

Again, this program's outcomes are contextual, a more traditional and expansive arts training program, housed within a School of the Arts, and leverages the significant arts training students receive by focusing on the entrepreneurial production of art. Following this thread, it is also more likely that these students will entrepreneurially replicate or innovate models existing in their own art mediums and those of their peers: non-profit arts business creation, portfolio careers and especially teaching. However, with changing markets and market demands, student expectations for what course content might hold change as well. For example, this author observed that family entrepreneurship emerged as a popular topic in the classroom, which may have little to do with the artistic discipline students pursue. As these students seek to gain from the mentorship and collective wisdom of faculty and peers, this author adapts to meet the demands of a student body appearing to think beyond an artistic discipline; they see themselves more holistically as "creators," as entrepreneurship is a process of creating.

Most would agree that context – however axiomatic – matters. First, the desired outcomes of these two programs are based on (to name just three): (1) the mission of institution; (2) the academic/professional trajectory and training of its students; and (3) the likeliness of students entrepreneurially replicating pre-existing arts business models after graduation based on institutional culture. Second, the authors see distinctions in programmatic focus helping students entrepreneurially: (1) produce art; (2) impact the production of art, its sale and distribution; and (3) attract audiences to art. Lastly – and importantly – the art the students either participate or are trained in differs, either: (1) "Fine" art; or (2) the popular arts, which at least partially drives the desire to set up for- or non-profit organizations. Thus, what is generated is a set of layered outcomes based on each program's institutional context and curricular designer.

To the question, "What are we (as a field) doing here, anyway?" one need only examine what is being done presently, given this chapter's assumptions. In short, arts entrepreneurship educators are simply "finding their way" in unique educational environments. Through these two examples, at least, it is obvious that many contexts are at play when developing these programs' outcome framework. "What are the authors doing here?" in our individual programs is responding to: (1) a desire to see our students succeed through the arts in whatever way they choose; (2) institutional context; and (3) a sensitivity to "the Fine Arts" and popular art. The larger issue, again, concerns whether the field as a whole desires an agreed upon set of curricular outcomes (similar to most existing academic arts disciplines) or should local context and curricular adaptively rule the day? More directly put: does, can or should one size fit all?

The arts entrepreneurship course in Julia's first semester required her to develop a feasibility study on a venture that she wanted to pursue but had no idea what kind of venture interested or inspired her. A part of her arts entrepreneurship classes focused on either creating or identifying niche markets, becoming specific about her market and articulating that service or product. She was taught two forms of niche creation, an "Outside/In" approach and an "Inside/Out" approach, both of which could help her identify not only something to write about, but also a hidden entrepreneurial passion.

Julia chose to use the Inside/Out approach. She wants to celebrate her colleagues, friends and other artists who produce remarkable work, but do not have an internet-based marketing platform to sell from themselves. Julia does this by creating her own artistic work and uses a website platform as a digital gallery to promote her own art while simultaneously serving others. Now, at least, she had something for the feasibility study she could get excited about: a web-based portfolio site similar to Etsy but much more interactive, local and visually appealing. The more innovative part of the venture was to drive the site's traffic to her new "brick and mortar" art gallery with the intention of attracting a more traditional arts consumer demographic to help a local economy. However, the most innovative part of her venture was that she could rent her gallery space as a "pop-up-shop" four nights a week, which would pay for almost all of the gallery's monthly expenses – if the location had a "pop-up-shop" culture.

As Julia worked on her class project, she developed a way her site could actually make money for both her featured artists and herself; given that this was a low profit endeavor, it was not all that difficult. Her gallery audience of choice (read: market) live in a 300-mile radius of her university, which fits her desire for "local flair." Julia likes this idea, as she feels it fulfills mutual needs – the needs of the local (state-level) artists to sell their work, those who would support emerging local artists and even Julia herself.

III. SO WHAT ARE STUDENT'S ENTREPRENEURIAL DESIRES? THESE ARE OUTCOMES AS WELL, RIGHT?

When considering educational outcomes for arts entrepreneurship programs, it is comfortable to approach the topic from an exclusively educators' perspective. That is, in this new "era of assessment" in higher education, thinking about an educator's desires for students and designing curricula to meet these desires seems logical. However, we must remember that students are involved. As this chapter assumes that educators want students to succeed, we must address the elephant in the room: do students want the same things we do? If they do not, why do they enroll in our classes? Further, what should be our response if students know they do not want to develop a career in the arts after graduation but appear in our classrooms anyway?

As the fictional vignette above illustrates, this student is thinking far beyond a traditional career as an arts producer. Julia desires to create a platform where both her art and the art of others are brought to market in service of both herself and a local community. In this case, Julia is trying to accomplish three critical tasks: (1) producing art (the revenue generated from the venture would allow her to produce more art); (2) impact the production of art (by providing gallery space for other artists); and (3) attract new audiences to art (by virtue of the gallery itself). There is no doubt that this is a laudable idea, though her desire to create such a venture poses a question for arts entrepreneurship educators: does Julia's desired outcomes meet or match the desired outcome of the field – much less her instructor's? Specifically, will the educational experience created by her instructor provide a solid curricular platform with which to build and sustain her project if she decides to launch the venture – assuming launching her venture is Julia's desired outcome?

If one addresses outcomes first, and applies the assumption made at the start of this chapter (which can serve as a potential ethical or philosophical touchstone for the field), we can interrogate how the assumption becomes a curricular outcome. If Julia's instructor truly embraced the assumption, then that educator would develop an outcome strategy preparing her to accomplish her three critical tasks: to consistently produce art through an entrepreneurial venture, to impact the production of art and lastly to attract new audiences to art. Abstracted, these outcomes might include the following:

1. In order to consistently produce art through an entrepreneurial venture, students should be able to:
    ● Describe the traditional or status quo methods contemporary artists use to sustain themselves
    ● Recognize opportunity in various arts markets
    ● Develop innovative launch and sustainability methods for entrepreneurial ventures outside their home arts discipline.
2. In order to impact the production of art, students should be able to:
    ● Describe the cultural and economic environments of both the Fine and popular arts
    ● Compare and contrast the most popular arts business models
    ● Articulate the differences between for- and non-profit arts businesses, startup procedures and sustainability strategies.
3. In order to attract new audiences to art, students should be able to:
    ● Compare and identify arts infrastructure in both urban and rural environments
    ● Recognize the role of arts policy in community development
    ● Analyze arts economic impact studies.

As these outcomes demonstrate, Julia's arts entrepreneurship education is quite broad. Though it includes aspects of New Venture Creation, it is decidedly arts based. Specifically, it focuses not on starting, growing and then selling a for-profit business, but instead considers a more holistic view of arts culture within an arts economic system. Further, it merges these broader-based ideas with more discrete (i.e., realistic or tangible) topics that some may consider "skills."

The challenge this fictitious set of outcomes presents falls squarely on both the educator and the field itself. In order to address these outcomes, the educator (or accumulative faculty within the department or program) must have (at least) a clear understanding of both the broader and more fine grained aspects of: (1) arts culture; (2) the arts economies; (3) arts business models; (4) New Venture Creation; (5) arts policy; (6) economic and community development through the arts; (7) economic sustainability strategies both in and outside the arts; and (8) the intersection of arts culture and economies as they are negotiated through geography. If Julia attends this course aligned with the desired outcomes of the instructor, then we should assume that both Julia and the field would expect the instructor to have some understanding of (at least) the eight broader topics listed above. At this point in the field's development, however, it may be a tall order for some of our educators to possess the entirety of this knowledge. As educators, we come to the field with a diverse set of disciplinary training, backgrounds and experiences. The strength this brings both to the classroom and the field is that educators can draw on this diversity as they develop curricula and participate in the field's theoretical and pedagogical development. However, this second generation of arts entrepreneurship educators does not come to the field as they were originally trained; there are no terminal degrees in arts entrepreneurship where graduates are trained in the field's theory, scholarship and pedagogy, which puts a tremendous amount of pressure on this generation's educators.

Repeating, as arts entrepreneurship educators we are not trained in a traditional academic context to be in an arts entrepreneurship classroom: no theoretical, educational or pedagogical training, other than experience in the field and our own arts education. Compared to our colleagues in established disciplines, the fact of the matter is that the field cannot at this point formally prepare its educators through a traditional paradigm. However, for many of the field's educators, real-world entrepreneurial experience coupled with our primary disciplinary training – and in some cases pure passion for the topic – provides a rich palette with which to build an academic field, develop outcomes and design impactful curricula. The classroom becomes, then, a grand improvisation in the construction of a discipline by virtue of ours – and our students' – aspirations to succeed through the arts. More simply put – as we see in Julia's desires – students highlight weaknesses and strengths in both the field and its educators. The partnership is striking and perhaps unrecognized: our students are helping us develop programmatic and discrete course outcomes, curricular content and delivery, our own personal knowledge base and the field's future educator training system.

Yet our own weaknesses are only part of the challenge. Both aligning desired outcomes between student and instructor and understanding the myriad of reasons why students appear in our classrooms is part of any educational paradigm. For arts entrepreneurship educators who have taught for any length of time, they have likely seen the entire continuum from "I'm only here because it fits my schedule" to "I've been wanting this education my entire life." Most educators have little control over their attendance sheets or the desires/preconceptions of students. The field, however, may have a responsibility to adapt to a student's desired outcome if it is determined that (for example) they lack the temperament or desire to develop an entrepreneurial arts career after graduation.

Knowing the field cannot be everything to every student, we can forge our curricular efforts towards at least two distinct student groups: those that desire entrepreneurial success in the arts and those that want a successful (and perhaps entrepreneurial) life in the 21st century, though not primarily through the arts.

As briefly mentioned above, preparing students for the realities of a new, intrapreneurial workforce, requiring different skills than demanded by their parent's generation, poses a significant opportunity for the arts entrepreneurship educator. Regardless of the disciplines our students pursue after graduation, there is a growing realization that the three well-worn entrepreneurial traits of creativity, innovation and opportunity recognition are increasingly desired by the world's 21st century economy. This global desire for entrepreneurial skills within diverse organizational and disciplinary modalities is explicit.[9] Further, when entrepreneurial skills are both recognized within organizational management structures and have the appropriate assessment metrics, higher education can play a significant role in meeting these demands.[10] The field can meet these demands by not only recognizing the need, but designing curricula for our students who may not desire to "entrepreneur" in the classic sense, yet might desire an organizational position allowing for a high level of creativity and risk taking.

By choosing a local audience, Julia appeals to her state's pride and her generation's sense of "contributing to the social good" trend making its way to both small and large communities. With this in mind, she develops a targeted marketing strategy focusing on aspirational and elitist markets employing technological and aesthetic consumption models.

Through research, Julia found ways to reach these markets via online newsletters and social media, which she knew was vital. Since Facebook has become an important interactive marketing platform, she knew her venture was more about driving Internet traffic to her website than directing that traffic to her gallery. She also needed a Twitter account, a personal LinkedIn account and blog, which would aid her in making discoveries around what it is she wishes to create: Emerging Visions.

Decision, Julia had come to find, was unequivocal choice making. This was an endeavor that would require a wide-range of her own personal resources, an expanded network, the goodwill of others and a lot of labor on her part. This decision-making process was difficult, but certain aspects of her arts entrepreneurship course made it easier. Regardless, making the decision to strike out on her own full-time and make her living from doing so was more an act of courage than anything else.

*Julia learned both new and standard entrepreneurship/business con-
cepts: bootstrapping, crowdsourcing and corporate, private and in-kind
support. Her arts entrepreneurship courses introduced her to for- and
non-profit startup and stressed venture piloting before making significant
time and resource investments. As Julia worked on her feasibility study, it
was becoming clear that Emerging Visions was emerging as a vision.
There was something about this process that was exciting, satisfying and
almost Romantic – in a 19th century way.*

IVA.   PEDAGOGY-SERVING OUTCOMES: DISCUSSION

Similar to most arts entrepreneurship educators across the country, the
authors of this chapter approach pedagogy uniquely, but agree on the
primary student outcome assumption outlined at the beginning of this
chapter. Though both authors concur that the classroom should be as
experiential and team-based as possible, one author leans towards a more
formalized and traditional approach focusing on the understanding of
economics and the relationship of "art and culture" in startup decision
making (hard concept), while the other sees the classroom as less
formalized and, thus, more dynamic, daring and experimental (leaning
towards a "soft concept" approach and working to "flip the classroom").
This should not surprise the reader as disciplines throughout our campuses participate in varying pedagogies serving a broader, unified curricular outcome – some more conservative, some more experimental.
Again, the field encounters a challenge, though more philosophical:
should the content of our pedagogy (in service of this chapter's primary
assumption) lean towards more traditional business concepts in service of
decision making to support entrepreneurial action or leverage creativity
in service of innovative thinking to this action.

Likely, the field would reject the choice and suggest that both are
critical – and not remarkably, the authors would agree. Yet this articulates
the critical philosophical and pedagogical issue mentioned above that the
field lacks the maturity in its own theoretic construct and pedagogical
analysis to address: how holistic should this field actually be? Academic
fields (especially as interdisciplinary as ours) cannot be everything to
every person: each mature field develops a unique answer to the question
– some embracing, some rejecting, some in between. What may help is a
simple reminder that disciplinary developments – including pedagogy –
are dynamic affairs subject to research, empiricism, innovation, application, passion, argument, failure, agreement, fad, success and assessment to name a few. The field is just now entering this process, and as a

field we should acknowledge that as Julia generates Emerging Visions, her professor likely shares her lack of clarity. Yet for her instructor, there is a decidedly unique pedagogical path complete with a desired outcome, and despite appropriate terminal-degree graduate training based in arts entrepreneurship, Julia's professor will introduce her to critical issues she simply would not have encountered in a typical arts training paradigm. The end of Section III is an abstract of what Julia's classroom experience would have been if co-taught by the authors.[11]

Anecdotally, there is a popular notion in the field that arts entrepreneurship can (and perhaps should) be taught through experiential means. The argument suggests that entrepreneurship is a process of risk-taking and no matter how full or dynamic the day's lecture, nothing compares to hands on experience. Experience leads to an owning of one's knowledge, as one has experienced it, rather than simply hearing or reading about the trials, tribulations and success of "real life" entre-preneurs. One effective model for providing experiential learning is to enable students to run or develop an entity while still in college. However, if the program does not allow for such a training modality, games may offer a next-best alternative. Games in the classroom, such as The Marble Game, played at the second author's university and now a subsequent school in Wisconsin, enables students to understand how value is relative and how one can amass resources from essentially nothing but one's story.[12]

Two weeks before Julia was to turn in her feasibility study, she knew that Emerging Visions was going to be a reality, piloted between her sophomore and junior year. Emerging Visions was simply accepted as her task in life – there was nothing else to do, discuss or debate. Having a close friend who could build a basic website for her was helpful and she knew a small crowdsourcing campaign through Kickstarter would cover her startup costs. Securing the art was easy. However, before she could pilot Emerging Visions, she needed a set of data – economic data she could understand – to best locate a temporary gallery (even as a "pop-up-shop" a few nights a week) and make sure her markets would engage both experiences: technological and "brick and mortar."

Within a 300-mile radius lie four small to medium-sized cities for Julia to locate the gallery. What was concerning her was the state of the broader economy – a well-worn topic in her arts entrepreneurship courses. Every month (just after the monthly unemployment data was released) her instructor took the class through the same 16 economic indicators, and by simply filling in some characters on a chart, the class developed a broad, monthly snapshot of the nation's economic health. Julia noticed the obvious trend, which impacted her markets significantly: the economy was slowly but steadily growing and so was disposable income – the economic key to her success. She created a set of more discrete and targeted economic indicators that would impact the success of Emerging Visions. Julia followed this data regularly and found that her targeted indicators were even more positive for Emerging Visions than her class's monthly tracking. By reading recent arts policy literature and analyzing economic impact studies for the cities she was considering locating the gallery, it was clear that one city in particular possessed the infrastructure, market and culture to support Emerging Visions as summer pilot.

IVB. PEDAGOGY-SERVING OUTCOMES: EXAMPLES

In order to achieve the goal of "increasing a student's chance of success," Julia engaged in both lecture- and experientially-based study, which offered a theory, industry vocabulary and expectations of knowledge to prepare her for market entry. When Julia encountered this newfound knowledge, she both discovered and owned such knowledge because of her classroom experience. Furthermore, she was engaged in experientially based learning (including games in the classroom, community engagement, speaking about fundraising and venture creation) primarily through the act of play. By playing, Julia came to know joy, which increases the speed and efficacy of the learning process. In the end, Julia was given permission to engage the artists' sensibilities: this partially identifies an arts entrepreneurship program. (As Jung opined, "The creation of something new is not accomplished by the intellect, but by the play instinct acting from inner necessity. The creative mind plays with the object it loves").[13] Some of the classroom games Julia experienced included the "The Paperclip Game," "Market Feedback, Speed Dating Style," a "Truck of Grapes" and "Market Research to Perceive Market Gaps," which are described below. Additionally, we outline the more unique aspects of our classroom efforts: "The Entrepreneurial Ecology of the Arts," Outside/In Approach to Niche Creation," "Inside/Out Approach to Niche Creation" and "Mentoring as Critical and Indispensable" below.

The Paperclip Game: This game parallels the story of a young man who traded up a paperclip in a limited number of trades, going from a paperclip to owning a house. Pedagogically, the intent is to teach the relativity of value by effectively engaging another person, communicating a story and convincing the other to trade something that each then owns.[14]

Market Feedback, Speed Dating Style: In this excursive, students begin with the question: "If you could create anything, regardless of money or struggle, what would you create?" This question helps students to imagine and not self-censor around perceived monetary restrictions and margin of difficulty of an imagined idea. Students are then divided into two groups, each facing the other. Each duo (A and B) has six shared minutes to describe their concept and receive feedback from each other. When time expires, group A stays stationary, while B moves a seat down (hence the speed dating reference). Typically one B group person then rotates to the beginning of the line where an A group person receives them.

A Truck of Grapes: Students are asked what they would do if willed or gifted a dump truck load of fresh grapes from a recently departed family member. There is no person to give the grapes back to and the student must do something with them. Chances are, to even dump the grapes, one will have to pay a fee at a waste receiving location. Students must then collectively (as a group) brainstorm as to how they might profit from these newly acquired resources. As grapes have a brief shelf life, there is a deadline of freshness they must consider. This exercise teaches students to think differently about what resources they may already possess and – hopefully – how resources might be deconstructed to create additional and previously unforeseen opportunities and resources. For example, various parts of grapes can be sold for health benefits. Seeds can be extracted and used for oil and the juice of the grape for drinking or other purposes. Any waste product remaining can be composted. This compost can be sold, used or donated. These activities could potentially generate income, if not a profit, if handled wisely.

Market Research to Perceive Market Gaps: In this game, students exit the classroom and enter into the larger body of the college or university. The students' job is to individually engage with those they encounter and ask them about the arts in their community and the nation at large: what is missing, what can be improved and so on. This feedback that students receive is often surprising. This experience is then discussed as a classroom group. Those who struggle for entrepreneurial ideas of their own are often inspired by the responses – to the point of developing new fundraising strategies or business models.

The Entrepreneurial Ecology of the Arts (EEA): As a complement to the experiential pedagogy outlined above, a contextually based business strategy is critical to the success of any emerging arts entrepreneur. Abstracted, the EEA curriculum helps students identify pertinent economic and cultural data sets supporting arts business decisions and sustainability strategies. By analyzing this data in five separate economic and cultural modalities, students can develop better and more informed business decisions, thus allowing more time for product development.

Outside/In Approach to Niche Creation: This technique asks students seven simple questions that focus on the external as it applies to the individual:

- Identify where you want to live.
- Look at the market and ask what is missing.
- Look to other communities and ask what they have, that one's own does not.
- Is there an audience for this concept in one's own community?
- How can you gather and engage with them?
- What makes what you are doing *different*?
- What makes what you are doing *necessary*?

Inside/Out Approach to Niche Creation: This second technique focuses on the individual student as it applies to the external and is more introspective:

- Answer the following: If you could create anything, regardless of money or struggle, what would you create?
- Consider and categorize your talents, interests, skills and experiences that afford knowledge or wisdom.
- Look at your lists and ask: How can these tools, techniques, knowledge and skills be 'repurposed' so as to be utilized in a host of ways?
- Synthesize each of these (image of funnel with each being placed within)
- Play with these discoveries with your imagination. What can you create out of these things? Pay particular attention to those things that are of interest to you.
- Whatever comes out of this imaginative play and synthesizing of talents, interests, skills and experiences that netted and process stimuli, take a hard look at that, as it may be a project that represents the possible engagement of your potential: numerous talents, skills and interests.
- If this idea is personally of interest, look to the market for competition and potential marketability.
- Imagine the resources, identify them, plan and startup.

Mentoring as Critical and Indispensable: For the authors, mentoring is vital to our students' experience. For Julia, this ancient mode of learning would be a critical aspect of her art entrepreneurship classroom. The authors see arts entrepreneurship education as much a mentoring experience as it is a classroom or even "experiential" endeavor. Though co- and non-curricular activities are important to our field, the authors find that investing the time to speak with (and learn about) our students is crucial to their success and our educational outcomes. Emerging entrepreneurs need mentoring as risks often create direct emotional and real-world impact, which for some is an important step in self-actualization.

V. LESSONS LEARNED

The authors identify significant trends in the development of their arts entrepreneurship training programs in a *cross-disciplinary* context (having a mixed classroom of arts and non-arts majors – including business majors). Perhaps the most compelling is that students often want to learn entrepreneurial skills through arts-based training. This provides (for lack of a better term) a more "product-based" approach for students who are more passionate about the value of an arts product for specific markets. Next, we find our programs are less formulaic and possess more variety, resulting in students seeing our programs as more creative than a traditional entrepreneurship training experience. Lastly, entrepreneurial training developed in an arts-based environment generates entrepreneurial ventures that lie on a continuum from "very traditionally arts based" to those that barely integrate the arts. We see this as a positive outcome as many of our non-arts students come to experiment with their own creativity for the first time in a significant way through our programs, and empowering students to do so – for these authors – is desired outcome; as these students enter the workforce we feel that allowing these students the opportunity to be creative helps to prepare a 21st century workforce. Anecdotally, as students come back to us a year or two after graduation, many state that their employers are excited to see that a new potential employee had an arts entrepreneurship course in college.

However, our experience with *exclusively* arts students yields a different set of observations. First, overall, the more technically and artistically adept, the more these students simply want to make a living with their art – extreme financial gain is NOT a goal. Contrastingly, those less skilled are looking for entrepreneurial options connected to the arts, which typically means that they recognize their artistic skill levels may not be as high as their peers and are looking for a way to make a living with, perhaps, more tangential arts skills. Again, these students are not looking to become rich, only to fill their refrigerator. Second, the pressure from their applied arts instructors to produce art at the highest level possible attenuates the time students can invest in our classes. Third, we see that many of our students are highly trained in creating art and desire an entrepreneurial lifestyle, yet do not choose to follow through on either. We have learned that despite the passion, effort and good intentions on both sides of the desk, our students still struggle with "crossing the line" into an entrepreneurial lifestyle.

VI. CONCLUSION

Some of the outcomes the authors witnessed during their own teaching career include the creation of theatre companies, galleries, film and media companies, serving as independent artists, pursuing careers as freelancers with an entrepreneurial mindset leading them into television, film, radio and a host of other professional and industry opportunities. Others include innovating and bringing to market products that impact the production of art such as dance tights with integrated joint support, color-coded guitar strings with matching color coded music to ease the process of learning standard musical notation and even a smart phone application to rate new music in real time – all three granted patents. Indeed, some students engage in an entrepreneurial lifestyle and others do not. When asked what the authors expect to see students doing after they graduate (tongue in cheek, but more so in truth), the reply is automatic: "Whatever they choose to do." As the field negotiates its theoretical and curricular relationship with both the business school, arts training and arts culture, a consensus on desired student outcomes – whatever they may be – must be a part of that discussion to achieve the moniker of "emerging discipline" and produce effective curricula.[15]

Entrepreneurship scholarship insists that entrepreneurs create opportunities, and, thus, arts entrepreneurship educators are inevitably tasked with helping students not only recognize and seize opportunities, but to provide them with the intellectual and experiential opportunities in the classroom to act entrepreneurially outside the classroom. In part, the authors report that our classrooms are not exclusively an "educational process serving measurable outcomes": we strive to develop a platform for "the testing of one's courage" – both intellectual and experiential, both student and instructor. Though this more philosophical stance may fly in the face of a traditional educational policy approach, it likely best mirrors and folds into a student's experience when faced with the prospect of realizing an idea in the arts marketplace: it takes a certain temperament to pursue an idea one believes will create value. Courage (intellectual and real) is required – as is a measure of mentoring.

It is critical to remind the reader that the authors do not suggest that starting an arts business is a primary outcome of arts entrepreneurship education. Though the abstracted outcomes mentioned at the beginning of Section II articulate these ideals, in the authors' programs, these are exceptional outcomes at this point in the field's development. Indeed, the majority of students engaged in our classrooms will not create businesses in a traditional sense, but will develop an understanding of how to "entrepreneur" and deliver value to employers and communities. Indeed, knowing how to create value is as important as creating it and an arts entrepreneurship classroom is a perfect platform to test students' propensity to "entrepreneur" in a space where risk is mitigated. Julia, it seems, is as much an arts entrepreneur as she is a passionate young woman in an economic environment allowing courageous play. Enrolling in an arts entrepreneurship course was her choice, yet one should acknowledge her professor who had the courage to engage in a field where there are no rules, roadmaps, theory or training: her instructor's experience in the arts marketplace, professional arts training and professional career provided both an educational and experiential classroom platform. The risks are great for both parties, and as a field we must recognize that without mutually assumed risk the classroom and our scholarship becomes a false shadow of what we preach.

Perhaps one of the most important lessons we can take from Julia's experience lies in the field's future negotiations concerning educational outcomes. Most conversations will certainly center on the core topic, yet orbiting issues will likely inform our results. One concerns our own knowledge and training. Mentioned above, Julia's instructors needed a significant knowledge base of at least eight distinct topics. In this example, that specific knowledge base was required. As we know, our classrooms are diverse affairs possessing a kaleidoscope of entrepreneurial desires. These eight topics are only the beginning of what we must intellectually possess as effective instructors and mentors. Soon the field will need to consider the academic and practical preparation of our future educators.

Another consideration concerns varying yet intersecting continuums that the field must negotiate in order to develop appropriate outcomes. One concerns "hard" versus "soft" knowledge, defined here as the tension between New Venture Creation (hard business and entrepreneurship knowledge) and more amorphous curricula (soft knowledge centering on mindset). Another concerns the weighting of for- versus non-profit topics. Yet another negotiation is outlined in this chapter: what is more important/effective – active student engagement or classroom intellectualism? Other continuums abound, yet now in context. How should we weight these three critical negotiations for differing institutional missions – conservatory, research-one, private and land grant? What about the art at these institutions: should a college that focuses on training students exclusively in the Fine Arts focus on non-profit entrepreneurial topics at the expense of New Venture Creation? Or should this institution rely on soft knowledge? Can outcomes be written that embrace both scenarios? Another level of complexity emerges: how do we develop appropriate curricular outcomes when a student's home is India, Saudi or China? How do we negotiate an arts/political/cultural/ economic continuum for these students? Should we? What about institutions in low-income rural areas? What is the correct curricular balance between for- and non-profit topics when that university's departmental mission focuses on community engagement, yet also possesses a strong arts administration program? How does the field prepare this entrepreneurial student group to best serve the community? As we negotiate these questions, the answer lies not in "oh, it's a little of everything" or "New Venture Creation or bust" but in defining how we want to intellectually and experientially prepare our students to successfully behave as entrepreneurs after they graduate – if that is their choice. The challenge is to develop robust, adaptive outcomes that can address a myriad of environmental contexts and support a myriad of curricular negotiations. To that end, the authors suggest that arts entrepreneurship educators possess (at a minimum) an intellectual understanding comprising the eight topics presented above (arts culture, arts economies, arts business models, New Venture Creation, arts policy, economic and community development, venture sustainability strategies in both the for- and non-profit realms and the impact of geography in the arts) to educate our students in entrepreneurially: (1) producing art; (2) impacting the production of art, its sale and distribution; and (3) attracting audiences to art[16]

Precise educational outcomes inform curriculum design and serves as the basis for accreditation. Consensus on what it is that educators desire students to learn (in conjunction with what they want to learn) is a critical step in creating curricula contextualized for the conservatory, private, public and other institutions. Oddly, for a field whose disciplinary prefix embraces collaboration and whose suffix celebrates innovation, we have yet to seriously engage in the painstaking work – the nuts and bolts – of our classroom. For a field whose prefix elevates itself through the aesthetic power of art and whose suffix calmly revels in the aesthetics of the market, arts entrepreneurship educators have yet to realize the beauty of a student's success through a contextual consensus. And for a field whose prefix rejects "the false" in art, yet whose suffix embraces value, we appear not to embrace our own authentic power in the classroom. As educators, we are up to the task of taking this critical first step for the students we profess to care about. Simply put, we must have the courage to fail and the passion to succeed. We must say that we do not know much of what we need to know and above all – for the field to advance and sustain – articulating our classrooms must be a shared responsibility.

NOTES

1. At this time, Fine Arts professional organizations (symphonies, ballets, museums, small and medium-sized performance venues, etc.) were beginning to experience financial pressures, which led to the shuttering of countless non-profit performing arts organizations. Generally speaking, this financial stress has market and demographics roots: as the popular arts consumed by a younger demographic enjoyed more commercial success (rock music, for example), these markets left the Fine Arts en masse. Remaining was an older audience demographic buying season tickets, participating in fundraisers and actively financing the Fine Arts and Fine Arts venues though endowments and estate gifts. In addition to ever increasing pressures on traditional non-profit arts funders (foundations and local philanthropy), this trend continues despite efforts to make the Fine Arts more relevant in 21st century life. See, for example, John Axelrod, *The Symphony Orchestra in Crisis: A Conductor's View*, Naxos Books, Kindle edition, 2013. Of course, the role of technology in Fine Arts consumption patterns since the 1970s cannot be ignored.
2. Note that the career development model remains a vital part of Fine Arts training at some institutions. See Angela Beeching (2010). *Beyond Talent*. Oxford: Oxford University Press, 2010. Also, see the Network of Music Career Development Officers http://www.music careernetwork.org.
3. Note that the field boasts three peer-reviewed journals: *Journal of Arts Entrepreneurship Research*, *Journal of Arts Entrepreneurship Education* and *Artivate*.
4. See The College Music Society's Outcomes for Arts Entrepreneurship Education (2012), http://www.ae2n.net/page6/styled-5/page26.html as the field's first attempt at developing educations outcomes, and Jason C. White (2013). "Barriers to Recognizing Arts Entrepreneurship Education as Essential to Professional Arts Training." *Artivate* 2(3): 28–39.
5. College Music Society Inaugural Summit, Blair School of Music, Vanderbilt University, January 16–17, 2010.
6. See, Pinchot, G. III (1985). *Intrapreneuring*. New York: Harper and Row for a discussion of the term.
7. The Conference Board (2006). *Are They Really Ready to Work? Employer's Perspectives on the Basic Knowledge and Applied Skills of New Entrants to the 21st Century Workforce.* Edited by J. Casner-Lotto, p. 49.
8. Ibid. p. 16.
9. See Menzel, Hanns, Aaltio, Iiris and Ulijn, Jan (2007). "On the Way to Creativity: Engineers as Intrapreneurs in Organizations." *Technovation* 27(12): 732–743 and Maorkovska, Monika (2008). "Intrapreneurship – Way of Working in Organizations for Improvement of Working Quality." (sic) Paper read at the 5th International Scientific Conference, Vilnius, Lithuania. May 16–17.

10. See Kennedy, Joseph W. (2010). "Empowering Future Organizational Leaders for the 21st Century." *International Business and Economics Research Journal* 9(4): 145–148, Antoncic, Bostjan and Hisrich, Robert D. (2001). "Intrapreneurship: Construct Refinement and Cross-Cultural Validation." *Journal of Business Venturing* 16(5): 495–527, Zahra, S.A., Kuratko, D.F. and Jennings, D.F. (1999). "Corporate Entrepreneurship and Wealth Creation: Contemporary and Emerging Perspectives." *Entrepreneurship Theory and Practice* 24(2): 5–9, Kuratko, D.F., Ireland, R.D. and Hornsby, J.S. (2001). "Improving Firm Performance through Entrepreneurial Actions: Acordia's Corporate Entrepreneurship Strategy." *Academy of Management Executive* 15(4): 60–71 and Morris, M.H. and Kuratko, D.F. (2002). *Corporate Entrepreneurship.* Mason, OH: South-Western College Publishers.
11. The authors currently teach the pedagogical and curricular practices described below.
12. The Marble Game is an offshoot of Kyle MacDonald's effort of trading up from a single red paper clip to an eventual house. At the second author's institution, The Marble Game is played in a course called Attracting Capital. In this case, students begin with a marble, as it has no apparent and obvious use. In the fall semester of 2013, one student traded up from her marble to over $1,700 in value.
13. Jung, C.G. (1970). "The World of Values." In J. Jacobi (ed.), *Psychological Reflections.* (2nd edition, p. 200). Princeton, NJ: Princeton University Press.
14. Second author's note: The first time I used this exercise in class, one student, after 45 minutes, returned with a working iPhone.
15. Beckman, Gary D. (2014). "Entrepreneuring the Aesthetic: Arts Entrepreneurship and Reconciliation." In F. Welter and T. Baker (eds.), *Routledge Companion to Entrepreneurship* (pp. 296–308). New York: Routledge.
16. Emerging from this suggestion is the question of experiential knowledge. At this point (anecdotally), it appears as if the field expects arts entrepreneurship educators to have real-world, entrepreneurial experience of some kind (either for- or non-profit) within an arts discipline.

9. The value of creativity: implications for industrial design and design entrepreneurship

Joyce Thomas and Lisa Canning

I. INTRODUCTION

> Creativity is an instinctive urge ... that gives creators an unusual euphoria and generates an unmatched sense of satisfaction. Creativity is the core of new ideas. It's the source for new products, new designs, and vision to see the world in a renewed way.[1]

For creatives and designers, using imagination and creativity to earn a living is frequently a lifelong love and fascination. Their ideas take them in every direction imaginable. They are community leaders, organizers, activists, and catalysts for change, as well as creators of products, graphics, images, films, books, poems, songs, and dances.[2] Business professionals historically have perceived designers and creatives as a soft asset that does not heavily contribute to their profit and loss statement. However, evidence of using creative, non-linear design thinking in business successes exists and has been the topic of a number of business thought leaders.

In *The Rise of The Creative Class* Florida explained that creativity is the most valuable quality of our times, 'the decisive source of competitive advantage.'[3] He suggests that creatives will become society's 'dominant class' in the 21st century.

Books like *Where Good Ideas Come From*[4] have contributed to 'innovation jams' at companies like Google and IBM where employees are given free time to brainstorm collectively and experiment with the things that are of interest to them. Kelley,[5] in *The Art of Innovation: Lessons in Creativity from IDEO, America's Leading Design Firm*, illustrated how IDEO tackled what would eventually become the Palm V and Polaroid's I-Zone camera by becoming 'anthropologists' tracking the behavior of people likely to use the products. Just shy of 20 years before

Kelley, *In Search of Excellence*, Peters and Waterman's management book[6] examining 43 of Fortune 500's top companies, described the success of 3M's Post-it Notes that was launched in 1977. Peters and Waterman wanted to prove how crucial people are to business success and has described the essential message of the book as 'people, customers, and action.' They illustrate that not only the bean counters' 'numbers' are crucial but that these soft factors, including embracing and understanding human needs, also become hard ones.

These success stories have become staples of marketing literature. Creativity is big business these days. Corporate and institutional giants such as Starbucks, IBM, General Electric, Citibank, the US Navy, American Express, Boeing (McDonnell Douglas), Pfizer, SC Johnson, Kohler, the World Bank, and others are recognizing the connectivity the creative arts hold as conductor for organizational transformative change and innovation to fuel profits.[7]

An IBM poll of 1500 CEOs identified creativity as the first 'leadership competency' needed for future success,[8] to help their corporations solve problems and innovate faster. A 2011 Martin Prosperity Institute study revealed that entrepreneurship levels may be connected to a region's underlying creativity.[9] These studies point to a need to cultivate creativity and entrepreneurship in post-secondary education. New generations entering the workforce need to be better prepared to fully contribute to the economic, social, and cultural growth of our communities.

According to the National Endowment for the Arts, industrial design is the largest segment of the creative class.[10] In order to begin to understand the broader role creatives can play in transformative change, we will explore how these creatives approach their craft and practice; traditional and emerging fields of industrial design entrepreneurship; the era of industrial designers as founders and key partners; design entrepreneurship education; and how this reflects on the broader field of arts entrepreneurship.

II. THE PRACTICE OF INDUSTRIAL DESIGN

Each and every moment of their days, people interact and engage with objects (products) that have been designed to enable, empower, or delight them – from cell phones, to furniture, to automobiles, to medical products, and beyond. Manufacturers mass-produce these products to solve the needs of large groups of people (e.g. Swiffers and Post-it Notes) that will ultimately produce profits for their companies. According to the Industrial Design Society of America (IDSA), '*industrial design* is the profession that determines the form of a manufactured product, shaping it to fit the people who use it and the industrial processes that produce it.'[11] Industrial design practitioners utilize 'design thinking' as one part of their methodology to innovatively solve complex or wicked problems. Drawing upon intuition, logic, and systematic reasoning, designers explore problems to discover and imagine new, desirable solutions that satisfy human needs, serving as the advocate for and the voice of the consumer in the product development process. At the same time, designers must also work across interdisciplinary boundaries with engineering, manufacturing, and marketing to ensure that what they design can also be manufactured sustainably and profitably for the company producing and selling the products.

Formosa of Smart Design tells us that design is less about generating products and more about creating positive experiences for the user.[12] In order to do that, this profession requires creative vision with an understanding of and empathy with users,[13] up-to-date knowledge about market conditions, excellent visual and verbal communications, and technical and manufacturing knowledge.

> Design has become the language with which to shape those objects and to tailor the messages that they carry. The role of the most sophisticated designers today is as much to be storytellers, to make design that speaks in such a way as to convey these messages, as it is to resolve formal and functional problems.[14]

Industrial designers frequently practice as employees working for in-house design/engineering studios within large or small corporations, or within independent design consultancies typically started by an individual or group of entrepreneurially minded industrial designers. The scope of an industrial design consultancy is very different than a manufacturing corporate structure. Consultants tend to focus on the design and creation of products/services whereas corporations deal with this as well as manufacturing, marketing, sales, legal ramifications, and more. The industrial design practice for both has evolved to creating a holistic package of designs from initial concepts to production-ready designs. In a corporate environment, designers often focus on a single product category, whereas in a consultancy, the range of product development projects may be more varied (e.g. medical products, lawn and garden, toys, housewares). In both cases, the end result is that the client/manufacturer owns the intellectual property and the designer's remuneration is based only on the original design. These forms of practice have been the 'norm' for this profession since its inception in the late 1920s.

Traditional roles for industrial design entrepreneurship emerged with design firms run by the forefathers of the industrial design profession, Norman Bel Geddes, Walter Dorwin Teague, Raymond Loewy, and Henry Dreyfuss, who created products for Kodak, Steinway, Bell Laboratories, Royal, Honeywell, Polaroid, World's Fairs, and more.[15] In these early years, industrial design was focused more on the styling and appearance of products than today's holistic practice of incorporating both human and manufacturing needs into refined, well-designed products.

Three of these original industrial design firms continue today. This form of design entrepreneurship (founders as entrepreneurs with employees) continues as a major form of practice today with firms like IDEO and frog design. These consultancies typically develop products under contract to a client (the client owns the intellectual property and arranges for the manufacture and distribution of those products).

A survey of the Core77.com design directory reveals that worldwide 2521 industrial design firms have registered in their comprehensive guide of design firms and creative agencies.[16] This listing includes 977 industrial design firms in the US. There are 5698 total firms across all design industries, including design management, apparel design, interaction design, architecture, engineering, and more, that range in size from large agencies to solopreneurs (an entrepreneur who runs a business alone).[17]

Today, new opportunities for designers exist due to the expansion of available technology and the rapid explosion of connectedness since the birth of the Internet in the 1990s. What industrial designer hasn't dreamed about becoming an entrepreneur? The appeal of being one's own boss, picking the clients and projects is undeniable. The potential for future earnings from the body of one's past creations (residual income) is compelling. Some of the hurdles to starting a business, like finding the necessary startup capital, can be very small compared to other businesses. The physical tools to practice this profession are now commodities; most designers already have a laptop and the software they need along with paper and pencils. Tie these together with the differentiating features of this craft – the design abilities of problem finding and solving, design thinking, ideating, and researching (e.g. ethnographic, empathic, participatory, and human-centered methods); the skills to rapidly visualize design solutions through low fidelity prototypes (sketches and drawings; 3D computer modeling; paper, foam core, foam, and wood models); and the understanding of material, processes, manufacturing and human factors – and a bit of space and you are ready to go as a solopreneur (entrepreneur founder as designer).

For designers looking for access to rapid prototype models, the website www.makexyz.com allows people to rent out the services of their personal/business 3D printer to anyone with printing needs.[18] 3D printing technology is coming soon to a FedEx/Kinkos near everyone. In the last three years alone there has been more progress in the 3D printing space than the previous 20 years combined.[19] For more high fidelity appearance prototypes, the design entrepreneur can purchase the services of a high-end rapid prototyping firm and professional model maker. Other components of new product development (e.g. engineering, marketing, product certification) equally can be outsourced or accomplished through partnerships (joint ventures) with other firms or solopreneurs.

For those looking to self-produce their own concept(s), crowdfunding or working/partnering with venture capitalists are resources that can provide startup capital. 'Crowdfunding involves an open call, mostly through the Internet, for the provision of financial resources either in form of donation or in exchange for the future product or some form of reward to support initiatives for specific purposes.'[20]

Through the participation of its investors, crowdfunding creates and expands networks that can be stronger than more traditional ones. The people who invest share in the developer's passion for the projects and participate because it is fun. The relationships built in these networks can be more on a personal level rather than professional, and the investors can benefit from the network when it comes to additional business opportunities or issues.[21]

Kickstarter, based in Brooklyn, New York, is one crowdfunding source in this space. It has become a hub of creativity for designers from around the world and has raised more money for creatives and their projects than the National Endowment for the Arts.[22] At the 2014 Industrial Designer Society of America (IDSA) National Conference in Austin, Texas, John Dimatos, partnerships lead for design and technology at Kickstarter, discussed the changes to product development when creators embrace transparency, collaborative funding, and community involvement, enabling their backers to become engaged throughout the creative process.

III. EMERGING FIELDS OF INDUSTRIAL DESIGN ENTREPRENEURSHIP

(a) Designer Founder as Entrepreneur: Industrial Design Consultancy

The top three reasons entrepreneurs have shared about why they start their own business are: the freedom to pursue new opportunities; the chance to follow their personal passions; and the ability to gain independence from others' control. Money ranks fourth.[23]

Following in the footsteps of the industrial design founders, entrepreneurial designers continue to give birth to new firms – often spinning off their new entities from corporate or consultant offices, capitalizing on their expertise gained in previous employment, and practicing in traditional modes of developing products under contract to a client. This form of design entrepreneurship is sometimes practiced as 'freelancing,' especially for recent graduates who have not yet succeeded in landing their first industrial design employment experience.

(b) Designer Founder as Entrepreneur: Design/Development/ Manufacturing

> When you first start off trying to solve a problem, the first solutions you come up with are very complex, and most people stop there. But if you keep going, and live with the problem and peel more layers of the onion off, you can oftentimes arrive at some very elegant and simple solutions. Steve Jobs[24]

Industrial designer Maria Boustead had an idea for stylish, functional bike bags for city commuters that was born from her own need. Living and commuting via bicycle in Chicago, Boustead discovered a product opportunity in the market – bike bag solutions that could be briefcases or purses for women. She founded Po Campo on a desk in her home, initially sewing her own prototypes prior to finding manufacturing in China. Po Campo has developed into a growing company with international distribution within a few short years.[25] Boustead is one example in a growing trend of designer entrepreneurs who retain control over the intellectual property of their designs, are part of the core founding team of startup companies, and who sometimes use resources such as Kickstarter to help launch their business.

The Designer Fund is another resource available to entrepreneurial designers looking to create businesses with meaningful impact. They seek 'Designer Founders,' believing companies can be more successful when the key design, engineering, and business talent collaborate from the beginning to create businesses that can craft better user experiences through higher quality products. Resources provided include angel funding, mentorship, and connections to help designers build their companies. This servant leadership based community fosters a positive virtuous cycle of successful designers giving back to the next generation of entrepreneurial designers.[26]

(c) Designer/Entrepreneur Supporting Startup Business Founder

Entrepreneurship isn't about being in a specific industry, having a distinct type of education, or dressing a certain way. If you're passionate about providing value and using your unique set of skills to solve problems for others, then yes, you are entrepreneur material.[27]

Designers are also helping to shape the direction of young startup companies from a non-founding position. For example, within the university supported business incubator EnterpriseWorks at the University of Illinois at Urbana-Champaign Research Park, industrial design students, mentored by the 'Designer Entrepreneur-in-Residence,' are working with startups that have been born through innovation across a variety of disciplines at the university. Through this program, these young startups (that are most frequently student-led operations) are exposed to the value of collaboration across disciplines as a foundational element that will help their venture succeed. This form of design entrepreneurship is also sometimes practiced by industrial design consultancies and solopreneurs and may result in joint ventures or partnerships.

(d) Designer/Entrepreneur Participating in Online Co-creation

Other online sources also embrace customer co-creation –'an active, creative and social collaboration process between producers (retailers) and customers (users), facilitated by the company.'[28] For example, at Threadless.com and Quirky.com, customers become active participants in an innovation process and take part in the development of new products or services. Both Threadless and Quirky use community-based innovation: the community suggests new concepts, votes on ideas, and collectively determines the products that go into production. The concept behind these platforms is to convert the creativity of sizeable audiences into alternative research and development labs – t-shirts for Threadless and a variety of objects for Quirky.[29] These types of ventures appeal to both industrial designers and armchair inventors, and embrace a new 'hacking' paradigm.

(e)   Designers Supporting Not-for-Profit Social Entrepreneurship

> Entrepreneurs are entrepreneurs for one reason: They love solving problems for people. Sure, they want to be successful. But to them, the real mission of their business is to help others.[30]

Industrial designer Nancy Perkins has taken a different route in design entrepreneurship. Following very successful runs as both corporate and consultant (solopreneur) designer, Nancy took on the role of President and CEO for the Dallas Lighthouse for the Blind (DLB), one of her former clients. As leader of this not-for-profit social entrepreneurship model, Perkins explores new design opportunities to enrich the business and to fulfill the needs of this factory that predominantly utilizes a blind and visually impaired workforce. Perkins says of the DLB, 'We are in the changing minds business – helping other people understand what people who are blind can actually do.' While the DLB is not a manufacturing source for entrepreneurs (the specialized fixtures and sewing/ manufacturing requirements for a blind workforce don't work well for short run customization), its officers must act entrepreneurially to discover new business opportunities outside of their traditional Federal government contracts as well as in innovating new ways for people with no or low vision to build quality products.

Her experiences as a corporate designer and a consultant provided Perkins with essential skills that apply to managing a complex organization that employs over 200 people. Consulting as a solopreneur gave Perkins a window to many types of company operations that have helped inform her professional practice: at the DLB she finds that she is always drawing on her entrepreneurial creative abilities to solve problems even when this has taken her beyond her original design field.

> In my current position, I have a different appreciation of the value of design to an organization whose purpose is not providing design services. My industrial design education and experience have been invaluable when managing and planning the future of our organization. I truly believe that designers have a distinct advantage in solving problems and driving organizations forward. Nancy Perkins[31]

IV. DISCUSSION: THE ERA OF INDUSTRIAL DESIGNERS AS FOUNDERS AND KEY PARTNERS

We're really in the era of the designer as founder, as entrepreneur, as a key partner in new businesses. ... 15 years ago, every meeting I had started with some CEO or somebody on the management team asking me, 'What's the [return on investment] on design?' Yves Béhar[32]

Today, Béhar says that venture capitalists are more likely to say, 'Well, if you don't have a designer on your team, I don't think we're going to give you money.'

The barriers to the designer as entrepreneur seem to be shrinking: we are becoming more receptive to new ways of doing, designing, and conducting business. In a 2011 article in FastCo, Nussbaum calls this a radical change that shows a new sophistication in business where non-designers can talk about design intelligently. 'Our industry is more about design in some ways today than European businesses are.'[33]

Nussbaum tells us that he believes that creativity is a more inclusive term than design. Business people, engineers, and venture capitalists could more easily accept the concept of creativity than design, in part because 'creatives' have long been part of the culture of advertising. Owners are growing 60 percent faster than other businesses when they give sales and marketing the right attention. By starting with the correct focus, they are seeing a return in increased profits and personal well-being.[34] 'One key to entrepreneurs' success is that they frame things differently, they connect existing dots in unique ways. The two guys who started Method, for example, frame-changed the market for sustainable cleaning products from a "suffering-is-good-for-you" space to a "cool-design-that's-good-for-the-planet" space.'[35]

Academic studies documenting the history of the fashion industry can provide some valuable insights towards the practice of entrepreneurship in other design fields such as industrial design. Wenting's work shows that successful young designers generally accumulate experience through job mobility prior to establishing their own firm. Creativity and tacit knowledge can be transmitted if two people work closely together within the boundaries of a firm as employees, suggesting that for these young designers gaining experience as an assistant of an established designer adds to their own value. 'Indeed, it appears that designers do not only use the knowledge they gained at previous employers in their own entre-preneurial venture, but also put their prior experiences to good use while working as an employee for other houses' (p. 599). This research indicates that spinoffs in the fashion industry inherit part of their parents' organizational fitness and ultimately outperform other entrants; the evolutionary theory of routine inheritance works across these cultural industries similarly to how it works in manufacturing industries. Alternately, Wenting suggests that more successful firms could be attracting better designers who ultimately were more likely to start their own firms and survive: successful firms might act as magnets for creative and entrepreneurial talent.[36]

> Fashion design entrepreneurs in Holland who produce for a large, mass-consumer market earn more steady and higher average incomes than designers who design unique pieces of clothing for small shifting market niches. The latter group often consider themselves as artists more than business people and accept a lower income for more artistic freedom.[37]

The study by Wenting's team showed that network ties with fellow designers and experience gained in the past explain economic success. Co-location affects economic success indirectly by facilitating learning through increased opportunities to gain valuable experience and socio-professional networking. Entrepreneurs in clusters tend to collaborate more and this networking enhances economic performance. Design students can be advised to learn first from established designers before venturing out on their own. Internships and active networking provides the opportunity for both new and current designers to share risks and exchange knowledge.[38]

An industrial design student posed this question in a discussion board forum on the industrial design website Core77.com: 'Why aren't there more industrial designers that go the entrepreneurship route?' This student suggested that the designer might want to create a business around the products they design rather than giving the credit to a large corporation. Responses to this question explored many different positions from the community – from suggesting that entrepreneurial mindset was as much about personality traits as it was about design skill sets, to the need for more experience for recent graduates (still learning about designing for production) prior to becoming an entrepreneur, to recognizing that running a 'shop' will take time away from the actual 'designing,' leaving perhaps only 10–15 percent of your time practicing the craft.[39]

In the article 'Why Aren't There More Designer Founders?', Alter suggests that 'designers want to design' and frequently have a single-minded dedication to their craft – a hypothesis borne out through personal conversations with designers. This is one reason designers often choose design agencies surrounded by a like-minded cohort of designers. At other corporations, and especially startups, the designer can practice as a lone designer for years. This can be due to the limited resources of the startup or the ability to outsource, purchasing design and other services under the counsel of the in-house leadership.[40]

Alter suggests that a founder's job is to lead, often doing the work no one else is excited to do (e.g. fundraising, recruiting) along with the cool stuff of product development. As a designer founder entrepreneur, there is a need to find clients, market products, understand and handle legal issues (including intellectual property), and to manage both at the project level and overall business level.[41]

Alter again reflects that as entrepreneurs, *founders* are often not actually amazing at performing any one thing, whereas *designers* practice to excel at their craft. Both, however, are iterative problem solvers who have to strike a balance between the needs of their customers (e.g. consumers, colleagues, and funders), which also includes investment into the design and development of their products. For people who live only for designing products, interfaces, or logos, it may not be a good fit to start their own company where they would spend significant time on business tasks that would take them away from their real passions. 'But if what they really love is the *process* around designing – around solving problems they are passionate about – then they are well-suited for entrepreneurship.'[42]

V. ENTREPRENEURSHIP EDUCATION FOR INDUSTRIAL DESIGNERS

So the big question is how do design schools help their students to become more entrepreneurial? In 2007, Beckman reported that most large institutions of higher education in the arts were tremendously complex and could be overwhelmed by the need to deliver the core skills of their disciplines. They could have too many competing agendas to be able to focus specifically on the fusion of creative skills with life sustaining competencies.[43] Since Beckman's report in 2007, we are beginning to see some changes in this landscape with new trends in philosophy, curricula, and outcomes.

The purpose of this review is to investigate design education to better understand how entrepreneurship is introduced and taught at the under-graduate and graduate levels in industrial design programs in the US. Post-secondary schools (universities) that teach towards a career in industrial design are the focus of this study. The industrial design program curricula from the top five schools as ranked by the Design Futures Council[44] and the top ten schools as ranked by US News and

World Reports[45] were reviewed. There is some overlap in these lists resulting in a survey of 13 of the highest ranked schools teaching industrial design in the US out of a total of 64 schools accredited by NASAD (National Association of Schools of Art and Design).[46]

The online curriculum presence for the following schools was reviewed for this study:

1. University of Cincinnati – BS and MID (design)[47]
2. Rhode Island School of Design – BFA and MID (industrial design)[48]
3. Art Center College of Design – BS (environmental design) and MS[49]
4. Syracuse University – BID and MFA[50]
5. Carnegie Mellon University – BDes and MA (design)[51]
6. Cranbrook Academy of Art – MFA (design)[52]
7. Savannah College of Art and Design – BFA, MA, and MFA[53]
8. California College of the Arts – BFA and MBA (design strategy), MFA (design), dual MFA/MBA (design strategy)[54]
9. Pratt Institute – BID and MID (industrial design)[55]
10. Ohio State University – BSD and MFA[56]
11. Rochester Institute of Technology – BFA and MFA[57]
12. School of the Visual Arts – MFA (products of design)[58]
13. School of the Art Institute of Chicago – BFA, MDes, and MFA (designed objects)[59]

The curricula for each school's undergraduate and graduate programs were reviewed and searched for the term entrepreneur in the course titles and descriptions. Course catalogue listings were also reviewed to understand if information related to entrepreneurship was imbedded in a course without being listed in the description. For example, programs including 'professional practice' course listings may or may not include a unit on design entrepreneurship depending on the faculty member responsible for teaching the course.

The 13 programs included in this overview study of design entrepreneurship education are shown in Table 9.1. Each school is preceded by their 2014 rankings by DesignIntelligence (DI) and US News and World Report (USN). Eleven of these programs grant undergraduate degrees in industrial design and 13 master's level degrees.

Table 9.1 Presence of entrepreneurship courses in industrial design curriculum in US schools

Ranking agency	School	Undergraduate program	Graduate program	Undergraduate entrepreneurship courses	Graduate entrepreneurship courses
DI (1)	University of Cincinnati	BS in Design	Master of Design	Optional elective?	Not definitive
USN (1) DI (4)	Rhode Island School of Design	BFA in Industrial Design	MID (Industrial Design)	Yes	Not definitive
USN (2) DI (2)	Art Center College of Design	BS in Environmental Design	MS	Yes	Yes
DI (3)	Syracuse University	BID – Bachelor of Industrial Design	MFA	Yes	No
USN (3)	Carnegie Mellon University	BDes – Bachelor of Design	MA in Design MDes, MPS (Master of Professional Studies) in Design for Interactions	No	Optional elective?
USN (4)	Cranbrook Academy of Art	None	MFA in Design	–	Not definitive
DI (5)	Savannah College of Art and Design	BFA	MA, MFA	No	Yes
USN (5)	California College of the Arts	BFA	MBA – Design Strategy, Public Policy Design, Strategic Foresight MFA in Design Dual MFA/MBA in Design Strategy	No	Yes

Table 9.1 continued

Ranking agency	School	Undergraduate program	Graduate program	Undergraduate entrepreneurship courses	Graduate entrepreneurship courses
USN (6)	Pratt Institute	BID – Bachelor of Industrial Design	MID (Industrial Design) GID: The Global Innovation Design Track	No	Not definitive
USN (7)	Ohio State University	BSD	MFA	No	No
USN (8)	Rochester Institute of Technology	BFA	MFA	Optional elective?	Yes
USN (9)	School of the Visual Arts	None	MFA in Products of Design	-	Yes
USN (10)	School of the Art Institute of Chicago	BFA – Designed Objects Pathway	MDes, MFA in Designed Objects	No	No
Core course on entrepreneurship offered			Yes	3	0
			No	6	2
Elective course on entrepreneurship offered in another field			Optional elective?	2	5
			Not definitive	0	4

Of the 11 programs offering an undergraduate degree in industrial design, only three programs offered courses specifically including entrepreneurship – Rhode Island School of Design,[60] Art Center College of Design,[61] and Syracuse University.[62]

Two undergraduate programs included elective courses to be taken in other programs (business, interdisciplinary studies, finance, and interactive games and media) at the students' discretion or with advisement from faculty – University of Cincinnati and Rochester Institute of Technology. These courses may or may not include entrepreneurship education.

Seven of the top 11 undergraduate programs evidenced no entrepreneurship education. All 13 schools offered master's level courses in industrial design. Two of these programs had no mention of entrepreneurship in the course offerings. Five programs offered specific courses including design entrepreneurship – Art Center College of Design,[63] Savannah College of Art and Design,[64] California College of the Arts,[65] Rochester Institute of Technology,[66] and School of the Visual Arts.[67]

Four additional graduate level programs (indicated on the chart with 'Not definitive') may include some entrepreneurship education; however, it is unclear to what extent these topics are covered from the course listings on their websites.

It is to be noted that although Carnegie Mellon University's course listings do not specifically include entrepreneurship, their design program is undergoing a significant revision beginning in fall of 2014, when they will launch new programs that respond to the increased demand for design's evolving role in the 21st century.

> 1. Design has become a highly interactive, collaborative, and trans-disciplinary activity that is integral to the success of businesses and institutions all over the world and, 2. these organizations are recognizing the need for new problem-solving approaches in light of mounting social and environmental challenges. Designers who understand and can solve for these complex 'systems problems' will be in increasing demand in the coming decades.[68]

Outside of these highly ranked industrial design programs, there are two additional programs that we would like to note that actually focus on entrepreneurship education in design and creative fields. Although the University of California at San Diego (UCSD) has no formal program in industrial design, they focus on melding entrepreneurship education into the core concepts of industrial design in their technical elective in product design and entrepreneurship.[69] This course focuses on developing new product concepts and performing marketplace analysis with the goal of starting a new company. Teams are selected to receive awards from a NCIIA (National Collegiate Inventors and Innovators Alliance) grant to further develop their project following the course.

Recognizing that mastering the basics of the creative's craft takes a minimum of four years of intense undergraduate study, the Institute for Arts Entrepreneurship[70] is a post-secondary program outside of higher education teaching 21st century creative entrepreneurial thinking and leadership skills. It draws an interdisciplinary group of students from the creative sector (e.g. performing artists, visual artists, designers, culinary artists, and architects) and emphasizes both cognitive and non-cognitive skill building, placing creativity, self-awareness, and empathy at the core of learning. The curriculum provides opportunities for creatives to advance their cognitive development relevantly to their area of expertise in ways they can apply in business.[71]

For many practicing industrial designers in the US, the bachelor's degree is their highest level of formal education. The practice of design education at the undergraduate level continues to promote design careers working for others (works made for hire). It is left to the learned and intuitive design/empathy thinking skills that are developed throughout their undergraduate education and then further honed through professional practice to help guide industrial designers in their path to entrepreneurship.

VI. IMPLICATIONS: BUILDING CREATIVE LEADERSHIP THROUGH ADVANCING ARTS ENTREPRENEURSHIP EDUCATION

> It's still early days, and the chasm between business and design yawns. Closer cooperation is necessary. Designers who exhibit business acumen can be involved at a more strategic level within a corporation. Executives who learn to apply design methods such as prototyping or brainstorming have a better shot at building a corporate culture that nurtures innovation – and the business' bottom line.[72]

While there has been some progress in design entrepreneurship education in the last ten years, relatively few designers and creatives are equipped with the mindset, skills, knowledge, and insight to realize their full potential in the marketplace when they complete their post-secondary or graduate degree in a creative field. Similar to any creative problem solving process, the way creatives learn is iterative and relies upon knowledge acquisition, reflection, and application. Creatives need to learn the language and tools of business to facilitate communication and employ design thinking skills to discover new solutions to satisfy human needs.

There are some good examples of courses in a few of the top industrial design programs, yet entrepreneurship tends not to be taught consistently across undergraduate and graduate degree programs. What is integrated into the curriculum can vary significantly depending on faculty who carry the baton for entrepreneurship.

Our contemporary educational experience is not designed to fully harness the ingenuity and resourcefulness of the creative community to create new small businesses or to fully contribute to the economic, social, and cultural growth of our communities. Creative entrepreneurship training should be integrated into all educational programs as a way of thinking, rather than be absent or partial as in the current curriculum.

By focusing on and investing in expanding the skill set of creatives, we ensure that our culture is enriched and opportunities are generated. Creativity plays a huge role in the value proposition of businesses – from the design and development of the products they produce to creative leadership building a healthy, profitable, and lasting corporate culture. It is the core of new ideas, enabling us to see the world in a renewed way and producing transformative change that allows us to leave it in a better state than when we found it.

NOTES

1. Canaan, D. (2003), 'Research to Fuel the Creative Process.' In Laurel, B. (ed.), *Design Research: Methods and Perspectives* (p. 236). Cambridge, MA: MIT Press.
2. Jackson, M. R., Kabwasa-Green, F., Swenson, D., Herranz, J., Ferryman, K., Atlas, C., Wallner, E., and Rosenstein, C. (2003), 'The Culture, Creativity, and Communities (CCC) Program at the Urban Institute,' available at http://www.urban.org/UploadedPDF/411311_investing_in_creativity.pdf (accessed 22 June 2014).
3. Florida, R. L. (2002), *The Rise of the Creative Class: And How It's Transforming Work, Leisure, Community and Everyday Life*, New York: Basic Books, p. 4.
4. Johnson, S. (2010), *Where Good Ideas Come From: The Natural History of Innovation*, London: Penguin.
5. Kelley, T. (2007), *The Art of Innovation: Lessons in Creativity from IDEO, America's Leading Design Firm*, New York: Random House, Inc.
6. Peters, T. J. and Waterman, R. H. (1982), *In Search of Excellence*, New York: Harper & Row.
7. Creativity at Work (n.d.), 'About Linda Naiman,' available at http://www.creativityatwork.com/about/linda-naiman/ (accessed 6 July 2014); Creativity at Work (n.d.), 'Selected Clients,' available at http://www.creativityatwork.com (accessed 6 July 2014); Creative Leaps International (n.d.), 'Projects of Creative Leaps,' available at http://www.creativeleaps.org/about/clientsandpartners.htm (accessed 6 July 2014); Johnson, M. L. (2014), 'When Art Meets Manufacturing,' *Winston-Salem Journal*, 12 June

2014, available at http://www.journalnow.com/home_food/home_garden/diy/when-art-meets-manufacturing/article_5b920de2-c0c6-573a-88e8-c3b14532546e.html (accessed 6 July 2014).

8. IBM (2010), 'IBM 2010 Global CEO Study,' available at http://www.ibm.com/services/us/ceo/ceostudy2010/index.html (accessed 17 August 2011).

9. Florida, R., Mellander, C., and Stolarick, K. (2011), 'Creativity and Prosperity: The Global Creativity Index,' Martin Prosperity Institute, available at http://martinprosperity.org/media/GCI%20Report%20Sep%202011.pdf (accessed 25 June 2014).

10. NEA (2013), 'Valuing the Art of Industrial Design: A Profile of the Sector and Its Importance to Manufacturing, Technology, and Innovation,' available at http://arts.gov/sites/default/files/Valuing-Industrial-Design.pdf (accessed 5 July 2014).

11. IDSA (2004), 'What is ID?' Industrial Designers Society of America, available at http://www.idsa.org/webmodules/articles/articlefiles/what_is_id_brochure.pdf (accessed 24 August 2008).

12. Formosa, D. (2006), 'Social Responsibility through Design: Smart Design Calls for a Wide-Angle View of Universal Design,' Smart News [homepage on the internet], available at http://www.smartdesignworldwide.com/news/article.php?id=98 (updated 2006, accessed 14 September 2009).

13. Thomas, J., McDonagh, D., and Strickfaden, M. (2012), 'Empathic Education in Design: Strategies for Healthcare Practitioners?' *Australasian Medical Journal*, 5(5), 292–300.

14. Sudjic, D. (2009), *The Language of Things: Understanding the World of Desirable Objects*, London: W.W. Norton, pp. 20.

15. Papanek, V. and Fuller, R. B. (1972), *Design for the Real World*, London: Thames and Hudson; Clark, P. (1998), 'Henry Dreyfuss, Industrial Designer: The Man in the Brown Suit,' *Journal of Design History*, 11(1), 105–106; Cooper, R. and Junginger, S. (2013), 'General Introduction: Design Management – A Reflection.' In Cooper, R., Junginger, S., and Lockwood, T. (eds.), *The Handbook of Design Management*, London: Bloomsbury.

16. Core77.com (2014), 'Design directory,' available at http://www.designdirectory.com/Search?tda_status=false&tag=&page_size=50&page_no=1&state=&msas=&cities=&budgets=0&specialty=&countries=&phrase= (accessed 26 June 2014).

17. Miller, G. S. (2005), Urban Dictionary.com, available at http://www.urbandictionary.com/define.php?term=solopreneur (accessed 27 June 2014); Zimmerman, E. (2011), 'A Small Business Made to Seem Bigger,' *The New York Times*, 2 March 2011; Rauch, J. (2012), 'You, Inc.,' *National Journal*, 7 June 2012; MacMillan Dictionary Buzz Word (n.d.), available at http://www.macmillandictionary.com/us/buzzword/entries/solopreneur.html (accessed 27 June 2014).

18. Falk, T. (2013), 'Where to Find a 3D Printer Nearby,' SmartPlanet blog, 17 March 2013, available at http://www.smartplanet.com/blog/bulletin/where-to-find-a-3d-printer-nearby/ (accessed 26 June 2014).

19. Bengtson, T. (2014), 'Why the Retail and Shipping Industries Should Fear 3D Printing,' Print.com, 20 April 2014, available at http://3dprint.com/2444/retail-shipping-industries-fear-3d-printing/ (accessed 26 June 2014).

20. Belleflamme, P., Lambert, T., and Schwienbacher, A. (2014), 'Crowdfunding: Tapping the Right Crowd,' *Journal of Business Venturing*, 29(5), 585–609.

21. Schwienbacher, A., and Larralde, B. (2010), 'Crowdfunding of Small Entrepreneurial Ventures,' *SSRN Electronic Journal*, 28 September 2010.

22. Boyle, K. (2013), 'Yes, Kickstarter Raises More Money for Artists than the NEA. Here's Why That's Not Really Surprising,' *Washington Post*, available at http://www. washington post.com/blogs/wonkblog/wp/2013/07/07/yes-kickstarter-raises-more-money-for-artists-than-the-nea-heres-why-thats-not-really-surprising/ (accessed 6 July 2014).

23. SOBO (2013), 'State of Business Owner 2013. The Pulse of Small and Midsize Business,' available at http://www.stateoftheowner.com/downloads/State-of-the-Owner-Full-Report-2013.pdf (accessed 6 June 2014).

24. Levy, S. (2006), 'Q&A: Jobs on iPod's Cultural Impact,' *Newsweek Technology*, MSNBC. com, 14 October 2006, available at http://web.archive.org/web/20061022014411/http:// www.msnbc.msn.com/id/15262121/site/newsweek/ (accessed 26 June 2014).
25. Becky (2011), 'Designer Interview: Maria Boustead, Founder of Po Campo,' DesignPublic. com, available at http://blog.designpublic.com/2011/06/23/designer-interview-maria-boustead-founder-of-po-campo/ (accessed 25 June 2014); Lubin, L. (2014), 'Po Campo's Maria Buostead Says: "On Yer Bike!"' Urbanful.org, available at http://urbanful.org/2014/ 06/12/po-campos-maria-boustead-says-yer-bike/ (accessed 25 June 2014).
26. DesignerFund.com (n.d.), available at http://designerfund.com (accessed 30 June 2014).
27. Tarkenton, F. (2014), 'Everything You Know about Entrepreneurship Is Wrong,' GoSmall-Biz.com Blog, 14 May 2014, available at http://gosmallbiz.com/everything-you-know-about-entrepreneurship-is-wrong/ (accessed 17 May 2014).
28. Piller, F. T., Ihl, C., and Vossen, A. (2011), 'Customer Co-creation: Open Innovation with Customers.' In Wittke, V. and Hanekop, H. (eds.), *New Forms of Collaborative Innovation and Production on the Internet* (pp. 31–63).
29. Piller et al. (2011), op. cit.
30. Tarkenton (2014), op. cit.
31. Perkins, N. (2014), in personal correspondence with the author.
32. Wieners, B. (2013), 'Yves Béhar: The Designer as Entrepreneur,' *Business Week/ Innovation & Design*, 24 January 2013, available at http://www.businessweek.com/articles/ 2013-01-24/yves-b-har-the-designer-as-entrepreneur (accessed 10 February 2014).
33. Nussbaum, B. (2011), 'Designers Are the New Drivers of American Entrepreneurialism,' FastCo/Business+Design+Innovation, 3 October 2011, available at http://www.fastco design.com/1665120/designers-are-the-new-drivers-of-american-entrepreneurialism (accessed 10 February 2014).
34. Nussbaum (2011), op. cit.
35. Nussbaum (2011), op. cit.
36. Wenting, R. (2008), 'Spinoff Dynamics and the Spatial Formation of the Fashion Design Industry, 1858–2005,' *Journal of Economic Geography*, 8(5), 593–614.
37. Wenting, R., Atzema, O., and Frenken, K. (2011), 'Urban Amenities and Agglomeration Economies? The Locational Behaviour and Economic Success of Dutch Fashion Design Entrepreneurs,' *Urban Studies*, 48(7), 1333–1352.
38. Wenting et al. (2011), op. cit.
39. Core77.com (2011–2012), 'Industrial Design Entrepreneurs?' available at http:// boards.core77.com/viewtopic.php?f=33&t=25732 (accessed 17 May 2014).
40. Alter, J. (2013), 'Why Aren't There More Designer Founders?' Wired.com, available at http://www.wired.com/2013/08/why-arent-more-startups-founded-by-designers/ (accessed 17 May 2014).
41. Crawford, T., Bruck, E. D., and Battle, C. W. (2005), *Business and Legal Forms for Industrial Designers*, New York: Allworth Communications, Inc.
42. Alter (2013), op. cit.
43. Beckman, G. (2007), '"Adventuring" Arts Entrepreneurship Curricula in Higher Education: An Examination of Present Efforts, Obstacles, and Best Practices,' *Journal of Arts Management, Law, and Society*, 37(2), 87–112.
44. DesignIntelligence (2014), 'America's Best Industrial Design Schools 2014,' Design Intelligence, 28 May 2014, available at http://www.di.net/articles/americas-best-industrial-design-schools-2014/ (accessed 4 June 2014).
45. Access2Knowledge.org (2014), 'What Are the Top Industrial Design Schools in the U.S.?' 15 April 2014, available at http://www.access2knowledge.org/jobs-education/top-industrial-design-schools/ (accessed 4 June 2014).
46. IDSA (2014), List of ID Schools | Industrial Designers Society of America – IDSA, available at http://www.idsa.org/list-id-schools (accessed 3 June 2014); Access2 Knowledge.org (2014), op. cit.
47. University of Cincinnati (2014), Academics, Industrial Design, available at https://web apps.uc.edu/DegreePrograms/

CurriculumGuideView.aspx?Program=280&Pasla=23BSDES-INDL&CurriculumGuideID =561 (accessed 15 June 2014); University of Cincinnati (2014), Master of Design, available at http://daap.uc.edu/academics/design/m_of_design/curriculum.html (accessed 15 June 2014).

48. Rhode Island School of Design (2014), Courses | Industrial Design | Academics | RISD, available from http://www.risd.edu/academics/industrial-design/courses/ (accessed 5 June 2014).

49. Art Center College of Design (2014), Environmental Design | Undergraduate | Programs | Art Center College of Design | Pasadena, CA, available from http://www.artcenter.edu/ accd/programs/undergraduate/environmental_design.jsp (accessed 15 June 2014); Art Center College of Design (2014), Course Descriptions | Product Design | Undergraduate | Programs | Art Center College of Design | Pasadena, CA, available from http:// www.artcenter.edu/accd/programs/undergraduate/product_design/course_descriptions.jsp (accessed 5 June 2014); Art Center College of Design (2014), Course Descriptions | Industrial Design | Graduate | Programs | Art Center College of Design | Pasadena, CA, available from http://www.artcenter.edu/accd/programs/graduate/industrial_design/course_ descriptions.jsp (accessed 5 June 2014).

50. Syracuse University (2014), Curriculum | Syracuse University College of Visual and Performing Arts, available from http://vpa.syr.edu/art-design/design/graduate/design-plus/ curriculum (accessed 15 June 2014); Syracuse University (2014), Curriculum | Syracuse University College of Visual and Performing Arts, available from http://vpa.syr.edu/art-design/design/undergraduate/industrial-interaction/curriculum (accessed 15 June 2014); Syracuse University (2014), Course Catalogue Industrial and Interaction Design, available from http://coursecatalog.syr.edu/2011/programs/industrial_and_interaction_design (accessed 15 June 2014); Syracuse University (2014), Course Catalogue Industrial and Interaction Design, available from http://coursecatalog.syr.edu/2011/programs/industrial_ and_interaction_design (accessed 15 June 2014).

51. Carnegie Mellon University (2014), Program Framework | Carnegie Mellon School of Design, available from http://design.cmu.edu/content/program-framework (accessed 5 June 2014); Carnegie Mellon University (2014), Master of Design | Carnegie Mellon School of Design, available from http://design.cmu.edu/content/master-design (accessed 5 June 2014); Carnegie Mellon University (2014), Master of Arts in Design | Carnegie Mellon School of Design, available from http://design.cmu.edu/content/master-arts-design (accessed 5 June 2014); Carnegie Mellon University (2014), Graduate Program | Carnegie Mellon School of Design, available from http://design.cmu.edu/programs/grad (accessed 15 June 2014); Carnegie Mellon University (2014), Bachelor of Design | Carnegie Mellon School of Design, available from http://design.cmu.edu/content/bachelor-design (accessed 5 June 2014).

52. Cranbrook Academy of Art (2014), Cranbrook Academy of Art: Academic Requirements, available from http://www.cranbrookart.edu/Pages/AcademicRequirements.html (accessed 5 June 2014); Cranbrook Academy of Art (2014), Cranbrook Academy of Art, 3D Design, available from http://www.cranbrookart.edu/Pages/3D.html (accessed 5 June 2014).

53. Savannah College of Art and Design (2014), Master of Fine Arts (MFA) in Industrial Design | SCAD.edu, available from http://www.scad.edu/academics/programs/industrial-design/degrees/mfa (accessed 15 June 2014); Savannah College of Art and Design (2014), Master of Arts (MA) Degree in Industrial Design | SCAD.edu, available from http:// www.scad.edu/academics/programs/industrial-design/degrees/ma (accessed 15 June 2014); Savannah College of Art and Design (2014), Courses | SCAD Industrial Design, available from http://www.scad.edu/academics/programs/industrial-design/courses (accessed 5 June 2014); Savannah College of Art and Design (2014), Bachelor of Fine Arts (BFA) in Industrial Design | SCAD.edu, available from http://www.scad.edu/academics/programs/ industrial-design/degrees/bfa (accessed 15 June 2014).

54. California College of the Arts (2014), Curriculum | California College of the Arts, available from https://www.cca.edu/academics/graduate/design-mba/curriculum (accessed 15 June 2014); California College of the Arts (2014), Curriculum | California College of

the Arts, available from https://www.cca.edu/academics/graduate/design/curriculum (accessed 15 June 2014); California College of the Arts (2014), Curriculum | California College of the Arts, available from https://www.cca.edu/academics/industrial-design/ curriculum (accessed 5 June 2014); California College of the Arts (2014), Design | California College of the Arts, available from https://www.cca.edu/academics/graduate/ design (accessed 15 June 2014); California College of the Arts (2014), Design MBA Programs | California College of the Arts, available from https://www.cca.edu/academics/ graduate/design-mba (accessed 15 June 2014); California College of the Arts (2014), Design MFA / MBA in Design Strategy | California College of the Arts, available from https://www.cca.edu/academics/graduate/design/dualdesign (accessed 15 June 2014); California College of the Arts (2014), Industrial Design | California College of the Arts, available from https://www.cca.edu/academics/industrial-design?page=1 (accessed 15 June 2014); California College of the Arts (2014), Three-Year MFA Option | California College of the Arts, available from https://www.cca.edu/academics/graduate/design/three-year-mfa (accessed 15 June 2014).
55. Pratt Institute (2014), Pratt Institute | School of Art and Design | Undergraduate School of Art and Design | Undergraduate Industrial Design, available from https://www.pratt.edu/ academics/art-design/art-ug/undergraduate-industrial-design/ (accessed 5 June 2014); Pratt Institute (2014), Pratt Institute | School of Art and Design | Undergraduate School of Art and Design | Undergraduate Industrial Design | Industrial Design B.I.D., available from https://www.pratt.edu/academics/art-design/art-ug/undergraduate-industrial-design/ industrial-design-bid/ (accessed 5 June 2014); Pratt Institute (2014), Pratt Institute | School of Art and Design | Graduate School of Art and Design | Graduate Industrial Design, available from https://www.pratt.edu/academics/art-design/art-grad/industrial-design-grad/ (accessed 5 June 2014); Pratt Institute (2014), Pratt Institute | School of Art and Design | Graduate School of Art and Design | Graduate Industrial Design | Master of Industrial Design, available from https://www.pratt.edu/academics/art-design/art-grad/industrial-design-grad/industrial-design-mid/ (accessed 5 June 2014).
56. Ohio State University (2014), Bachelor of Science Degree Programs in Design, available from http://design.osu.edu/sites/design.osu.edu/files/Design_UG_Feb_2014.pdf (accessed 5 June 2014); Ohio State University (2014), Application for Graduate Studies, available from http://design.osu.edu/sites/design.osu.edu/files/graduate_application_11.13.pdf (accessed 15 June 2014).
57. Rochester Institute of Technology (2014), Industrial Design MFA | Programs of Study, available from http://www.rit.edu/programs/industrial-design-formerly-industrial-and-interior-design (accessed 9 June 2014); Rochester Institute of Technology (2014), Industrial Design BFA | Programs of Study, available from http://www.rit.edu/programs/ industrial-design-0 (accessed 9 June 2014); Rochester Institute of Technology (2014), Industrial Design – Design – RIT: College of Imaging Arts & Sciences, available from http://cias.rit.edu/schools/design/graduate-industrial-design (accessed 9 June 2014); Rochester Institute of Technology (2014), RIT Planning Sheet, available from http://cias.rit.edu/ media/uploads/curriculum/sod/planning_sheet.pdf (accessed 9 June 2014); Rochester Institute of Technology (2014), RIT Undergraduate Course Descriptions, available from www.rit.edu/upub/pdfs/Undergrad_Course_Descriptions.pdf (accessed 9 June 2014).
58. School of the Visual Arts (2014), Business Structures | Products of Design, available from http://productsofdesign.sva.edu/curriculum/first-year/spring/business-structures/ (accessed 9 June 2014); School of the Visual Arts (2014), Industrial Design Program Curriculum | Products of Design, available from http://productsofdesign.sva.edu/curriculum/overview/ (accessed 9 June 2014).
59. School of the Art Institute of Chicago (2014), SAIC – Architecture, Interior Architecture, and Designed Objects: Courses – School of the Art Institute of Chicago, available from http://www.saic.edu/academics/departments/aiado/courses/ (accessed 4 June 2014); School of the Art Institute of Chicago (2014), SAIC – Master of Design in Designed Objects – School of the Art Institute of Chicago, available from http://www.saic.edu/academics/ graduatedegrees/mdesob/ (accessed 15 June 2014); School of the Art Institute of Chicago

(2014), SAIC – Master of Fine Arts in Studio – School of the Art Institute of Chicago, available from http://www.saic.edu/academics/graduatedegrees/mfas/ (accessed 15 June 2014); School of the Art Institute of Chicago (2014), SAIC – Master of Fine Arts in Studio: Curriculum Requirements –. School of the Art Institute of Chicago, available from http://www.saic.edu/academics/graduatedegrees/mfas/curriculumrequirements/ (accessed 15 June 2014).

60. Rhode Island School of Design undergraduate courses: Business Principles: Design and Entrepreneurship (ID-2382).

61. Art Center College of Design undergraduate courses: Design Management 1 (PRD-351), Design Management 2 (PRD-401), Project Management (PRD-461).

62. Syracuse University undergraduate courses: Industrial Design: Professional Practices (IND 578).

63. Art Center College of Design graduate courses: Entrepreneur Methodology (IND-605), Entrepreneur Studio (IND-606).

64. Savannah College of Art and Design graduate courses: Entrepreneurship for Designers (IDUS 733).

65. California College of the Arts graduate courses: Business of Design (seminar).

66. Rochester Institute of Technology graduate courses: Interactive Games and Media: Innovation and Invention (IGME-581).

67. School of the Visual Arts graduate courses: Dynamics of Strategy and Design, Business Structure, Service Entrepreneurship.

68. Carnegie Mellon Design (n.d.), available at http://design.cmu.edu/programs (accessed 5 June 2014).

69. University of California San Diego undergraduate course: Product Design & Entrepreneurship (MAE 154).

70. The authors of this chapter who are members of the arts and design community and experienced educators, professional practitioners, and arts entrepreneurs have generated the framework and curriculum for this program.

71. Thomas, J., McDonagh, D., and Canning, L. (2014), 'Developing the Arts Entrepreneur: The "Learning Cloud,"' *Design Journal*, 17(3), 425–444.

72. Wong, V. (2009), 'How to Nurture Future Leaders,' *Business Week*, available at http://www.businessweek.com/stories/2009-09-30/how-to-nurture-future-leadersbusinessweek-business-news-stock-market-and-financial-advice (accessed 4 June 2014).

PART IV

Bridging the disciplinary perspectives

10. Towards a cross-disciplinary understanding of entrepreneurship

Satish Nambisan

I. INTRODUCTION

Entrepreneurship is not merely "a thing that business people do to start companies." It is a *way of thinking* – an approach towards discovering and pursuing opportunities (solving problems) in ways not constrained by the present – that finds application in diverse contexts and institutions (new and old; public and private). It emphasizes imagining new possibilities in the face of high uncertainty, committing one to putting valuable ideas into practice and finding a broader meaning in one's ideas and actions. As such, entrepreneurship can be practiced (and indeed has relevance) in careers and contexts in a wide range of fields – from engineering, science, and technology to arts and design to health and medicine. It also has equal relevance whether one works in the private, non-profit, or public sector. No wonder then programs and courses on entrepreneurship have taken root in schools and institutes across the disciplinary spectrum. This is definitely good news.

At the same time, there seems to be little consensus in the different fields on how we should help our students develop skills and capabilities for entrepreneurial pursuits. One approach has been for students in various disciplines to register for entrepreneurship and innovation management courses offered by business schools. Such courses would definitely help them gain a business perspective and a sound understanding of the more general entrepreneurship-related activities (e.g. developing a business plan). However, business school entrepreneurship courses typically do not pay much attention to the unique contextual characteristics of a particular discipline or domain (e.g. music, medicine) and as such may offer only limited discipline-specific guidance to students (e.g. entrepreneurial pursuits in music and arts may differ much from that in a more regulated environment such as medicine or healthcare). Another approach has been for faculty in specific disciplines to develop entrepreneurship-related courses and programs tailored to a given discipline. While rooted firmly in the disciplinary context, by and large such courses have tended to adopt an ad hoc approach towards incorporating entrepreneurship-related content. Left to the perspectives, biases, and personal experiences of the instructor, these courses vary widely in their learning objectives, content, and structure. As Beckman and Hart suggest in Chapter 8, without a consensus among entrepreneurship educators in a field on the desired student outcomes, the entrepreneurship curricula may lack the key and basic components critical to student success in entrepreneurial pursuits. Simply adding on a few entrepreneurship-related topics would not help to serve the students' goals and objectives. What is lacking in all of these efforts is a more coherent approach towards integrating entrepreneurship with the curriculum of a particular discipline.

As I stated in Chapter 1, it has become imperative that we view entrepreneurship not simply as an add-on to the curriculum (or as a set of "good-to-have" topics) but as comprising a more fundamental set of skills that must be imbued throughout the curriculum. In this final chapter, my goal is to initiate a conversation on this by offering a cross-disciplinary view of entrepreneurship, one that brings a focus on both the context- (or discipline-) specific characteristics as well as the core skills and capabilities. I believe such a conversation structured around the entrepreneurship context and the entrepreneurship skills would enable us to build cumulative knowledge on entrepreneurship – as it is practiced and taught in the different disciplines – and thereby facilitate developing a shared or cross-disciplinary understanding of entrepreneurship.

In presenting this framework, I borrow heavily from the ideas and concepts advanced by the different contributors to this book. And, by doing so, I hope to demonstrate the potential to gather a rich set of insights from the different fields and disciplines in our effort to develop a better approach to fostering entrepreneurship among our students. I also discuss some of the implications of the framework presented here. Apart from the obvious implications for developing a more coherent entrepreneurial curriculum in the different fields and disciplines, I also consider the need to start entrepreneurial education early on in student life (in freshmen year at universities or even in high schools and middle schools) as well as the critical need to find venues to continue this conversation on a cross-disciplinary view of entrepreneurship.

II. A FRAMEWORK FOR A SHARED UNDERSTANDING OF ENTREPRENEURSHIP

As I briefly noted in Chapter 1, the prevalent view of entrepreneurship involves the creation of a new company or a start-up. Given this, curricular initiatives in entrepreneurship often emphasize the set of activities that one must carry out towards this end. Such an activity-based and new-venture-focused view of entrepreneurship is no longer relevant in many fields and disciplines.

A broader view of entrepreneurship may simply relate to the undertaking of an initiative or an endeavor that creates value but without the assurance of success and, consequently, with the bearing of risk. It has also been suggested that the root words (from French) "entre" (to be in) and "prendre" (to take) together mean not just "to undertake" an activity but "the act of immersion into something that also takes hold of you or possesses you."[1] All of these interpretations take us away from the contemporary notion of entrepreneurship as starting companies and to a more general notion of entrepreneurship as pursuing an opportunity (that creates value) with passion and endurance. In turn, this implies an emphasis on the underlying skills and capabilities rather than merely on a set of activities or processes to follow.

Such a focus on skills and capabilities is also relevant when one looks at the nature of opportunities that we are presented with in the world today. Not all entrepreneurial activities lead to starting new companies. Many entrepreneurial pursuits are undertaken within established organizations and other institutional contexts (public, for-profit, and non-profit). The end goal is not a start-up but the solution to a problem in a context that is burdened with uncertainty and risk and the creation of value (economic, social, etc.). Often, this requires discovering the problem (or opportunity), marshaling the resources needed to solve it, and then getting that solution to the market. It may call for navigating uncertain and risky terrains and persevering in the face of short-term failures. It may also imply the need to go beyond one's immediate domain and comfort zone and to span multiple disciplines and integrate knowledge and resources from afar.

To further develop such a cross-disciplinary understanding of entrepreneurship, I suggest a focus on two interrelated aspects: the *context* for entrepreneurship and the portfolio of entrepreneurship *skills and capabilities* (see Figure 10.1). These two aspects together shape an individual's entrepreneurial behavior and as such should gain our attention while designing the entrepreneurship curriculum in schools and universities

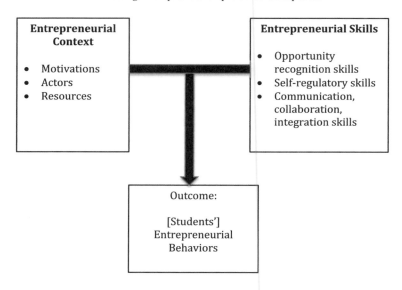

Figure 10.1   Entrepreneurial context, skills, and behavior

(note: the outcome of entrepreneurship programs should be the demonstration of desired entrepreneurial behaviors among the students).

I identify critical elements of these two aspects of entrepreneurship and briefly discuss them. My objective here is not to present an exhaustive list of contextual characteristics and skills and capabilities but to illustrate the promise of considering such a framework to develop a broader understanding of entrepreneurship and its place in the curriculum in the different disciplines.

III.   ENTREPRENEURIAL CONTEXT

I identify three important elements of the entrepreneurial context: (1) the motivations that drive the entrepreneurial pursuit; (2) the actors that are involved in and/or shape the entrepreneurial pursuit; and (3) the resources that form the basis for the entrepreneurial pursuit. I discuss each below.

(1) *Motivations*: Prior research has shown that people get engaged in entrepreneurial pursuits for a wide range of reasons such as financial benefits, non-financial (e.g. reputation, lifestyle) benefits, psychological needs (e.g. need for independence).[2] Research has also shown that the perspective or the worldview one brings to entrepreneurial pursuits is partly shaped by these motivations.[3]

Importantly, the motivations and drivers of entrepreneurship also vary with the context. For example, as Butler and Anderson note in Chapter 4, for most physicists entrepreneurial pursuits are a means to another end, rather than an end in itself. Statements such as "This is the way that I can make this thing happen" and "It has become a means to getting somewhere and doing something that otherwise I couldn't do" imply that the broader rationale for engaging in entrepreneurship is more intrinsic than extrinsic (at least within the population of scientists studied by Butler and Anderson). On the other hand, in the music arena, as Beeching notes (Chapter 7), the motivation for pursuing entrepreneurial ventures is driven largely by the "brave new world" that musicians find themselves in – a world of disruptive technologies that has transformed the ways in which music is created, produced, and distributed. One is left with few options other than to venture out on one's own in this new landscape. In the healthcare arena, two key contextual factors have radically shaped the motivations for physicians and other healthcare professional to engage in entrepreneurship. As Meyers (Chapter 5) and Patterson and Kant (Chapter 6) all note, the Affordable Care Act (healthcare reform) and the emergence of new information technologies (e.g. mobile technologies, social media) have both already shown the potential to radically transform the scope and the nature of entrepreneurship in healthcare.

Why should we be interested in entrepreneurial motivations as educators? If we want to design a curriculum that would foster an appropriate set of entrepreneurial skills among our students, then we should understand these motivations that are likely to shape students' entrepreneurship-related goals and behavior. In other words, the learning objectives of the curriculum should be related to or at least acknowledge the motivations that underlie the particular context.

(2) *Actors*: The nature of the individuals and institutions that populate the entrepreneurial context form another important element. They include the entrepreneurs, the organizations they are affiliated with, funding agencies, and regulatory bodies. These actors collectively set the culture and the value system that will shape the entrepreneurial activities.

Importantly, the value system adopted (and sometime enforced) by the actors in an entrepreneurial context tends to emphasize certain skills and deemphasize certain other skills. For example, as Beeching notes (Chapter 7), an "anti-business" thinking pervades some parts of the music world (i.e. business is seen as the antithesis of creativity and art) and this inhibits a musician-entrepreneur's ability to connect and collaborate with other actors in the industry (e.g. promoters, club managers). Similarly, as Meyers notes (Chapter 5), biosciences and healthcare is one of the most highly regulated industries in the US (given the primacy of patient safety). This, however, makes entrepreneurial pursuits in healthcare lengthy, expensive, and highly uncertain. These two contexts illustrate the need to emphasize different types of skills. While in the former case one has to be quite adept at collaborating with partners with different value systems, in the latter case tolerance for ambiguity and some of the self-regulatory skills (discussed in the next section) assume considerable significance.

Clearly, entrepreneurs need to possess a wide range of skills and capabilities. However, the relative significance of the different skills and capabilities in a given context (as shaped by the actors that reside in that context) could inform on the entrepreneurship curriculum.

(3) *Resources*: The third element relates to the nature of the resources that one has to deal with to find success in an entrepreneurial context. Resources include domain knowledge, skills/talent, and technologies: they can be structured or unstructured and dispersed or concentrated.

The context-specific characteristics of the resources dictate the nature of the entrepreneurial processes and activities. For example, when the resources are highly dispersed across various types of boundaries (disciplinary boundaries, geographical boundaries, institutional boundaries), it calls for a greater extent of collaborative and structured processes. It may also call for a greater level of integration skills and capabilities. For example, as Brown notes (Chapter 3), much of the entrepreneurial pursuits that he and his students have been engaged in over the years originated from the collaborative arrangements with industries: typically, a company in the process of solving a problem would find that a faculty has a key missing skill set or technology and will go about trying to integrate that with the rest of its in-house resources. Similarly, when the resources are ill structured and complex, more flexible processes and a greater level of experimentation (and tolerance for ambiguity) may be needed. An understanding of the nature of resources that are most likely to matter in an entrepreneurial context can thus inform on the types of entrepreneurial activities as well as the associated skills that a student will need to master.

IV. ENTREPRENEURIAL SKILLS

I next consider the portfolio of skills and capabilities that is critical to engage in entrepreneurial pursuits – what I collectively refer to as *entrepreneurial thinking skills*. Here I focus on three entrepreneurial thinking skills: (1) opportunity recognition skills; (2) self-regulatory skills; and (3) communication, collaboration, and integration skills.

Before I discuss each of these in detail, I must note that all of these are skills that can be acquired. Studies show that the related cognitive skills can be enhanced and refined through frequent exposure to entrepreneurial experiences.

(1) *Opportunity recognition skills*: The first set of skills relate to identifying, discovering, and/or evaluating promising entrepreneurial opportunities. In some cases opportunities might already exist and may just need to be discovered, while in some other cases opportunities may need to be created by reconfiguring existing resources in a new context.[4] Whether opportunities are discovered or created, opportunity recognition often involves cross-pollination of ideas from different fields and finding patterns in seemingly unrelated problems and solutions.

Obviously, opportunity recognition skills are important in all entre-preneurial contexts; however, the nature of opportunity recognition and the associated skills would likely vary with the context. For example, in relatively structured contexts (such as in the sciences), one may be able to map out new opportunities by systematically considering solutions to a well-known or well-defined problem or by looking for ways to deploy a resource (new technology or technique). Consider Brown's description (Chapter 3) of how he discovered new opportunities by looking for the potential application of optimization techniques in various industrial contexts. In other contexts, there may be a need to look for opportunities by studying or observing human behavior in different situations, and the associated skills (e.g. ability to empathize) may be different.

Similarly, in fields such as arts and music, the opportunity may be much more hazy and ill defined. Sometimes the introduction of new actors may generate new opportunities (e.g. Beeching's description in Chapter 7 of how Kickstarter upended the music creation process). In other situations, a more effectual process – one that starts with the existing means rather than the predefined goals – may be the way to create new opportunities.

A critical element of opportunity recognition is a focus on the "why." For example, engineers are trained to solve problems, but they are rarely asked to identify the problems that they want to solve. As Melton notes (Chapter 2), a focus on the "why they are doing what they are doing" underlines the significance of two related behaviors (or skills): curiosity about the changing world (which would then point to the problems that need to get solved) and making connections among disparate data points (in ways that reveal potential opportunities). These are skills that are quite important in entrepreneurship in engineering but are largely absent in existing engineering curricula.

The underlying issue here then is the need for entrepreneurship educators to carefully consider the nature of opportunity recognition that their students are likely to be engaged in (in the respective disciplines) and to focus on cultivating the associated skills and behaviors.

(2) *Self-regulatory skills*: Self-regulation relates to cognitive processes through which individuals monitor, evaluate, direct, and adjust their own behavior so as to progress towards desired goals.[5] Self-regulatory behavior assumes significance in contexts where critical choices must be made, especially under relatively high time pressures – as is true in most entrepreneurial pursuits. Prior research has documented the importance of self-regulatory processes in the domain of entrepreneurship.[6]

There are several self-regulatory skills: here I identify some of the more important ones. Self-control is a basic and important aspect of self-regulation: it relates to the extent to which individuals can do what is necessary for attaining progress towards key goals and, at the same time, refrain from doing what will distract from these goals and attaining them.[7] Another such self-regulatory skill is metacognitive skill – metacognition involves individuals' awareness of and control over their own cognitive processes.[8] It includes what individuals know about themselves as cognitive processors of information as well as the knowledge and experience that individuals draw upon in devising or selecting the most effective cognitive strategies to employ in a given situation. Both aspects of metacognition can assist individuals in choosing or developing the most appropriate strategies to employ in performing important tasks involving cognition in entrepreneurship (e.g. solving complex problems or adjusting effectively to rapidly changing environmental conditions). Another self-regulatory skill relates to our ability to maintain consistent focus on clearly defined long-term goals and to demonstrate persistence in actual efforts to achieve these goals. Called Grit, psychologists have extensively studied this (including in the context of entrepreneurship).[9]

As I noted earlier, prior research has established the importance of all these skills for entrepreneurial pursuits. More importantly, all the self-regulatory skills discussed here are ones that can be acquired or strengthened. And, several techniques have been identified that could be used to help individuals build or strengthen these skills. These include simple priming procedures, in which individuals are reminded of key goals they wish to reach; mental contrasting, which requires individuals to think about their goals, outcomes, and obstacles; and implementation intentions, which involves individuals having to think about how they will actually implement their goals.[10]

These and other techniques can be incorporated into curricula to develop self-regulatory skills. (Incidentally, these skills have a wide range of applicability beyond the context of entrepreneurship.) Further, careful consideration of the context may inform on the relative importance of these (and other) self-regulatory skills.

(3) *Communication, collaboration, and integration skills*: The third set of skills directly relate to the nature of the opportunities (problems and solutions) most entrepreneurs find themselves dealing with (regardless of their discipline or field) – increasingly complex and interdisciplinary – and the ensuing need to communicate and collaborate with diverse actors and to integrate a diverse set of resources. For example, as Thomas and Canning note (in Chapter 9), industrial designers are now engaged in entrepreneurial opportunities in areas that traditionally have not appreciated the value of design. Similarly, opportunities in the interactive entertainment area (e.g. video gaming) have brought together entrepreneurs and professionals in a wide range of disciplines – artists, musicians, computer scientists, designers, behavioral scientists, etc. Indeed, one can identify many other such opportunities – think climate change, energy, healthcare – where ideas and concepts from STEAM (Arts + STEM) disciplines have to be integrated to transform knowledge into value.

All of these emphasize the set of skills related to communication, collaboration, and knowledge integration. These skills include the ability to view the problem (or the solution) from different disciplinary perspectives and to entertain contrarian interpretations of both problems and solutions; the ability to work together in teams with members from diverse fields holding different worldviews; and the ability to develop and communicate compelling narratives of the problem (opportunity) and/or the solution.

A whole set of new techniques and approaches have emerged in recent years to facilitate the development of these skills. For example, the design thinking approach that has its roots in industrial design (Thomas and Canning's discussion in Chapter 9) has introduced many novel techniques to enable entrepreneurs to adopt a more holistic view of opportunities. Similarly, design thinking also emphasizes going through cycles of divergent and convergent thinking, and analysis and synthesis.

In some disciplines, the inherent characteristics of the activities lend themselves to cultivating these very same skills. For example, as Beeching notes (Chapter 7), in music education, ensemble training and performance work allows musicians also to hone their communication, collaboration, and presentation skills. Similarly, from working intensively with both the art and craft repertoire, musicians develop analytical and synthesizing skills and the ability to appreciate multiple interpretations of the same text. These are all skills that have direct relevance to entrepreneurial pursuits.

Before discussing the implications of the framework, I must note that the above is not an exhaustive list of entrepreneurial thinking skills. My objective in discussing these three important sets of skills was to demonstrate the need to examine the relevance of various skills in the context in which students are likely to be engaged in entrepreneurship.

V. IMPLICATIONS OF THE FRAMEWORK

(a) Imbuing Entrepreneurship in the Curriculum

As I had noted in Chapter 1, there is considerable consensus among most fields and disciplines on the important need to cultivate an entre-preneurial mindset among students. Entrepreneurial mindset relates to a state of mind that orientates one towards entrepreneurial opportunities, activities, and outcomes. It is evidenced by the collection of attitudes, values, and behavior that one maintains towards entrepreneurial pursuits. As the various chapters in this book indicate, entrepreneurial mindset is a construct that all of us can relate to regardless of our particular disciplinary perspectives and biases (e.g. see the discussion of entre-preneurial mindset in engineering in Chapter 1 and in biosciences in Chapter 5). However, developing such a mindset has become a critical challenge.

The objective of this book and the framework offered in this chapter is to help us address this challenge. In particular, it is hoped that the collection of ideas and concepts advanced in the different chapters would help us to gain a broader and shared understanding of entrepreneurship and the related mindset. I believe a stronger focus on entrepreneurship skills (that can be acquired through practice) will help us address this challenge in more concrete terms. At the same time, the nature of such skills and their relative importance may vary with the field. In the framework presented here, I suggested that a focus on the entrepreneurial context (motivations, actors, and resources) would likely help us to adopt a more systematic approach towards deciding which set of entre-preneurial skills to focus on in each discipline.

A second implication of the focus on entrepreneurial skills is the ability to imbue the entire curriculum of a given discipline with oppor-tunities for students to practice and develop these skills. We should not merely add on a couple of courses on entrepreneurship in the curriculum and expect students to develop these skills. Instead, efforts should be made to see how techniques to develop the relevant entrepreneurial thinking skills can be integrated with discipline-specific content in the different existing courses. Such efforts are ongoing in some fields. For example, as Chapter 2 shows, the Kern Family Foundation is working on integrating entrepreneurship in engineering curricula through new pedagogical approaches such as Entrepreneurially Minded Learning (EML). Similarly, Thomas and Canning (in Chapter 9) provide another excellent example of such integration. They note that although the University of California at San Diego (UCSD) has no formal program in industrial design, UCSD has focused on melding entrepreneurship education into the core concepts of industrial design in their technical electives in product design and entrepreneurship. As Beeching notes (in Chapter 7), while many of the entrepreneurship-related concepts and skills are applicable for musicians, they need to be discussed in a context appropriate to musicians' values and priorities.

Another approach is to go beyond the traditional curriculum and to use cross-campus initiatives to inculcate these entrepreneurial skills. Such initiatives should not be limited to the entrepreneurship competitions and contests that already exist in most campuses. As Beckman and Hart note (in Chapter 8), such collaborative cross-campus opportunities might include dedicated workshops for engineering students interested in bringing their arts-based inventions to the arts markets or three-day innovation jam sessions that allow students from multiple disciplines to throw ideas together in pursuit of solving some big problems. Such forums meld together the entrepreneurship context and the entrepreneurship skills in ways that accelerate the adoption of desired entrepreneurial behaviors among students. At the end, as Beckman and Hart note, the objective should be to generate larger and more profound cross-campus, cross-disciplinary entrepreneurial collaborations.

(b) Starting Early: Entrepreneurship Education in Freshmen Years

If we accept the fact that an entrepreneurial mindset is critical for students in all disciplines and that the associated skills can be acquired over time, then shouldn't the effort at developing those skills start early on itself? In most universities, students are exposed (either through course work or competitions) to entrepreneurship, if they are at all, only in the latter years of their stay on the campus (i.e. when they are seniors or graduate students).

An interesting finding from the study conducted by Butler and Anderson (Chapter 4) was that for all the 136 physicist entrepreneurs they interviewed, entrepreneurship was more like a learned habit rather than something that genetically drove them. Indeed, most physicists are not naturally entrepreneurial, and the ones that do become entrepreneurs do so because they have become socialized in ways that change their attitudes and skill sets. This is borne out by the experience of Robert Brown and his numerous students at Case Western Reserve University (Chapter 3) – the more you interact with peers engaged in entrepreneurship, the more likely you are to be inclined towards it. It is then a tragedy that many scientists are exposed to entrepreneurial skills only when they are well into their careers, robbing them of the opportunity to acquire and refine those skills when they are much younger.

As I noted earlier, studies have shown that entrepreneurship-related cognitive skills could be enhanced and refined through frequent (repeat) exposure to diverse entrepreneurial experiences. Thus, the more we expose our students – in schools and universities – to varied types of entrepreneurial experiences earlier on in their life, the better. It is this thinking that has led some schools to explore and experiment with entrepreneurship education in the freshmen year. For example, Babson College (a private business school located in Wellesley, Massachusetts) has for years required their freshmen to take an entrepreneurship course. Similarly, the university that I work at (University of Wisconsin-Milwaukee) has started an experiential entrepreneurship course for freshmen in business, engineering, and arts. While it is too early to predict the efficacy of such courses, there is no doubt that a greater number of opportunities to experience and practice entrepreneurship will definitely lead to a better acquisition of these skills.

The broader point here is to start entrepreneurship education early, and this includes entrepreneurship education in K-12 institutions too. As Robert Brown notes (in Chapter 3), asking young students to ponder energy and climate issues and their solutions will inevitably bring forth questions about how the solutions might be carried out and the connection to entrepreneurship.

High schools and middle schools can employ diverse platforms (project-based courses, idea competitions, internships, summer camps, etc.) for students to experience entrepreneurship with different levels of complexity.[11] Importantly, schools don't need to do this all on their own. Several large universities across the nation – including the university that I work at – have launched entrepreneurship outreach and mentoring programs aimed at nurturing the entrepreneurial interests and skills among middle and high-school students. Similarly, organizations such as the Network for Teaching Entrepreneurship (NFTE) and the Kauffman Foundation offer rich sets of resources for teaching entrepreneurship in schools.

(c) Venues to Develop a Shared Understanding of Entrepreneurship

Given the discussion so far (not just in this chapter but in the other chapters as well), it is evident that the promise and potential for developing a shared and cross-disciplinary understanding of entrepreneurship exists and is high. It is equally evident that such a shared understanding can help us considerably in developing more coherent entrepreneurship educational efforts in the different fields and disciplines – efforts that focus on a core set of entrepreneurial skills that is informed by the unique characteristics and demands of the particular disciplinary context. The question remains: how will we develop such a shared cross-disciplinary understanding of entrepreneurship?

To a great extent I believe this process has been hampered by the lack of communication among entrepreneurship scholars and educators in different disciplines. As I briefly noted in Chapter 1, entrepreneurship research (and pedagogical approaches) by business academics are published in journals and books that cater to scholars and practitioners in the business community. Similarly, publications by entrepreneurship scholars and educators in other disciplines have largely been limited to conferences and the few journal outlets tailored to those disciplines.

Given the broader relevance of entrepreneurship, it is imperative that we break out of these discipline-specific venues and forums and start talking with each other instead of past each other. And there are some outlets that facilitate such discussion. One that immediately comes to mind is the annual conference organized by United States Association for Small Business and Entrepreneurship (USASBE) that has in recent years attracted a considerable number of participants from non-business disciplines. Similarly, the flagship management conference, the Academy of Management Annual Meeting, presents another suitable venue to host cross-disciplinary conversation on entrepreneurship education.

At the same time, there are also a number of entrepreneurship-focused organizations that could provide equally valuable platforms for such a cross-disciplinary debate and conversation. For example, Venture Well (previously NCIIA) has attracted people from engineering, science, and business disciplines in efforts to develop entrepreneurship programs for engineers. Organizations such as the Kauffman Foundation, Coleman Foundation, and Schwab Foundation also provide venues (both physical and virtual) to socialize entrepreneurship-related findings and insights across disciplinary boundaries. And, as Melton notes in Chapter 2, while the KEEN Network (funded by the Kern Family Foundation) focuses on promoting engineering entrepreneurship, recently it has started reaching out to a broader set of participants to develop new pedagogical

approaches. A missing voice in many of these cross-disciplinary entrepreneurship conversations is that of those in the biosciences and the
healthcare arenas. Organizations such as the one Arlen Meyers leads (the
Society of Physician Entrepreneurs – see Chapter 5) could help broaden
the dialog to those participants too.

VI. CONCLUSIONS

As we rapidly transition towards a global innovation economy that
demands in equal measure novelty, sustainability, affordability and effectiveness, our success in solving problems will be marked by the entrepreneurial mindset that we bring to apply the knowledge that we hold.
Clearly then, an education in entrepreneurship – or more specifically in
entrepreneurial thinking skills – is going to be fundamental for all
disciplines and fields. It is this thesis that has motivated this book.

When I set out the rationale for this book, I had identified a few key
objectives (see Chapter 1). Here I would like to briefly re-examine some
of those objectives in light of the various chapters.

- In the individual chapters, the authors have identified a set of core
  themes, concepts, and frameworks related to how entrepreneurship
  is viewed and/or practiced in their particular discipline/field (e.g.
  entrepreneurial mindset in engineering, students' desired outcomes
  in arts entrepreneurship). By building on these themes and concepts, future entrepreneurship research can facilitate the development of cumulative knowledge that has relevance to all fields and
  disciplines.
- The chapters also serve to share entrepreneurship-related insights
  and best practices across fields. In particular, the innovative programs and practices described here (programs in physics entrepreneurship, in bioscience entrepreneurship, in arts entrepreneurship,
  etc.) may provide valuable templates for entrepreneurship educators
  in other disciplines.
- The discussion in the various chapters could also help inform the
  evaluation of entrepreneurship programs in schools and universities.
  As I noted previously, we should focus not just on a general set of
  entrepreneurial skills but also on how context-specific characteristics shape the entrepreneurial pursuits and thereby the relevance of
  those skills. Program outcomes (e.g. student entrepreneurial behavior) that are closely linked to such context-relevant entrepreneurship

skills will be crucial to truly evaluate entrepreneurship programs and initiatives in various disciplines.

In addition to the above, and more broadly, I hope that this book will fuel a greater level of debate and conversation on entrepreneurship among scholars and educators in all fields and disciplines – a debate that would bring us closer to a truly cross-disciplinary understanding of entrepreneurship. If so, this book would have served its purpose well.

NOTES

1. As mentioned in the talk given by Kavita Ramdas, President and CEO of the Global Fund for Women at Stanford University's Entrepreneurship Corner, available at http://ecorner.stanford.edu/authorMaterialInfo.html?mid=216 (accessed on 1 Oct. 2014).
2. Carsrud, A. and Brännback, M. 2011. Entrepreneurial motivations: What do we still need to know. *Journal of Small Business Management*, 49(1), 9–26.
3. Shane, S., Locke, E., and Collins, C. 2003. Entrepreneurial motivation. *Human Resource Management Review*, 13, 257–279.
4. For more on opportunity recognition, read: Alvarez, S.A. and Barney, J.B. 2007. Discovery and creation: Alternative theories of entrepreneurial actions. *Strategic Entrepreneurship Journal*, 1(1), 11–26. Also read, Baron, R.A. 2006. Opportunity recognition as pattern recognition: How entrepreneurs "connect the dots" to identify new business opportunities. *Academy of Management Perspectives*, 20(1), 104–119.
5. Forgas, J.P., Baumeister, R.H., and Tice, D.M. 2009. *Psychology of self-regulation: Cognitive, affective, and motivational processes*, New York: Psychology Press. Also read, Zimmerman, B.J. 2006. Development and adaptation of expertise: The role of self-regulatory processes and beliefs. In Ericsson, K.A., Charness, N., Hoffman, R.R., and Feltovich, P.J. (eds.), *The Cambridge Handbook of Expertise and Expert Performance*, New York: Cambridge University Press, pp. 705–722.
6. Mitchell, R.K., Busenitz, L., Bird, B., Gaglio, C.M., McMullen, J.S., Morse, E.A., and Smith, J.B. 2007. The central question in entrepreneurial cognition research. *Entrepreneurship Theory and Practice*, 31(1), 1–27. Also read, Baron, R.A. and Henry, R.A. 2010. How entrepreneurs acquire the capacity to excel: Insights from basic research on expert performance. *Strategic Entrepreneurship Journal*, 4, 49–65.
7. Baumeister, R. and Alquist, J. (2009). Self-regulation as a limited resource: Strength model of control and depletion. In Forgas, J.B., Baumeister, R.F., and Tice, D.M. (eds.), *Psychology of Self-Regulation*, New York: Psychology Press, pp. 21–34.
8. For a good introduction to metacognition, read Flavell, J. 1979. Metacognition and cognitive monitoring: A new area of cognitive-developmental inquiry. *American Psychologist*, 34(10), 906–911.
9. For more details read the work by Duckworth and her colleagues. Duckworth, A.L., Peterson, C., Matthews, M.D., and Kelly, D.R. (2007). Grit, perseverance and passion for long-term goals. *Journal of Personality and Social Psychology*, 92(6), 1087–1101.
10. For example, read Stadler, G., Oettingen, G., and Gollwitzer, P.M. 2010. Intervention effects of information and self-regulation on eating fruits and vegetables over two years. *Health Psychology*, 49, 274–281. Also read, Papies, E.K and Hamstra, P. 2010. Goal priming and eating behavior: Enhancing self-regulation by environmental cues. *Health Psychology*, 39, 384–388.

11. For more on the need to broaden entrepreneurship education, read Nambisan, S. 2014. Make entrepreneurship a part of education. *Milwaukee Journal Sentinel*, 27 Feb. 2014, available at http://www.jsonline.com/news/opinion/make-entrepreneurship-a-part-of-education-b99214666z1-247680431.html (accessed on 1 Oct. 2014).

Index

Undercofler, James 109
United States Association for Small
   Business and Entrepreneurship
   (USASBE) 185
universities
   faculty entrepreneurship 35, 38, 42,
      42–50
   flipped classes 35
   healthcare entrepreneurship 93–5
   startups 94–5
   see also faculty entrepreneurship
University of California at San Diego
   (UCSD) 163–4
University of Cincinnati 160, 161, 163
US Food and Drug Administration
   (FDA) 79–80, 95, 96
US News and World Reports 159–60

value
   adding through innovation 74
   capturing 22
   definition 17
   engineering entrepreneurship 17–18
   Entrepreneurial Minded Learning
      (EML) 25–9

entrepreneurial mindset 21–2
   healthcare entrepreneurship 77, 86
   healthcare value chain 96–7
venture capitalists (VC) 99, 100
Venture Well 185
ViewRay, Inc. (VRI) 46
VIPCO (Virtually Integrated
   Pharmaceutical Company) model
   87
In Vitro Diagnostics (IVD) 96

Wallas, Graham 20
Waterman, Robert H. 150
Webb Young, James 20
Wenting, Rik 157–8
*Where Good Ideas Come From: The
   Natural History of Innovation*
   (Johnson) 149
Wolfe, Julia 117–20
Wolfensohn, James 111
Wong, V. 164
World's Fairs 152
Wyatt, Philip 54–5